A

HANDBOOKS

OF

ENGLISH LITERATURE

EDITED BY PROFESSOR HALES

THE AGE OF ALFRED

LONDON: G. BELL AND SONS, LTD.
PORTUGAL STREET, KINGSWAY, W.C.
CAMBRIDGE: DEIGHTON, BELL & CO.
BOMBAY: A. H. WHEELER & CO.
NEW YORK: THE MACMILLAN CO.

THE AGE OF ALFRED

664-1154

BY

F. J. SNELL, M.A.

AUTHOR OF 'THE AGE OF CHAUCER,' 'THE AGE OF TRANSITION,' 'HANDBOOK TO THE WORKS OF DANTE,' ETC.

LONDON

G. BELL AND SONS, LTD.

1912

CHISWICK PRESS: CHARLES WHITTINGHAM AND CO.
TOOKS COURT, CHANCERY LANE, LONDON.

CONTENTS

THE AGE OF ALFRED

INTRODUCTION

ERRATA

Page 65, last line but one, *for* Prince *read* warrior.
Page 65, line 12 from below, *for* hero *read* latter.
Page 97, last line, *for* Mersey *read* Humber.
Page 183, line 17, *for* Amazons *read* Cwenas.

of the language, which strikes him as having a foreign appearance, like Dutch or Swedish. The fact that it is the parent of his everyday speech, his *mother* tongue, the fact that its sounds are 'as strong as they are sweet and beautiful,' does not do away with the practical difficulty of understanding words and phrases which centuries ago became obsolete, does not teach an accidence not very elaborate, it is true, but much more complex than the irreducible minimum of inflectional changes to which we are accustomed. The difficulty is somewhat lessened for those who know German, but not by any means entirely removed, for every language, every dialect, has its idioms, and a German dictionary would prove of little use for deciphering the meaning of an Anglo-Saxon composition. It is not too much to say that the comprehension of an Old English poem frequently calls for as much acumen as a Latin epic or a Greek play, though, as in all languages, the prose is simpler.

It is evident, then, that this volume stands apart from its fellows in the series, which suppose easy reference to the texts. In the preparation of the work due regard has been had to this very important difference. Not a few may seek to learn whether it is worth while to set about the perhaps ungrateful task of conquering the stubborn, uncorrupted speech of our remote ancestors in order to enjoy the repast to which it gives access. Others, it may be, have already made up their minds that, however, rare the repast, they cannot afford the time or trouble necessary for gaining possession of the key. Still, they are not unwilling to acquaint themselves with the leading ingredients and behold the banquet, as it were, afar off.

The requirements of these two classes explain the presence of rather numerous quotations, supplemented by translations. Occasionally translation or paraphrase has been substituted for the original, notably when a double citation would necessitate too large a draught on our space. Wherever possible, the author has availed himself of the renderings of representative scholars, in every instance indicating the source. Where there is no acknowledgement it may be assumed that he is himself responsible.

Thanks are due to Professor Gollancz, who has not only been good enough to permit free quotation from his excellent versions, but has also kindly revised them for the present work.

The main object of the book is to serve not merely as an introduction, but as an aid to the study of the Old

English writings themselves. If there are those who have not leisure to master the language, but would fain taste the quality of the literature, there are many who have made some progress with the acquisition of the language, and stand in need of a guide to the prose and poetry of the age of Alfred, or, in other words, the pre-Norman period of our national life.

For the behoof of resolute students, as distinct from mere 'general readers,' it has been deemed advisable, and in fact imperative, to incorporate a novel feature in the guise of a chapter on Old English versification—a truly fearful and wonderful growth. In other volumes of the series no such discussion has been necessary for the reason that the principles of prosody involved are those which obtain now. The mechanical basis of Anglo-Saxon poetry, being utterly different from the rimed and blank verse, which at present are the poet's sole choice, it would be expedient on this ground alone to render some account of it. But there is another reason for taking that course. The structure of the verse produced a profound effect on the style of the writers. Most of the verbosity of Anglo-Saxon poetry is directly attributable to this cause. To the need of alliteration must be ascribed also the occurrence of half meaningless formulae, the sway of conventional phraseology, which would be otherwise an enigma, and at best detracts from the freshness of poetical experiments.

Apart from this factor, Old English literature was conditioned by two potent influences—a state of war which was almost normal owing to internal dissensions and the attacks of the Danes; and the conversion of the nation to Christianity, which had a tendency to divert all intellectual energy into religious channels. The former circumstance was the cause of the crude delight in tales of savagery, and the grotesque imposition of warlike motives on the pacific errands of saintly apostles, leading sometimes to the complete disguisement of the character and aims of the servants of God.

Uncertainty is the law of life, and, conspicuously, the law of conflict, as is manifested by the familiar phrase 'the fortune of war.' The accidents of armed rivalry, conducted in the way which then seemed natural, were accompanied with dire results to individuals and communities; and from the fierce exultation aroused by victory it was not uncommon for warrior and minstrel to be plunged into the lowest depths of misery and despair in the hour of failure and disappointment. These alternations are reflected in the poetry of the age, which descends from an ecstasy of grim triumph to a mood of ineffable pessimism. The reception of Christianity provided but a partial remedy for this wantonness of joy and grief. In one sense it shared and added to it, for while the lay mind was preoccupied with the 'excursions and alarums' of earthly warfare, the clergy were enslaved with presentiments of the coming of Antichrist and the Day of Doom.

The fact that literature became, to so large an extent, the affair of the monks or of cloister-bred scholars militated against the display of originality. Writers were too much inclined to draw upon repertories like the Lives of the Saints to the neglect of secular traditions. *Beowulf* appears a brilliant exception, but it has been plausibly surmised that the poem is no more than an English rendering of a Latin composition hatched in some Frankish monastery. The homilies for which Ælfric is famous—and justly so, for he is master of a pellucid style—are avowedly borrowed from, or modelled on, the discourses of great doctors who wrote in Latin.

These conditions were not, perhaps, incompatible with the production of works of genius, if there had arisen a poet of surpassing intellect. As it is, we scan the landscape in vain for a Dante or a Milton; and the name that inspires most interest is that of Cynewulf.[1] He was of the true school of the prophets—that is certain; but his dithyrambic strains exhibit more passion than imagination. Intent on self-expression rather than self-discipline, he will not accept the common limitations of art, which is concerned as much with little as with great things, with picturesque detail no less than sweeping generalisations, with the concrete no less than the abstract. Measure in language is a virtue in which, like all his fellows, Cynewulf is singularly deficient. It is not requisite, or even desirable, that all writers should be as thrifty as Tacitus or Dante, but no really great poet or prose-writer ever allowed himself to be mastered by the glamour of mere words or the subtleties of ingenious paraphrase. All true artists, again, aim at the steady evolution of their themes. Cynewulf's progress is cyclonic, and he attains his goal not by evolution, but by revolution—at any rate, in his more characteristic effusions, his *Guthlac* and his *Crist*. When he has a definite tale to tell, he clothes it with an atmosphere of mystic fervour, and riddles it with subjective suggestions. The facts are never suffered to speak for themselves, the lyrical note always rising above and forming a harassing accompaniment to the narrative. From a temperamental standpoint, however, Cynewulf repays attention; his eloquence, if too luxuriant, is impressive, and his motives transparently sincere.

Save Cynewulf it is hard to find a single Anglo-Saxon writer who inspires us with a sense of his personality.

[1] If *Beowulf* be received as the product of a single intellect, its author was, of course, a very great genius, but, even so, we do not know his name, nor even his nationality. For the tangle of questions relating to the poem see the chapter on the subject.

Cædmon is more or less a shadow, a tradition. Once acclaimed as the father and prototype of Old English singers who were also devout, he has bequeathed nothing, or very little, that can with certainty be assigned to him, while the miracle of his poetic awakening under a seraphic touch is too stupendous for these prosaic days, when incredulous scepticism lies in wait for such a story with the spear of pitiless negation.

The great names of the Old English period—names known to all—are those of Bede and Alfred; and neither of them owes his distinction to the enrichment of the language with a masterpiece whether of prose or poetry. Bede's merits as a historian are incontestable, but his history is a Latin history. As for Alfred, he would not have achieved renown on the strength of his translations alone. But Alfred was a king and a soldier, and, secure in his exalted station and the peace he had won by the sword, he had the wisdom to give an impulse, by both precept and example, to the civilizing mission of humane letters. In this connection it would be improper not to mention Dunstan, who in his own person did considerably less for the language and literature than the West-Saxon monarch, and whose name does not occur in our list of writers. Indirectly, however, by his encouragement of learning, he was the cause of the recovery of Old English prose from the decadence to which it had sunk through political disorders; and to him, ultimately, we owe Ælfric—the most easy and elegant of Anglo-Saxon prose-writers.

Old English literature, then, divides into two main branches corresponding, to some extent, with successive chronological periods, although there was doubtless much overlapping. These branches consist of heroic and ballad verse, dedicated to adventure; and moral and didactic works. The former are more primitive in type, and some of it, presumably in time, but the lateness of the MSS. occasions a great deal of obscurity, and, as regards *Beowulf*, the theory of several redactions does not command universal assent. The *Anglo-Saxon Chronicle*, on the other hand, has unquestionably undergone a number of revisions and enlargements.

On the whole, the *Chronicle* is the most valuable compilation the Anglo-Saxons have handed down to us, regarded in a purely material aspect. As a contemporary record of events it is unique: no European literature can show anything like it. The simplicity of the style affords a sharp contrast with the turgid quality of most of the verse, and is, generally speaking, a guarantee of honesty. It is our chief authority for the periods over which it extends, and although we have to deplore the scarceness of particulars, the loss of these annals would have been a grave disaster, especially if it had occurred before the Latin chroniclers of the post-Conquest era had been able to examine their contents.

The study of Anglo-Saxon literature, resuscitated during the earlier decades of the last century, has since made enormous strides both in this country and on the Continent. Grein's *Bibliothek*, which is constantly receiving additions, forms an admirable collection of texts, each volume being equipped with an *apparatus criticus* which could hardly be bettered. The publications of the Early English Text Society comprise a number of Anglo-Saxon writings, most of which have the advantage of introductions and translations by competent scholars. These editions, and the writings of the lamented Professor Ten Brink, have greatly facilitated the task of the present writer, but he has derived much assistance from other sources. The most recent edition of *Beowulf*—that of Professor Sedgefield—is one of the best, being recommended by an almost exhaustive bibliography. Professor Ker's *Dark Ages* contains brief but excellent sketches of Anglo-Saxon literature in its European setting, and his crisp criticism will be keenly relished by all who have any acquaintance with the topics. The idea of the present work is somewhat different, its aim being to inform even more than to appraise; and there is no room for epigram—were the gifts ours—in attempts to expound complicated rhythms! Some hints have been taken from Jusserand's *Histoire Littéraire*; and the writer has explored with interest, and it is to be hoped, profit, B. Symons's erudite account of northern mythology in Paul's *Grundriss der germanischen Philologie*, more particularly those sections which bear upon the problems of Old English poetry.

In conclusion, gratitude demands warm acknowledgements to the Editor of the series for his most courteous and valuable assistance. From him have come numerous suggestions, nearly all of which have been adopted, to the great advantage of the book.

PART I. HEROIC POETRY

CHAPTER I

THE STAGES

It is a frequent complaint against literary history that it is too often encumbered with a huge and unnecessary mass of extraneous matter, the writer being so preoccupied with the setting that he is content with mere passing allusions to his professed and proper theme. Protracted incursions into the realms of ethnology and sociology, geography and topography, war and politics, are hard to justify; and in no instance, it may be said, ought the accidents of the study to overlay the substance on the scale to be found in some otherwise very agreeable narratives. But if any writer may be excused for granting himself licence with regard to side-lights, the indulgence may be claimed for the historian of Old English poetry, seeing that the atmosphere is so obscure, the ground so strange and unfamiliar.

It is a truism to remark that the English is a mixed race—

> Saxon and Norman and Dane are we;

and this circumstance explains the phenomenon of the language, as it has existed from Chaucer's time down to our own day: a language with a Germanic grammar—what grammar it has—and a cosmopolitan vocabulary. It cannot, however, be deemed to have much bearing on the condition of the English tongue prior to the Norman Conquest, for, whatever dialectal differences it may have exhibited, it preserved up to that period the purity of its 'word-hoard' and the fabric of its simple accidence. The sweeping character of the Norman triumph is attested by no evidence more eloquent than a comparison of the English of Chaucer with the English of Alfred; they are, to all intents and purposes, distinct languages. But the English Conquest, some centuries earlier, was still more drastic, still more terribly complete. The Britons were extinguished and effaced—laws and customs, architecture and commerce all submerged in a ruthless cataclysm of fire and sword. Arguments have been advanced to the contrary, but to all such arguments a conclusive reply is furnished by the fact that words denoted in our dictionaries as of Celtic origin are so few in number that they may almost be counted on the fingers of one hand.

The invaders transplanted to their settlements beyond the sea their entire culture, institutions, dialects and traditions, and, in the literary sphere, instead of beginning afresh and deriving inspiration from the valorous deeds attending the expropriation of the Britons, they resigned this field to the vanquished, and themselves turned to the memories of Continental heroism, clinging with passionate loyalty to the common heritage of Teutonic myths. The oldest specimens of our literature are epics or fragments of epics enshrining these myths, and, what is just as singular, they are without a parallel in Germany, which had to wait many ages for compositions like the *Nibelungenlied*, though it is possible, and indeed probable, that this famous poem was heralded by, and grew out of, songs and ballads, in which, as commonly, its topics were perpetuated. No wonder, therefore, if Old English poetry is regarded by German scholars as in many senses their own, and excites their elation as a survival of primitive minstrelsy, much of which, having been simply oral, has of necessity perished. The Saxon *Heliand* cannot compare in interest with the Anglo-Saxon *Beowulf*—the most precious of pre-Norman lays—but its language, as Professor Ker has pointed out, is full of phrases that are customary in Anglo-Saxon verse, and are, in fact, part and parcel of a common stock.

From these remarks it is manifest that a large and significant remnant of our older literature will be unintelligible if we bind ourselves to a purely insular retrospect. Our ancestors, as we have seen, had no taint of narrowness. They were eager for recitals of the brave 'days of yore'; the 'wide ways' beckoned their willing feet. Accordingly we shall do well, before making trial of Old English poetry, to train our imagination on the epoch of the migrations—that great popular unrest terminated finally by the firm rule of the Norman.

Nothing can exceed the pathos and indignation with which Gildas the Wise recounts the advent of the cruel adventurers in the midst of a superior but decaying civilization. Listen to his accents of despair:

> A multitude of whelps came forth from the lair of this barbaric lioness in three cyuls, as they call them, that is, in three ships of war, with their sails wafted by the wind and with omens and prophecies favourable. . . . They first landed on the eastern side of the island by the invitation of the unlucky King [Vortigern], and there fixed their sharp talons, apparently to fight in favour of the island, but more truly against it. The mother-land, finding her first brood thus successful, sends forth a larger company of her wolfish offspring, which, sailing over, join themselves to their base-born comrades. . . .
>
> The fire of vengeance, justly kindled by former crimes, spread from sea to sea, fed by the hands of our foes in the east, and did not cease until destroying the neighbouring towns and lands, it reached the other side of the island and dipped its red and savage tongue in the western ocean. . . . All the columns were levelled

with the ground by the frequent strokes of the battering-ram, all the husbandmen routed, together with their bishops, priests and people, whilst the sword gleamed, and the flames crackled around them on every side. Lamentable to behold, in the midst of the streets lay the tops of lofty towers tumbled to the ground, stones of high walls, fragments of human bodies, covered with livid clots of coagulated blood.

Some, therefore, of the miserable remnant, being taken in the mountains, were murdered in great numbers; others, constrained by famine, came and yielded themselves to be slaves for ever to their foes, running the risk of being instantly slain, which truly was the greatest favour that could be offered them; some passed beyond the seas with loud lamentations instead of the voice of exhortation. 'Thou hast given us as sheep to be slaughtered, and among the Gentiles hast Thou dispersed us.' Others, committing the safeguard of their lives, which were in continual jeopardy, to the mountains, precipices, thickly-wooded forests, and to the rocks of the sea (albeit with trembling hearts), remained still in their country.[1]

Gildas, who probably felt scant interest in the tribal divisions of these Berserkers, speaks of them under the collective or generic name of Saxons, just as the coast-line from Portsmouth to Wells in Norfolk had been known, before the exit of the Romans, as the *Litus Saxonicum*, and formed the special charge of an officer—the Count of the Saxon Shore. Both the creation of the office and the designation of the province were due to piratical expeditions dating back to the third century, and directed especially against the south-west portion of Britain as the fattest and richest to spoil. It was not until the fifth century, when the Romans were compelled to withdraw their protection, that the yearly apparition of the hostile fleet was transformed into a still more terrible menace. The 'Saxons,' against whose ravages there was no longer any effectual curb, now came to stay.

[1] Giles' tr.

The fact that Roman and Briton described their importunate foes as 'Saxons' may be taken as proof that in the hordes which accomplished these descents there was always a considerable element of that nationality, but the name bestowed on the country after the establishment of their sway, and which it still bears, makes it equally certain that the term would not have been accepted by the victors as fully defining their composition. It is likely that the selection of the name 'England,' as applied to the whole of the conquered territory, was more or less of an accident, but it shows that others—not only the Saxons—bore a prominent part in the winning of Britain. If we may follow the testimony of Bede, the confederacy embraced quite a medley of different, though, for the most part, cognate peoples. There were Jutes, and Angles, and Old Saxons, Frisians and Danes, Prussians and Rugians, and even Huns. According to this statement, all the fiercest and most warlike nations of northern Germany seem to have contributed their quota to the ruin of the unfortunate islanders. Nor is there anything at all improbable in Bede's account.

'This contracted territory,' says Gibbon, 'the present Duchy of Sleswig, or perhaps of Holstein, was incapable of pouring forth the inexhaustible swarms of Saxons, who reigned over the ocean, who filled the British islands with their language, their laws, and their colonies; and who so long defended the liberty of the North against the arms of Charlemagne. The solution of this difficulty is easily derived from the similar manners, and loose constitution, of the tribes of Germany, which were blended with each other by the slightest accidents of war or friendship. The situation of the native Saxons disposed them to embrace the hazardous professions of fishermen and pirates; and the success of their first adventures would naturally excite the emulation of their bravest countrymen, who were impatient of the gloomy solitude of their woods and mountains. Every tide might float down the Elbe whole fleets of canoes, filled with hardy and intrepid associates who aspired to behold the unbounded prospect of the ocean and to taste the wealth and luxury of unknown worlds.'

Amidst the conglomeration of forces three tribes stand out incontestably distinct—a circumstance which must be imputed to their greater numerical representation combined with military ardour and efficiency. These are the Jutes, the Angles, and the Saxons. Of the three peoples the Jutes appear to have furnished the smallest contingent, but, as against this, it must be borne in mind that they were probably the first to effect a permanent settlement in Britain. About the middle of the fifth century they colonized Thanet, and thence spread over the whole of Kent, the Isle of Wight, and a part of Hampshire. The parent stock—the Old Jutes, as they may be called—occupied the so-called Cimbric Chersonese, or that part of Denmark which is attached to the mainland and named after them Jutland (to-day, Jylland). The Angles were their neighbours; they dwelt in what is now the duchy of Schleswig, a corner of which is still known as Angeln. The Saxons held land to the south of the peninsula. They are usually localized in the districts between the Rhine and Elbe, but there was a westward movement of the populations on the Continent as well as in the direction of Britain; and, to judge from the evidence of Ptolemy, the country inhabited by the Saxons before the era of displacement was more restricted in area and contiguous with that of the Angles—'on the neck of the peninsula.' They were associated with the Franks in attacks on the Roman Empire; and Franks and Frisians were associated with the Saxons in attacks upon

Britain. It is notorious that of all the Low German dialects Frisian is that which has the closest resemblance to English.

Having given some account of the distribution of the three principal tribes on the Continent, it is desirable to show how the England they won with the sword was parcelled out among them. Of the Jutes we have already spoken. The Angles seized Northumbria, part of the Midlands, and the north-east coast from Scotland as far as Essex. As regards extent, theirs was the 'lion's share,' and thus little wonder need be felt at the extension of the name Ængla-land or England to the country as a whole. The Saxons established themselves in the south, and the names 'Essex,' 'Sussex,' 'Middlesex,' and 'Wessex' (the last half-forgotten till the novels of Thomas Hardy brought it again into use) remain to mark their possessions. Then, as now, Wessex was the most ill defined of provinces—especially its western boundary, which was finally the Tamar. To the Germans on the Continent the 'Welsh,' or aliens, were the Italians; to the Germans in England, the Britons, who maintained their independence in the west and south-west, the Cornish being known as the West Welsh. It may be observed, in passing, that in Old English the same word *wealh* was employed indifferently of a Welshman and a slave, thus pointing to the fate that awaited any of the British race who might fall into the hands of the victorious foe.

The Jutes may be considered as a connecting link between the larger divisions of the 'army,' their language approximating in some respects to that of the Angles, whilst in other respects it was more akin to Saxon speech. But Jutes, Angles, and Saxons all spoke forms of Low German, between which the differences were not wider than, nor perhaps so wide as, those between Scottish and English vernaculars, between Burns and Barnes. We are compelled to say 'Scottish' now, but in Anglo-Saxon times, when Northumberland extended to the Firth of Forth, the term would have been a singular misnomer; and from the standpoint of comparative philology Dunbar wrote purer English than Shakespeare. We may say then that the invaders used the same language, and the fact was recognized by the people themselves, since the Angles, holding the preponderance in number, or influence, or both, imposed their name not only on the country, but on the tongue. Before as well as after the Norman Conquest the language was known as English (*Englisc* or *Ænglisc*), and nothing else, but until recently scholars, and the public generally, were addicted to the term 'Anglo-Saxon' as descriptive of laws, language, and literature in England down to the date of the Battle of Hastings. In spite of the efforts of Freeman, Stubbs, and others to substitute the expression 'Old English,' in contradistinction to 'Middle' and 'Modern English,' the epithet 'Anglo-Saxon' has not yet passed into desuetude, nor perhaps is it desirable that it should. It has the merit of being at once understood, whereas 'Old English' is in danger of being confused with 'Middle English'—a term which is never employed save in a linguistic or literary context. Moreover, it contains the false suggestion that there was no break in the continuity of our literature, whereas nothing is more certain than that the Norman Conquest was, for the time, fatal to the intellectual life of our nation. Nor can it be alleged that the phrase 'Anglo-Saxon' is entirely without contemporary sanction. If it was not used of the language, it was certainly used of the people, for Alfred in one place designates himself as 'gratia Dei Angol-Saxonum rex.' Of the two 'Old English' is scientifically preferable, and it is further recommended by sentiment. Though to modern eyes its vocabulary appears strange and almost barbarous, it was nevertheless the language of Englishmen, the English language, and cannot by any possibility be treated as a foreign tongue. On the other hand, 'Anglo-Saxon' not only has the virtue of lucidity, but it is so firmly established by prescription as to impart an air of pedantry to systematic rejection. The consequence is that scholars, even those who in theory are strongly in favour of the term 'Old English,' are not always consistent in practice, and probably many years will have to elapse before anything like uniformity is attained in this particular.

Reference has been made to Alfred's assumption of the title 'King of the Anglo-Saxons,' and this may remind us that no sooner had the conquest of Britain been achieved than the question of overlordship became an apple of discord between the new kingdoms. The prize fell in the first instance to Northumbria, which in no long while was supplanted by the central Anglian kingdom Mercia. Wessex first grasped the hegemony in 827, when Ecgberht proclaimed himself 'King of the English.' The early supremacy of the Angles and the wide extent of their domains explain much—explain, amongst other things, how it came to pass that the language was called by their name. In these circumstances it would be natural to expect the growth of a flourishing native literature, and there are excellent reasons for believing that such a literature did, in fact, exist. But the political troubles of Northumbria and Mercia led to a total eclipse, and the fruits of Anglian poetic genius have been preserved to us only in West-Saxon dress.

To this it may be added that the two centuries which elapsed between the primacy of Northumbria and that of Wessex must have witnessed a great advance of culture. When the English conquered Britain, they were in possession of no proper alphabet—simply runes, the application of which was very circumscribed. They were used for divination, for charms, for the marking of houses and household utensils, but for none of the higher purposes subserved by writing—for laws and treaties, the propagation of religion and learning, and the transmission of elaborate poems in a complete form, and free from corruption. Strength of memory at all times bears a definite relation to the degree of exercise; like other faculties, memory can be braced to the performance of feats which strike the uninitiated with wonder and amazement. But it would be absurd to pretend that memory, though strong by nature and made yet stronger by practice, can discharge all the functions of penmanship, if only because it dies with its possessors. But the art of writing admits of the indefinite multiplication of copies, one of which at least may survive to distant ages.

CHAPTER II

THE RÔLE OF THE SCÓP

The relevance of the contents of the preceding chapter becomes obvious the moment we approach the epic or quasi-epic compositions in Old English which are still extant. Without some such preparation, the perusal of these poems would produce sensations of surprise and perplexity even beyond those which must still affect the reader, and that no amount of antecedent discussion can entirely remove. A poem like *Widsith* presents a problem of enormous interest and important enough to justify the most lavish pains that we can bestow upon it. The language is Old English, but in every other sense it appears as detached from insular associations as it is possible for a patriotic poem to be. Patriotic it certainly is, but the prowess it parenthetically extols was displayed not in conflict with the Britons, of whom we do not hear a sound, but on the fields of the Continent. Similar remarks apply to *Deór's Lament*, to *Finnsburg*, to *Waldere*, and to the chief legacy of all—to *Beowulf*. *Brunanburh* and *Byrhtnoth* are national, but, though instinct with martial sentiment, they are to be regarded rather as ballads than as epic poems. In form neither *Widsith* nor *Deór's Lament* is an epic, but both are epic in groundwork and suggestion, treating not of an isolated incident, real or imaginary, but of an accumulation of legends and traditions drawn from the common repertory of the German world, and assumed to be familiar to the audience, for of details there are exceedingly few.

Widsith derives its title from the initial word of the poem, which is also the ostensible name of the author. Literally 'wide-path,' we may construe it 'traveller.' It thus strikes the keynote of the poem as an apotheosis of the profession of the wandering minstrel. Whether Widsith was ever a proper name, or merely an ornamental epithet, cannot be determined, but it may be confidently affirmed that here at least it has a symbolical import, and that Widsith is to be considered rather as a type of his order than as a singer of flesh and blood. At first sight indeed it seems as if we can gather from the poem plain proof of his actual existence, since he does not stint to mention name and nation and certain passages in his peripatetic career. These statements, if they could be accepted, would testify that, like Alcuin, the poet was more at home in Germany and France and Italy than in England, in which—unlike Alcuin—he, on his own showing, could only have set foot as a stranger. His father, he tells us, was a noble Myrging, which intimates that he and his ancestors were domiciled in what is now Holstein. Faring to Burgundy, he had there enjoyed the favour of the celebrated Gunther, who had loaded him with acceptable gifts. He had been with Ælfwin (Alboin) in Italy, and praises his munificence in no measured terms. Ælfwin's sister Eadhhild was the consort of Widsith's own sovereign Eadgils, and the 'gold-wreathed queen' had surpassed even the monarchs who have just been named in the profusion of her bounty. It was in the company of this princess that the poet first visited the court of the mighty Eormanric (Hermanric), who, though acknowledged to be a king of savage temper and a treaty-breaker, did well by Widsith. The tyrant of the Goths presented him with a gold ring of the value of six hundred shillings, which on his return home he gave to his liege-lord, Eadgils, in token of his kindness in bestowing upon him land which had been the property of his father.

To any one unacquainted with the chronology of those times, this narrative must appear so plausible as almost to bear the impress of truth, notwithstanding the fact that in one place Widsith paints Eormanric in the dark colours assigned to him by historians, whilst in another he frankly records private benefits received from him. Considering that a greater than Widsith—Dante—has manifested equally dubious candour, this eccentricity cannot be deemed serious evidence against the genuineness of the story, but a cursory examination of dates is damning. Eormanric—'the great Hermanric,' as Gibbon calls him—was one of the Napoleons of the Dark Ages, and governed Europe from the Baltic to the Black Sea. This was towards the close of the fourth century. The conquest of Lombardy by Alboin—the Ælfwin of the poem—occurred just two hundred years later. Unless, therefore, we are prepared to credit Widsith with a patriarchal longevity, his autobiography collapses—it is plausible no more.

We have adverted to those passages of the poem which appear like oases in a desert of extravagant fiction, but, on closer examination, prove to be fallacious mirages. The anachronisms to which attention has been drawn do not stand alone; throughout, there is no clear sense of historical definition and perspective. The composition is designedly egotistic, although—and this is passing strange! —the hero is an abstraction. It is indeed an apt illustration of *gielpcwide*, or vainglorious utterance, akin to those sometimes discountenanced, sometimes applauded, in warriors like Beowulf. The puppet boasts of his peregrinations, of his exalted patrons, of his supereminent skill as a glee-man, and if he turns aside here and there to render hyperbolical tributes where they have been deserved, these are not usually of a character to cause us to forget the essential theme, which is the worth of Widsith and his likes, one of whom, Scilling, is mentioned by name. The minstrel's life is portrayed as something like a triumphal progress through the earth, and the minstrel himself as indispensable to the grace and dignity of courts, the increase of virtue, and the perpetual fame of noble warriors.

After a brief exordium introducing the speaker, Widsith begins his monologue by laying down the proposition that princes who wish their thrones to prosper must order their lives aright. From what follows one is tempted to conclude that, in Widsith's view, the whole, or main, duty of eorls is to appreciate the minstrel's art, and to see that it is suitably rewarded, although they would be justified in conducting the defence of their country—a course of which he highly approves. Out of the abundance of his learning Widsith furnishes a long list of rulers with their respective subjects—most of them obscure kinglets of obscure tribes. In the present state of our knowledge it would be futile to essay a complete revisal of this list with a view to the detection of possible error, but when Widsith digresses into the region of classical antiquity, he exposes himself to captious criticism. Alexander was a famous conqueror, but ought he to be dogmatically proclaimed the most powerful of men? Perhaps Julius Caesar may have a better claim to the distinction, but here he is set down as a ruler of the Greeks and marches with the princely rank and file. Does it not savour of injustice, and even insult, to pair that colossus with one Cælic, King of the Finns?

A minstrel was nothing if not courtly, and the intention of the poet in this enumeration seems to be no more than to demonstrate his acquaintance with the names and jurisdictions of monarchs, always with the implication that he could say more concerning them if he listed. They may, of course, be cited as models of their kind, and indeed, in those rough times the bare fact of kingship may have passed as a testimonial of merit. It was clearly a testimonial of popularity, for later in the poem Widsith naïvely avows that in the course of his journeyings it has been his invariable experience that the best beloved of mortals are those to whom God has vouchsafed sovereignty over men for the term of their lives.

At length there comes a break in the monotonous recapitulation, and the poet is pleased to tell us something of the valour of Offa, and the staunch and fruitful alliance of Hrothwulf and Hrothgar, who punished the race of vikings, routed the vanguard of Ingeld, and cut in pieces the army of the Heathobards at Heorot. Of Offa and Heorot we shall hear more hereafter. Meanwhile the extraordinary favour shown to the King of the Angles in selecting him for particular mention has been thought to demand explanation, and the reason has been found in the place that he occupied in the pedigree of the kings of Mercia. Although Widsith the man is confessedly a Myrging, *Widsith* the poem is plainly an Anglo-Saxon composition, and it has been conjectured that the actual writer discerned, and profited by, the opportunity to pay a delicate compliment to an insular prince, whose subject he may have been, and before whom the poem may have been recited. Having quitted formula for a more expansive style of narration, Widsith is tempted to dilate on the exploits of the Danish heroes, but he quickly recollects himself. Laudation of gallant leaders is his chief business in life, but for the moment his task is to affirm and illustrate the extent of his travels, and this he does with a will. He has been everywhere; and, although at the outset he is satisfied with naming European communities, he presently takes heart of grace and informs us solemnly that he has wandered into Bible lands—'has been with the Israelites and the Syrians, with the Hebrews'—and penetrated even into Egypt, and Persia, and India. These pretensions are quite in keeping with Widsith's character as an embodiment of travel, but, in predicating such things of himself, he impairs his status as a typical gleeman, for people of that class could have had no conceivable inducement to wend so far beyond the limits within which alone they could look for hospitality and largesse. But his elvish fancy did not pause to weigh unimportant details like these, and an ignorant, uncritical auditory was more likely to sympathize with his extravagances than stumble at his ineptitudes.

Widsith has been on intimate terms with the fellowship of Eormanric, and has not forgotten the meed of praise that is due to the incomparable thanes who battled for the defence of their metropolis with the host of Attila. He had previously passed high commendation on the excellent singing and harping with which he and Scilling had delighted the court of his victorious lord. Many gallant knights of good understanding in such matters bore testimony that they had never heard better song.

In an epilogue the writer of the piece sets forth the conclusion. Nature has ordained that gleemen should traverse many lands, should discourse to the accompaniment of the harp, and utter grateful acknowledgements, but their lot is far from unhappy. Wherever they go, be it north or south, they are sure to meet with generous patrons, connoisseurs in minstrelsy, who are glad to enhance their glory in the eyes of their retainers, and perform noble deeds until the dark day when 'all vanishes, light and life together.' Thereafter they are assured of an immortality of fame.

Such is *Widsith*, as it has come down to us, and it is safe to surmise that it is in no way the sort of poem by which the student expects to be greeted on the threshold of research into Anglo-Saxon literature. The main difficulty is to reconcile the contents of the poem with its existing dress. And here it may be observed that the chronology of Widsith does not transcend the sixth century—that is to say, of all the events and personages to which allusion is made, none can be found later than the year 600—while the poem itself, as we have it, must have been written in England considerably later. It has been preserved in a West-Saxon version, but, like other poems in the Exeter codex, probably had an Anglian predecessor.

The difficulty referred to seems to be capable of solution in one of three ways only. We may suppose the poem to be, frankly, a translation. Somewhere in North Germany, and in Myrging-land, an Englishman may have discovered a *Widsith*, been struck with it, and produced a version of it in his own language. This is possible, but not likely. A sense of form underlies the idea of translation, and art had not yet reached that stage of discrimination which suggests the enrichment of one language with the intellectual treasures of another. We refer, of course, to the various 'vulgar tongues,' which, from the standpoint of culture, were on a common level. Latin, the language of the Church, stood on a different footing; and the fame and sanctity of the Vulgate and other edifying scriptures familiar to scholars provoked experiments in translation, of which notice will appear in due time. But translation of contemporary verse more properly pertains to an age like Chaucer's, wherein the masters are bilingual and one of the two languages is distinguished by a relative perfection which marks it out for imitation. Anglo-Saxon was not behind any of the dialects of the Continent in literary culture; indeed, to judge from the only available evidence, it had attained its fullest bloom and already entered on its decline before they began to germinate.

Appropriation of material is another thing, although the original of *Widsith*, assuming such to have existed, is not exactly the source to which a poet in search of romantic episodes would naturally have repaired. He could obtain ampler information elsewhere. On the other hand, it is possible, if not probable, that the writer was an Englishman, who had been much abroad, so much so as to become steeped in German traditions. The poem is full of exaggerations and inaccuracies, but on one point its testimony may be trusted—namely, that communication was maintained between the scattered branches of the Germanic race, and the sentiment of kinship was kept alive very largely by the agency of wandering minstrels, to whom such travel served all the purposes of a liberal education. In the absence of books they may be forgiven for not always apprehending the succession of events; history, as far as they were concerned, was in its infancy, and the ruling motive of their performances was not so much instruction as pleasure—hence the name 'gleeman.'

If *Widsith* be treated as the offspring of a single brain, we may well conceive of it as a burlesque dating from a period when the minstrel's art had fallen into some disrepute, as a satire on the boastful propensities of the vagabond, illiterate, gain-seeking race of gleemen. Probably, however, we should be nearer the mark if we understood it as the effusion of a *scóp* who, for some personal end, parades his acquirements under the cloak of an impossible Widsith. We can perceive no objection to the acceptance of one or other of these alternatives, for, however bizarre, the poem has an internal consistency which may be attributed to the inspiration of some one bard. The mass of unadorned allusions appears like the débris of former ages, and may be symptomatic of fatigue and exhaustion in the particularization of narratives familiar to the verge of nausea. We shall see ere long that this is not the sole instance of such apparent débris of historical or legendary material in the sphere of Old English poetry. This, however, is not the way in which German criticism attempts the solution of the problem; and, as its proffered explanation has undeniable interest, as well as some degree of plausibility, it is necessary to state it.

Instead of regarding *Widsith* as a late individual caprice, we are invited to find in it something composite, something traditional, on which the last touches have been bestowed by a not too capable editor. We say 'not too capable' because the prologue implies that the Ostrogoths occupied territory to the west of the Angles. Such a traveller as Widsith boasts himself to have been—and it must be remembered that his contribution begins at l. 10 and ends at l. 134—would have known better than so to invert facts, but an editor—perhaps a Mercian—might have fallen into such a mistake from carelessness or sheer ignorance. This geographical misconception points to the composition of, at any rate, parts of the poem at a distance from the central scene, which would have been Holstein. Similarly, the anachronisms of Widsith's speech show pretty plainly that the poem, as a whole, must have been put together at a much later date than the close of the sixth century. Some considerable interval must have elapsed before the memory of Alboin, or Ælfwin, could have faded sufficiently to enable him to pass as a contemporary of Attila.

Still, there is no gainsaying the fact that the historical references are bounded by the sixth century, and there must, it is contended, be a reason for this horizon. A satisfactory reason is forthcoming if we may suppose that the elements of the poem were transferred to the new soil of Britain in the last migration of the Angles—about 575 —and there began to undergo modifications. Traditions, originally distinct, became fused; much was forgotten, much added. The entire process, it is imagined, covered a period of nearly two hundred years. The theory is propounded that what we have here is the residuum of a number of kindred songs in which the Widsiths and Scillings of successive ages recorded their gratitude for favours received, and that this explains the chaos of historical allusions. The original hero, it is thought, may have been Gunther, of whom Alboin is a sort of reproduction.

There are believed to be at least three primitive elements, and these have been subjected to intercalation. Neglecting the prologue and epilogue, and confining ourselves to that portion of the poem in which Widsith 'unlocks his store of eloquence,' we have first a list of famous kings jumbled together on no discoverable principle and including mythical as well as actual personages. Lines 10-13 are conjectured to be a later addition on the ground that they do not form a suitable introduction to a catalogue of monarchs, not all of whom can be supposed to have exemplified the maxims of conduct which these lines lay down. Möller suggests ll. 11 and 12 should change places, and it is further proposed that, as Offa and the Danish kinsmen were model princes, the lines properly belong to that portion of the narrative, which is also held to be comparatively modern. It is considered, too, that ll. 131-134 should follow immediately ll. 14-17, since in their present position the sentiment which they express is sheer bathos. We cannot accept this argument. The lines in question define the normal relations betwixt king and people, and are no more than an expansion of the term *wine*, so often used in Anglo-Saxon as a synonym of 'lord,' but properly signifying 'friend.' It may be that a modern poet might not give such crude expression to the attraction of rank, but it is to be feared that no experience is more common than the polarity of position; and therefore a travelled minstrel, who had been a *persona grata* at many courts, might feel constrained, at the close of his retrospect, to utter the truth that had been borne in upon him more than any other. If David said in his haste 'All men are liars,' Widsith implies in his leisure that all men are sycophants, but without sin. The suggested transpositions, then, do not appeal to us. They disturb not only the form, but the sense and unity of the poem, and may well be dispensed with.

The remainder of the composition is represented as consisting of two elements—an Eormanric catalogue and a lay of Ealhhild. The former is made up of two parts: a list of the peoples with whom Widsith professes to have been conversant and a roll-call of Eormanric's followers. The lay of Ealhhild, named after the generous princess, comprises practically all of what may be termed the narrative portions of the poem, commencing with ll. 50-58 and resumed in ll. 64-67, 70-74, 90-108, 135-143. It is claimed for this analysis that it gives us a complete poem, but it involves considerable violence to the text. The Eormanric list, in so far as it may be deemed to include the table of nations visited, breaks right into the Ealhhild lay as reconstructed by modern scholarship, but the connection of that table with the list of warriors is not self-evident, especially if we look at the Biblical races included in ll. 82-87. This section, however, may have been inserted late in the day, after the poem had, in other respects, assumed its present shape.

These hypotheses are no doubt ingenious and plausible, and, if accepted, go some way to clear up the mystery of this singular effusion. But, after all, *Widsith* may have been the creation of some Anglo-Saxon Puck, some wanderer in the night of vanished times, endowed with artistic and rhetorical instincts and a wide outlook on the world, which he had known how to serve, and had served him well. In *Deór's Lament*, which can hardly have been a case of polycephalic authorship, we have a similar example of the exploitation of Germanic traditions on a lesser scale.

Before turning to that poem, however, it is desirable to direct attention to another composition contained in the Exeter codex, and named the *Wanderer*. The hero is described in expressive Old English as an 'earth-stepper,' and he has that much in common with Widsith—he has been in many lands. But there the analogy ceases. For the buoyant optimism of Ealhhild's favourite comes a profound melancholy born of far other experiences and constitutional temperament. The lore in which Widsith wallows has no charm for this afflicted soul, wholly absorbed with his own griefs and hardships. The two poems are therefore opposed as positive and negative, as obverse and reverse, and that for a very good reason. *Widsith* is, to a great extent, ideal and imaginary, but the *Wanderer* is a document setting forth the grim realities of enforced exile. Probably the writer was a professional *scóp*, or gleeman, although the art of minstrelsy was known to courtiers as well as to its regular practitioners. Hints to that effect occur in *Widsith*, where something like technical accomplishment, not mere vague admiration, appears to be conveyed by the expressions *þa þa wel cuþan* and *gydda gleawne*. But passages in *Beowulf* (*see* especially ll. 2107-8) place the matter beyond a doubt. In this connection it may be remarked that the social status of the *scóp* was so high, that they seem to have been practically on a par with the warriors, who 'touched the game-wood,' *i.e.*, the harp. Both *Widsith* and the *Wanderer* refer to nobility of origin; the former speaks of *mines fæder eþel, frea Myrginga*, the latter deplores the parting from *freo-mægum* as one of the ingredients of his bitter cup.

The *Wanderer* is an elegy—a species of composition in which the Anglo-Saxons excelled, and of which they may lay claim to the honour of invention amongst Teutonic peoples. In a writing of this description designed to express welling emotion facts are necessarily few, but the situation which it discloses is that of a retainer—a domestic minstrel—who has lost his *gold-wine*, or patron, and been thus thrown on the charity of a cold world.

So must I often bind in fetters
My soul's thoughts, miserably wretched,
Deprived of country, far from my noble kin,
Since the day, now long ago, when earth's darkness
Covered my bounteous friend, and I went abject thence,
Stricken with winters, over the frozen waves,
And sought I the hall of some giver of treasure,
Some place, far or near, where one I might find
Who in the mead-hall would show me love,
Would comfort me in my friendlessness
And cheer me with delights. He knoweth who trieth
How dire is care as comrade
To him who has few trusty friends.
His portion is the exile's track, not twisted gold;
A body chilled with frost; nought of earth's bliss.
He remembers the retainers and receipt of treasure,
How in his youth his generous lord
Regaled him at the feast; but all delight has fallen away;
For this knows he who missed long ago
The wise counsels of his dear lord and friend
That often when sorrow and sleep both together
Bind him, poor solitary wretch,
It seems to him in fancy as though he clasps
And kisses his great lord, and on his knee lays

Hand and head, even as when erewhile
In former days, he shared the gift-stool's bounty.
Then wakes again the friendless wight,
Sees before him sea-birds bathing and spreading their wings,
Falling hoar-frost and snow mingled with hail.[1]

The Wanderer is a landsman. He deplores the necessity of traversing the watery ways and stirring with his hands 'the rime-cold sea.' A companion poem, the *Seafarer*, breathes a different spirit, and exhibits a sportive delight in the stimulus of rough weather and boisterous seas. As another piece in the same codex reminds us, the endowments of men vary, and, if the Wanderer discovers in the discomforts of a voyage the outward reflection of his inner woe, here is a picture of a bold viking in his heritage and element.

One o'er the dusky wave
Steers the prow; the stream-road knoweth he,
Guider of a host o'er the wide deep,
When bold seamen, quick of strength
Tug at their oars near the vessel's side.[2]

This is more the temper that we expect in a member of that sturdy race that swarmed over the sea to dispossess the Britons, but the Wanderer is a thorough pessimist and can see no good in anything earthly. He laments his own fate and that of his fellows, but the case of eorls, he finds, is hardly better. Utter despair makes him conceive of the whole 'middle-earth'—the world is often so termed in Old English poetry—as perishing, as sinking down in irreclaimable ruin. He conjures up visions of crumbling wine-halls, and prostrate corpses of warriors, the prey of hovering vulture or gray wolf, and shudders at the destiny

[1] Gollancz' tr. [2] *Ibid.*

of one whom a sad-faced lord has imprisoned in an earth-cave.

In a world so unstable and fast hastening to decay boastfulness is out of place—a fact of which Widsith does not appear to have been aware. Patience, control of the temper and of the tongue, reasonable courage, avoidance of avarice are commended, but these are ordinary counsels, and the point on which this Solomon lays especial stress is the folly of boastfulness. Vainglory is a vice which is very obviously unseasonable when all of which a man boasts will shortly tumble down.

The poem, like *Widsith,* may have been edited, for it, too, has a prologue and an epilogue, the former introducing the speaker and the latter summing up. On this supposition the editor appears to have been dissatisfied with the moral already drawn, and perhaps dissatisfied with the 'earth-stepper' as a garrulous, whining pagan. Certain it is that the central portion, which may once have been an independent lyrical composition, has no Christian teaching. The epilogue repairs this defect.

A man must never too rashly
Divulge his bosom's grief, unless he know beforehand
Bravely to find its cure. Well is it with him who seeks grace,
Solace of the Father in Heaven, with Whom rests all our security.[1]

In *Deór's Lament*—quite a short lyric—the case supposed is much the same, with the lyrically important difference that, while the 'hero'—if the irony may be suffered—of the previous poem has been the victim of some dark tragedy, which has left him without home or friends, Deór, to his disgust, has been forced to make way for a rival. But, like Milton, he bates not a jot of heart

[1] Gollancz' tr.

or hope; he has the consolations of philosophy and forestalls the question 'What supports me, dost thou ask?' with the words of the refrain:

þæs ofereode, þisses swa mæg.

That passed, so may this.

Deór's Lament, one of the treasures of the Exeter codex, if connected with the *Wanderer* by its setting of circumstance, has many ties with *Widsith*. All three poems bring before us the relations of domestic minstrel and patron. *Widsith* displays to us the happy gleeman returning to his native country, where he is honoured by his sovereign and receives from him a grant of land. *Deór's Lament* reverses the picture. There the poet has spent a long series of years at court apparently in secure enjoyment, only to be suddenly thrust out and deprived of his land, the outward and visible sign of his lord's esteem and the equivalent of a pension. The Wanderer has lost his kind protector by death, and, unconsolable, ceases not to mourn for him in vain and passionate strains. Between the three poems there is undeniable affinity and equally undeniable contrast, but *Widsith* and *Deór's Lament* approach each other more nearly. They share the same predilection for history and mythology, and the *Lament*, being unquestionably an artificial product, may—if we reject the theory of fusion—shed light on the genesis of *Widsith*, both being explained as scholastic exercises or poetical diversions.

Deór's Lament, in its present form, is clearly defective, and, if parts have been omitted, there are signs also of interpolation. According to the original design it appears to have consisted of strophes of six lines, or fewer, followed by the refrain above quoted. The key to the meaning of the poem is to be found in the last strophe, of which the refrain is anticipatory. 'I was for a while *scóp* of the Heodings, dear to my lord; my name was Deór; many a winter I had good service, a gracious lord, till now Heorrenda, a man skilled in song, has received the land right, which erst the lord's patronage gave me. That passed, so may this.' The situation is embarrassing, but Deór reflects that others before him have had to encounter difficulties. He thinks of Weland oppressed by Nithhad, of Beadohild, on whom and on whose brother Weland revenged their father's oppression; of Hilde; of Theodric, of the wolfish Eormanric—that grim king. The world is full of vicissitudes, so Deór refuses to be dismayed: 'That passed, so may this.'

The writer has not chosen his instances too skilfully, since he has seen fit to include the case of 'Maid Hilde,' which, so far from illustrating his point, contradicts it. On various grounds it will be advantageous to outline this legend—a primitive Germanic myth which was widely known both in Norway and on the shores of the Baltic and the North Sea. Naturally, there is some variation in the forms of the names, as they appear in Old Norse, Old English, and Middle High German, but the Anglo-Saxon forms will serve as well as any. Two of them are to be found in *Widsith*:

> Hagena [weold] Holmrygum ond Heoden Glommum.

Now Heoden was a young and handsome prince, the son of Heorrenda, and own brother of Hagena, his senior in years, who was of a gloomy and saturnine temper. Heoden falls hotly in love with Hagena's daughter, the lovely Hilde, whom he carries off, and with her, apparently, her father's treasures. Hagena, in a great rage, pursues the lovers, and overtakes them at one of the southernmost of the Orkney islands—Hoy. Hilde, on behalf of Heoden, tenders a gold necklace to her father by way of peace-offering, but the morose parent is not so easily reconciled, and a fierce conflict is kindled, which continues till nightfall. The kings then withdraw to their ships, and the corpses of the slain, who with their weapons have been turned to stone, lie motionless on the battle-field. The conflict, however, is unending, for every night Hilde, by her knowledge of magic, awakens the dead warriors to new life, and on the morrow the game is resumed, and so it will be till crack of doom.

It will be understood now why it is inapposite to allude to Hilde's elopement and its consequences as past and gone. Interest in the story, however, does not cease here. In the concluding strophe of the *Lament* Deór speaks of himself as formerly the *scóp*, or minstrel, of the Heodings, and names Heorrenda as his successful rival. In the Old Norse version, given above, Heorrenda is Heoden's father. At first sight we may be tempted to impute this alteration to some error or confusion on the part of the Anglo-Saxon poet, but, on comparing the later German legend of Kudrun, in which characteristic traits of the more ancient myth are reproduced, it is certain that the story of Hilde was remodelled in some particulars, and Hôrant (Heorrenda) now figured as a singer endued with the miraculous faculty of bewitching all living beings—a faculty which he turned to account by winning for his nearest kinsman Hetele (Heoden) the affections of Hilde.

That under the circumstances Deór should have been thrust aside need excite no surprise, but the character of the legend shows plainly enough that the circumstances are imaginary. It is doubtful indeed whether the writer of the piece had a clear conception of the myth, at any rate in its original form, but it would be extremely rash to assume that the names were chosen at random. Deór, for example, may have been the name of a traditional minstrel —not just a chance appellation. Be that as it may, it is well to be in possession of one of the legends—and that the principal and most essential—which form the background of the lyric. Without such knowledge the poem itself cannot be properly or adequately understood; and, in addition to that, the topic is closely related to other matters which will engage our attention hereafter.

CHAPTER III

SCÓP-CRAFT

Before proceeding to epic compositions proper it seems necessary, or at least desirable, to give some account of the principles of Old English versification, which a glance at *Widsith*, *Deór's Lament*, or the *Wanderer* is sufficient to show, are strikingly unlike the rules of metre with which we are familiar in modern poetry. It was in the deft application of those principles to the unfolding of his subject that the *scóp* displayed his *cræft* or cunning—his mastery of technique; and the mechanical conditions of his work profoundly influenced its literary quality. This being so, we must seek to obtain an insight into the rhythms which preceded the introduction of strict prosody and its usual accompaniment, rime. Not that rime was entirely strange to Old English poetry, but it was differently understood, and in the ordinary sense so sparsely employed as to be almost a negligible factor in the art and mystery of the accomplished minstrel.

In the preceding chapter the terms minstrel, *scóp*, and gleeman have been used indifferently with reference to professors of the poetic art; and in early times, at any rate, when poetry was chiefly associated with light entertainment and assumed the form of song with instrumental accompaniment, it is unlikely that attempts should be made to differentiate them. In theory, the originator of a song—it is needless to point out that the Greek ποιητής, the Old English 'scóp,' and the Middle English 'maker' not only mean the same, but testify to the priority of poetry to prose for literary purposes—may have been distinguished from the singer or reciter, but literary property is a conception of much later times. The gleemen themselves, trained to sing and play on the harp, and also, it may be believed, to invent new songs, both words and music—we know this to have been the case in Provence—probably attached little importance to artistic monopoly and were content to contribute anonymously to the common stock, while their audiences would be still more incurious. This explains the survival of so few names of poets. It was not as authors that they won most esteem and the largest rewards, but as good singers and effective reciters, and no reputation could have been so evanescent as that of a wandering minstrel or a *scóp* retained by a local lord or petty potentate, whose breath or death could unmake him.

That the terms *scóp* and *gleomann* were virtually identical in meaning during the earlier ages, if not always, may be considered proved by passages in *Beowulf* referring to Hrothgar's minstrel, whose story of the rape of Hildeburh is introduced by the words:

> ðonne healegamen Hroþgares *scop*
> æfter medobence mænan scolde; [1]
>
> When Hrothgar's scóp should revelry proclaim
> Along the mead-benches.

while its conclusion is indicated thus:

> Leoð wæs asungen,
> gleomannes gyd.[2]
>
> the song was sung,
> The gleeman's strain.

[1] ll. 1066-7.

[2] ll. 1159-60.

This is clear evidence that *scóp* and *gleomann* might be one and the same, and that recitation was not distinguished from song. Moreover, since the versified tale is described as 'disport in hall,' the general position of poetry in the scheme of things, before stated, is aptly confirmed. It is when we come to long and elaborate poems like *Beowulf* itself that we are tempted to draw distinctions which may be purely logical. Just as Shakespeare was dramatist and actor, so the minstrel was poet and reciter. The gleeman may be defined as the *scóp* in action; the *scóp* as a potential gleeman, whose services were called into requisition on suitable occasions. Hrothgar's minstrel and Deór, the minstrel of the Heodings, are both designated *scóp* in their permanent capacity and personal relation to their employers, whereas in the latter of the two passages cited above, and also in *Widsith*, the term *gleomann* is used with direct reference to the exercise of song. The minstrel had, in fact, a dual personality. He was at once *littérateur* and musician; and the word *scóp* seems more applicable to him in the former character, the word *gleomann* in the latter.

With music we are not here concerned, but metre concerns us much. We learn from *Beowulf* that laymen shared in the rendering of songs and lays, but the metrical difficulties of Old English verse must have tended to deter unprofessional folk from attempting original composition otherwise, perhaps, than on a small scale. Here the *scóp* had, in a great measure, the field to himself.

Any one taking up a volume of Anglo-Saxon poetry for the first time will be immediately struck with the appearance in each line of two and usually three syllables beginning with the same letter, with the division of the lines into equal parts, and with the fact that the first half has commonly two alliterated words as against one in the second. Unless he has come across something analogous in the alliterative romances of the post-Conquest period, this will come to him as a revelation of a new principle of versification. Hitherto lines with rimes and lines without rimes in their terminating syllables or any recurring pause, but subject to more or less rigid laws of metre—these will have appeared to him as the only possible forms that poetry can assume: he is now brought face to face with a system which he may be apt to deem considerably more complex and exacting.

Stabreim, as the Germans call it, can be termed novel only in a subjective way, from the standpoint of the novice, for, in reality, the method is one of hoar antiquity. Ten Brink regards it as an heirloom descended from the remotest times of Indo-Germanic civilization. Certainly it is the common property of the Teutonic peoples, and in no way peculiar to the Anglo-Saxon race. It might be a gain if the word 'staff-rime' could be naturalized in the terminology of literary study. It may be censured as uncouth, but 'staff' or 'stave' in this connection was technical all through the north of Europe, and the combination would remind us that 'end-rimes' and 'head-rimes' are different forms of the same artistic expedient.

'When,' says Guest, 'the same modification of sound recurs at definite intervals, the coincidence very readily strikes the ear, and when it is found in accented syllables, such syllables fix the attention more strongly than if they merely received the accent. Hence we may perceive the importance of rhyme in accentual verse. It is not, as is sometimes asserted, a mere ornament: it marks and defines the accent, and thereby strengthens and supports the rhythm. Its advantages have been felt so strongly that no people have ever adopted an accentual rhythm, without also adopting rhyme' (*History of English Rhythms*, vol. i, p. 116).

Now Old English rhythm is essentially accentual, and the design of alliteration is precisely to '*strengthen* and *support* the rhythm'—hence the term 'staff' as applied to the alliterated syllables, which sustain the structure of the verse. 'Head-rimes,' in the nature of the case, have not the efficacy of 'end-rimes,' since they require the repetition of a single letter instead of a complete syllable. Doubtless for this reason they occur at briefer intervals and serve to knit up the halves of the same line divided by the caesura rather than to connect two or more whole lines. Normally (as Sievers conceives, invariably) the line consists of four accented syllables, two in the first, and two in the second half, with an indefinite number of unaccented syllables. Both accented syllables in the first half may be alliterated, but only the first accented syllable in the second half, which, however, was known as the 'head-staff.' In Old Norse the predominance of the *hofuðstafr* (or 'head-staff') is emphasized by the bestowal of a distinct, though roughly synonymous, name on the alliterated accented syllables of the first half of the line. They were described as *stuðlar* (or 'stays'). There were commonly two, but where only one syllable is alliterated, it is that which has the stronger accent. The importance of the 'head-staff' may have been due to the fact that, while a composition naturally began at the commencement of the line, a fresh sentence was frequently begun after the caesura. Often, too, the first half consisted of words forming merely an echo or paraphrase of some expression in the second half of the preceding line. The following passage will serve to exemplify these statements:

Ic on Higelace wat
Geata drihtne, þeah ðe he geong sy,
folces hyrde, þaet he mec fremman wile
wordum ond worcum, þæt ic þe wel herige

ond þe to geoce garholt bere
mægenes fultum, þær ðe bið manna þearf.

Beowulf, ll. 1830-5.

I know of Hygelac,
Lord of the Geats, although he be but young,
Guardian of the folk, that he will help me
In words and works, thee well to glorify
And to thy succouring bear shaft of spear,
Mighty support, where (or, if) thou hast need of men.

Here the sense is carried on almost entirely by means of second half-lines. Of the first at least three might be omitted without danger to the meaning, and such phrases as 'folces hyrde' and 'wordum ond worcum' are purely conventional tags. Such undertones or asides are a regular, but not admirable, feature in Old English poetry. They impede the progress of the narrative, and are a fruitful cause of that prodigality of language which is a notable failing of Anglo-Saxon poets. In many cases they are doubtless inserted for the sake of alliteration, the writer having already in view the sentence or clause with which he proposes to continue his deliverance.

This leads us to say something of alliteration as understood and practised by Old English versifiers. Everybody, of course, is aware of what is usually signified by alliteration, and there are probably few who will not recall in this connection the well-known illustration:

Apt alliteration's artful aid.

For our present purpose this instance is somewhat inapposite, since in Anglo-Saxon poetry the vowels were considered mutual or equivalent, as, for example in the line

eald ond infrod, ænige gefremman.

old and prudent, any [help] render

As regards the consonants, perfect alliteration would seem to demand the repetition not merely of single letters, but of combinations of letters where they occur. And this is sometimes found, *e.g.*

breostweorthunge, bringan moste.
breast-ornament, must bring.

But it is compulsory only in the case of *sc*, *sp*, and *st*, neither of which may be alliterated with a simple *s* or other *s* group. On the other hand, the combinations *hl*, *hn*, *hr* and *hw* may be alliterated with a simple *h*; and *c*, *k*, *qu* (or *cw*) are naturally treated as identical, *c* being always hard, and *k* and *qu* seldom used. The same remark applies to *s* and ʒ. The latter is not strictly a part of the Anglo-Saxon alphabet, but it is found in some foreign words, such as proper names. It may be added that *s* had generally the soft sound of ʒ, which would therefore have been superfluous.

Cases occur of cross alliteration, *e.g.*:

winia bealdor, ða se wyrm gebeah
Lord of comrades, whe the dragon coiled.

but they are not common, and are indeed rather incompatible with the principle of alliteration in relation to accent.

The tendency was to introduce the first accented syllable as early as possible—generally at the commencement of the line. This imparts to Old English verse a prevailingly trochaic character, so much so that we are tempted to look upon any unaccented syllable that may precede as *extra versum*. The effect is undoubtedly abrupt, and probably the fact that there are so few definite and indefinite articles in Old English poetry compared with Old English prose is associated with the nature of the metre, which, although rude, has the compensating merit of vigour and *élan*, and that in proportion as it adheres to the trochaic type of verse, which appears normal, original, fundamental. But too rigid an adherence to the trochaic tetrameter would unquestionably produce a sense of monotony, and either for this reason or, as is morely likely, because it would be too grave a tax on the ingenuity of poets to compose at any length in a measure only approximately trochaic, we encounter almost infinite variations of type. It must be recollected that there was no prescribed limit to the number of unaccented syllables before and between the accented ones—hence the necessity of 'staves,' of accents defined and strengthened by alliteration, stemming the rush of vocables.

We have spoken of an almost infinite variety of types—and perhaps the expression is not too strong as applied to the combinations and permutations possible within the assigned limits and under the very free conditions—but there is no doubt that the rhythms have a tendency to sort themselves into certain large classes or categories, these being again divisible into smaller classes. It is hardly supposable that Anglo-Saxon versifiers invented these genera and consciously availed themselves of them to obtain flexibility in their rhythms. More probably, they grew out of the exigences of a method of composition in which the coincidence of main stress and alliteration was obligatory. This point having been secured, what was left conformed itself to the sole remaining condition, viz., that the unaccented syllables should not be so numerous or so placed as greatly to disturb the balance of the parts, obscure the position of the caesura or pause, and impose on the 'staves' a heavy and unnatural strain in supporting a rout of parasitical syllables.

A world of trouble would have been saved if scholars had been content to accept the 'staves' and 'stays' as the only vital element in the verse and the rest as so much inorganic matter, but the study of rhythms has been carried far enough to have become a science with which the name of Professor Sievers is inseparably connected. In a work like the present it would serve no useful purpose to state the conclusions, or points at issue, in full; suffice it to note the most salient features.

The accent naturally attaches itself to a long syllable, but it may fall on a short syllable followed by another syllable, short or long, provided that it is not stressed. It is then said to be in resolution. An unaccented syllable is indicated by a cross – × – and short and long by the familiar signs ⏑ and – respectively. An acute accent (′) denotes a full stress; a grave accent (‵) a secondary stress. Thus a resolved accent would be specified by the formula ⏑́ ×. Besides the strongly accented syllables marked by alliteration, which receive the rhetorical emphasis, there are others which, by their nature, are subject to a relative degree of stress. These have a subordinate position, but are still not without significance or influence as regards the rhythm. Where the first half line has only one alliterated syllable the subordinate accent steps into the place of the missing 'rime'; and it must never be forgotten that the second half-line, though it has two accents, has only one alliterated syllable—the 'head-staff.'

Sievers distinguishes five primary types named alphabetically in the order of their comparative frequency. The following are examples:

A	–́ × | –́ ×	hýran | scólde
B	× –́ | × –́	him Grén | del wéarð
C	× –́ | –́ ×	oft Scýld | Scéfing

To these symmetrical types he adds two others syllabically unequal.

D	´ | ´ ` ×	(scheme: 1 + 3)	féond ǀ máncỳnnes
	´ | ´ × `		flét | ínnanwèard
E	´ ` × | ´	(scheme: 3 + 1)	wéorðmỳndum | þah
	´ × ` | ´		mórðorbèd | stréd

Besides primary types there are sub-types, of which Professor Kaluza has adduced ninety. It is needless to quote many instances here, but a few variants may be given by way of illustration. Thus, while A 1 is the normal form of the type, A 2 and A 3 represent by-forms, and these are subdivided into fresh sets. Thus

A 2 a	´ ` | ´ ×	wísfæ̀st | wórdum
	´ ` | ⏑́ ×	gúðrìnc | mónig
A 2 b	´ × | ´ `	Gréndles | gúðcræ̀ft
A 2 a b	´ ` | ´ `	gúðrìnc | góldwlànc

C 2 affords an instance of resolution (see above). Here the formula is × ⏑́ × \| ´ ×, of which an example occurs in the half-line, *in wórold wócum.*

It is a strong point with Sievers that there can be no more than two full stresses in each half-line, and that the natural accent of any other word receives the character of a thesis, as *fýrst* \| *fórd gewàt.* This, it will be observed, is a half-line of the D type. In order to obviate the violence thus done to ordinary modes of speech, Kaluza proposes a modification of Sievers' scheme by the admission of three feet in two of the types, which may then be considered identical. In this process type D practically disappears, one of its forms being assigned to a new version of type B, and the other associated with another reading of type C. Kaluza has four main types, which are formulated thus:

I. (2+2).	Type A	´ × | ´ ×	lánge | hwíle
II. (1+2+1).	Type B	× | ´ × | ´	þurh | míne | hánd
	Type D	´ | ´ × | ´	blǽd | wíde | spráng

III. (3+1).	Type E	´ ` × | ´	wéorðmỳndum | þáh
IV. (1+3).	Type C	× | ´ ` ×	him | sé yldèsta
	or	× | ´ ◡̀ ×	in | géardàgum
	Type D	´ | ´ ` ×	féond | máncỳnnes
	or	´ | ´ ◡ ×	léof | lándfrùma

Alliterative verse, whatever we may think of these amendments, is best explained on the principle that the ideal or standard half-line consists of two trochees, and that all others deflect from it. According to our view, which may possibly meet with acceptance, one trochee will serve, and its position in the half-line may vary, but in every instance where it stands alone it forms the pivot of the rhythm, and the mind is not satisfied until it is overtaken. The syllables in Kaluza's scheme which precede and follow the dominant trochee are in the nature of ballast, assisting to fill out the compass of the half-line. But sometimes, notably in the E type, the slurred syllables are so numerous that instead of merely steadying and completing the half-line they strain and overburden it. Take, for example:

fæderæþelum onfon

which requires to be scanned ´ × ` × × × | ´.

We do not propose to enter more deeply into this branch of the subject, which will probably impress most readers as bearing a greater resemblance to vegetable morphology than to prosody in the strict sense of the word. It is right to add that this was the only system of versification known to the Anglo-Saxons, unless we except what the Germans term *schwellvers*. That, however, differs from the normal verse in no other respect than in having three equal limbs with two caesuras instead of two half-lines with one caesura. Occasionally no caesura occurs in the normal alliterative line, which is then called a full verse.

Having shown the nature of alliterative verse in its

essential or fundamental aspects, it seems necessary to refer to its embellishments. Rime in the ordinary sense was not unknown to the Old English poets any more than alliteration is unknown to their successors, but in the course of time these artifices may be said to have changed places—that is, their relative importance has become inverted. Rime at that period was something optional—generally, perhaps, exactly what Guest declares it is not, 'an ornament or superfluity,' its true function being discharged by alliteration. In some instances indeed it seems to have been employed advisedly for the sake of a special effect. There is a passage in the *Crist* relating to man's earthly probation, in which rime and alliteration are associated in enforcing a series of contrasts.

swa helle hienþu, swa heofonas mærþu;
swa þæt leohte leoht, swa ðа laþan niht;
swa þrymmes þræce, swa þrystra wræce;
swa mid dryhten dream, swa mid deoflum hream;
swa wite mid wraþum, swa wuldor mid arum;
swa lif, swa deað, swa him leofre bið.

[Each man
While he is dwelling here, must now make choice]
Be it hell's shame, or heaven's fame,
Be it the shining light, or the loathsome night;
Be it majestic state, or the rash ones' hate;
Be it song with the Lord, or with devils discord;
Be it toil with the grim, or glory with cherubim,
Be it life or death, as it should liefer be.[1]

In the same poem we meet with a single line, with riming half-lines:

bruca þ mid blisse, beorhte mid lisse.

Enjoy with bliss, radiant with grace.

[1] Gollancz' tr.

Here the motive may be to emphasize the close connection between the ideas of happiness and Divine favour, but it is just as likely to be an ornament pure and simple —this echoing of one word by another with like ending. That rime was commonly regarded in this light is a fair deduction from its sporadic employment. In those rare instances in which it was employed continuously, it was not always handled with the artistic skill displayed in the *Crist.* The Exeter codex comprises a 'Rhyming Poem,' which is obviously an experiment. Taking the half-line as basis, the rimes may be considered to have been arranged almost necessarily in couplets, but they are also strung together in irregular sequences. The same rime is retained in sets of three, four, six, and as many as fourteen half-lines. Here and there are interposed rimeless half-lines, or the poet is content with mere assonance.

The 'Rhyming Poem' is a puzzle in more ways than one. Thorpe says of it: 'The conjectures formed with regard to its subject have been manifold; and it was only recently that the present editor, having taken up the poem in the almost hopeless attempt at illustration, was struck by its striking resemblance to some parts of Job; when on reading over the latter, he soon felt convinced that it was a very free paraphrase from the above chapters. *That words have been misspelt for the sake of the rime,* seems unquestionable; and all attempts at interpretation by comparison with the Vulgate, have proved far from satisfactory. The beginning of the poem corresponds with Job, xxix, 2.'

As the instances adduced thus far have been derived from religious poems, it may be imagined that the precedent of church hymns had some influence on versifiers, and this may well have been the case, but, broadly speaking, the use of rime may be traced, so far as Old English poetry is concerned, to a desire to gratify the ear. Rimes are found not only in religious verse, but in heroic poems, in which ecclesiastical influence was at its lowest. A plain instance occurs in *Beowulf*, l. 1014:

fylle gefægon, fægere geþægon,

joyed in the feast, partook of [many a] fair [mead-cup]—

which is strictly parallel with the examples previously cited. Sometimes, however, instead of the two half-lines of the same line riming, the rime is between the corresponding half-lines of consecutive long lines, as in the case of the following examples:

Ða ic furþum weold folce Deniga
ond on geoguðe heold gumena rice.[1]

When erst I ruled the people of the Danes
and in my youth held kingship over men.

hwæþre him gesælde ðæt þæt swurd þurhwod
wrætlicne wyrm, þæt hit on wealle ætstod.[2]

natheless it happened to him that the sword pierced through
the dragon quaint, so that it stuck in the wall.

Another ornament is assonance or half-rime. The paraphrase from Job supplies several instances: *geteoh, onwrah*; *wægum, wongum*; *beofode, lifade.* Others are: *wæf, læs; gebunden, geþrungen.* The same principle expresses itself in such jingles as *wordum ond worcum, swelan ond swellan, wigum ond wæpnum*, etc.; and even in compounds like *wordhord.* Many alliterative or riming combinations constantly recur and possess the character of formulae standing for ideas in some instances related, in others directly opposed. Such are *leoht ond lif, wer ond wif, ord on ecg, hond ond rond, habban ond healdan, singan ond secgan, leof ond lað, innan ond utan.*

[1] *Beowulf*, ll. 465-6. [2] *Ibid.* ll. 890-1.

This suggests the remark that convention is rampant in Old English poetry which boasts a vast multitude of circumlocutions and figurative terms—trite metaphors which are introduced as alternative expressions. Thus *Widsith* opens with the line:

> Widsið maðolade, wordhord onleac.
>
> Widsith spoke, word-store unlocked.

Here 'wordhord onleac' signifies exactly the same as 'maðolade,' the only difference being that, to us, it is more picturesque. But we should be much deceived if we thought of the addition as anything more than a typical instance of verbal redundancy. We shall find a parallel use of it in *Beowulf*, ll. 58-9:

> Him se yldesta ondswarode,
> werodes wisa, wordhord onleac.
>
> Him the eldest answered,
> Leader of the troop, word-store unlocked.

The phrase has a touch of poetical fancy, but it has evidently become a commonplace of speech, a mere humdrum *façon de parler*. A somewhat analogous example occurs in the lines:

> Him þa ellenrof ondswarode,
> wlanc Wedera leod, word æfter spræc,
> heard under helme.
>
> Then him answered brave,
> Proud prince of Wederas, word after speech,
> Stern under casque.

In this instance 'word æfter spræc' is as obviously superfluous as 'wordhord onleac,' while 'heard under helme,' though more graphic than 'ellenrof' is a stereotyped expression used twice later in the poem, and each time in the weaker half-line. This, as we have seen, is pre-ordained for the reception of the less essential elements of a sentence, but the foregoing examples show that the stronger half-line may hold the redundant phrase.

Old English is rich in synonyms, especially in the case of the simplest ideas, objects, and experiences. A word like 'mann,' for instance, has many substitutes—'wer,' 'guma,' 'ceorl,' 'secg,' 'sawolberend,' etc.; while verbs that signify dying, going, speaking, etc., exist in plenty. In some passages substantives which are quite or nearly synonymous take the place of pronouns, and the gust of the writer induces him to load person or thing with descriptive expressions of identical or similar tendency. If we turn to the passage in *Beowulf* in which the pestilent Grendel is first introduced, we shall be struck with the fact that the persecuting goblin is belarded with terms like 'a dark death-shadow,' 'hideous,' 'a solitary monster,' 'a demon,' 'an enemy of mankind,' several of which perform the function of pronouns.

Equivalents may be used in apposition to each other, or they may be used singly to avoid the repetition of some common word, or in preference to it. Thus 'hranrad,' 'swanrad' ('whale road,' 'swan road'), alternate with 'sæ' ('sea'); 'wundenstefna' or 'bundenstefna' ('ornamented prow') and 'sundwudu' ('sea-wood') with 'scip' ('ship'); 'gomenwude' ('game-wood') or 'gleobeam' ('glee-beam') with 'hearpe' ('harp'). When the word 'hearpe' does occur, it is often associated with 'sweg' ('hearpan sweg'='noise of the harp')—the two having become welded into a formula. The office of king or leader is very commonly indicated by the complimentary terms 'helm' ('helmet') and 'hleo' ('guard') respectively. Beowulf, as a prince of royal blood, and captain of a band of adventurers, is called 'hleo wigrenda' ('guard of warriors') or 'eorla hleo' ('guard of eorls'). On succeeding to the throne he is described as 'Wedra helm' ('helmet of the Wederas'). Thrice King Hrothgar is called 'helm Scyldinga' ('helmet of the Scyldingas' or Danes). 'Helm,' therefore, is clearly a synonym for 'cyning.' When men of birth, princes or lords, are named, it is a frequent practice to mention their parentage, as in the line

> Hunferð maþelode, Ecglafes bearn.
>
> Hunferth spake, Ecglaf's child.

Several of the synonyms cited are what are known in Old Norse lore as *kenningar*—that is, terms, usually composite terms, bringing forward some characteristic, external or internal, and in that way defining the person or thing in question. A warrior is one holding a shield ('lind-,' 'rond-,' or 'bordhæbbend'), 'one wearing a helmet' ('helmberend'), or 'one carrying a spear' ('gar-' or 'æscberend'). Or his exceptional fierceness may cause him to be described as 'battle-wolf' ('hildewulf') or 'sword-wolf' ('heorowulf'). This usage may be considered the poetical counterpart of the cognizance—'swin ofer helme' ('boar-image on helmet')—worn by warriors and burnt with their corpses.

Finally, we come to the *scóp's* style of narration with respect to the marshalling of his facts. Here we light upon an undoubted weakness of Anglo-Saxon poetry, in which there is seldom any regard for the gradual development of a plot, the character of the actors being always thought of as vastly more important than the circumstances leading up to the critical points of a relation. This may be due to the lyrical origin of the epic. It seems to be generally admitted that long poems like *Beowulf* were evolved from shorter ones—songs, dirges, tales, and the whole field of artistic speech covered by the comprehensive word 'giedd.' It cannot be imagined that guests in hall would always, or often, be prepared to accord the *scóp* the privilege of reciting an epic poem in full. The minstrel would have to be content, in most instances, with a 'rhapsody'—that is, a portion of some epic, or *résumé* of some myth, nicely calculated for the occasion. Thus in *Beowulf* the *scóp* beguiles the journey to Heorot by recounting Sigemund's slaughter of the dragon. As the hero was on his way to a similar adventure, this was a happy inspiration. The *scóp* had an ample store from which to draw. He was

cyninges þegn,
guma gilphlæden, gidda gemyndig,
se ðe ealfela ealdgesegena
worn gemunde.

the king's follower,
A famous man, mindful of tales,
Who minded very many old legends
Galore.

The tale of Sigemund is given only in the briefest outline, and not as a formal *giedd*, but, to judge from the recital of the story of Finn at the banquet following Beowulf's arrival, the *scóp* conceived of an *ealdgesegen* as already well known to his hearers, and therefore felt at liberty to dwell capriciously on certain features without entering into the motives or antecedents. But we cannot be certain that we have here a typical 'rhapsody,' since it forms part of a longer poem, and may well have been curtailed, to prevent too great an interruption of the principal theme. Be that as it may, there is an undeniable tendency in Old English poets to fasten on important moments of a narrative without due preparation, to neglect the provision of suitable links or transitions, and to over-elaborate the subjective element at the cost of picturesque description.

CHAPTER IV

BEOWULF

Now that some idea has been afforded of the art of versification and literary mannerisms of the *scóp*, we may turn our attention to what is left of the epic poetry of the Anglo-Saxons, of which the most considerable, and only perfect, example is *Beowulf*. There are a few other remains, including certain fragments which it is reasonable to suppose formed part of poems on a scale as large as *Beowulf*, and suggest the melancholy reflection that many more compositions have been irrecoverably lost. Still, it is a cause for thankfulness that we are not limited to such unsatisfying performances as *Widsith* and *Deór's Lament*. If the former reveals consciousness of an historic past, and the latter of a cycle of sagas, the heritage of the northern peoples, they tell us next to nothing of the legends themselves, and produce a sensation akin to the disappointment experienced on entering a church and finding in the painted windows a chaos of colour and riddles of broken images. Some portions of *Widsith* do not merit even this compliment; they are like strata of dry bones. *Beowulf* is different. Full of vitality, it unfolds not only the legend which is its main subject, but the historical incident out of which it apparently grew.

We have not to proceed far with the narrative before its mythical character stands plainly revealed. Monsters like Grendel do not belong to any order of created beings; they are pure figments of the imagination. However, three times in the course of the story mention is made of an affair which there are excellent reasons for regarding as real. In a sense, therefore, it is possible to attach an approximate date to the action of the poem; we are able to say that the events which it describes took place in the sixth century. In the poem itself the episode is hardly distinguishable from the legendary contents, especially as fabulous elements are blended with it, but the tale is corroborated by historical writings as early as, or earlier than, the poem which supplies the following version. Hygelac, King of the Geats, made a raid on the Hetware, a tribe of Franks, in which expedition he was slain and his army routed. Among those who shared the adventure was Beowulf, Hygelac's sister's son, who escaped by swimming across the sea to his home—in Sweden? This incredible feat is rendered still more miraculous by the additional touch that he entered the sea bearing thirty suits of armour. Although his countrymen were worsted, Beowulf himself performed prodigies of valour, and of the Hetware who assailed him very few survived. He was thus distinctly the hero of the occasion. Exaggerated accounts of his exploits were circulated far and near, and, as time went on, the figure of the dauntless warrior attained the proportions of a demigod—the vanquisher of Grendel. The incident is first named *à propos* of the presents made to Beowulf on his arrival at Heorot, calling up memories of the famous necklace of the Brisings, which, after being the treasure of Eormanric, Hama, and Hygelac successively, passed into the possession of the Franks; secondly, on the eve of Beowulf's conflict with the dragon; and thirdly, after the hero's death, which augurs ill for the people of the Geats faced as they are with the prospect of a renewal of the feud with the Franks and Frisians.

Now for the confirmation. In his *Historia Francorum*, written towards the close of the sixth century, Gregory of Tours alludes to a certain King Chochilaicus, who sailed with an array of Danes to the shores of Gaul, disembarked in a part of Theudoric's domains, and ravaged it. He hoped then to return with the spoil, but Theudoric having despatched his son Theudobert against him, the prince defeated the Danes in a sea-fight and slew their leader. This account infers that the disastrous expedition took place between A.D. 515 and 520.

The story is repeated in a *Liber Historiae Francorum* of unknown authorship, composed about 729, with the noteworthy addition that the Danes assailed *Attoarios vel alios*, the *Attoarii* evidently corresponding with the Hetware of the poem. The Hattuarii, a branch of the Franks, were located on the lower Rhine.

Lastly, an *Historia Monstrorum etc.*, likewise anonymous, speaks of a gigantic King Hugilaicus, who bore rule over the Getae (Geats), and was so enormous that 'from his twelfth year no horse could carry him.' This Hugilaicus, it is said, was slain by the Franks.

For the reasons already stated, special importance attaches to this episode, although it has no necessary connection with any of the three adventures with which the poem is properly concerned. But the raid into the 'land of the Frisians' is not the only historical feature of the composition. We have seen that in *Widsith* exceptional attention is bestowed on Offa, King of the Angles. Here he figures as a brave young prince who beats off the attacks of the Myrgings from his paternal kingdom and delimits its frontiers, which Myrgings and Suabians had thenceforth to respect. The names of this monarch and his son Eomer occur in the list of the Mercian kings who claimed descent from the kings of the Angles, but it may be noted that Eomer, though called Offa's son in *Beowulf*, is there given as his grandson. In his legendary Life of Offa, Matthew of Paris states that Offa's queen was a woman of violent temper, who was banished from her own country and crossed the sea to Mercia. He calls her Dryda. In ll. 1931-44 of *Beowulf* we have a portrait of a queen which would suit Offa's consort as she is depicted by Matthew of Paris. The poet has been praising the virtues of Hygd, the wife of Hygelac, when he suddenly passes—apparently there is a lacuna in the text—to a princess of quite another complexion.

> A proud spirit showed
> The bold queen of the people, a terrible sin.
> Not one of her dear clansmen save the great lord
> Durst venture to look her full in the face.

If he did, he was first cast into prison and then executed with the sword. The word *þryðe*, here translated 'pride,' has been construed by some interpreters as the name of the queen in question, which, in that case, sufficiently resembles the 'Dryda' of Matthew of Paris to be regarded as identical. Ten Brink is one of those who accept this account of the word, but there are difficulties in the way, and Professor Sedgefield goes so far as to say that it has been shown to be impossible as a proper name.

That, however, is not a vital matter. This girl of ungovernable temper—an expression of maiden chastity in its hardest guise—was to be the wife of Offa; and, as for her murderous resentment of notice, 'the kinsman of Hemming put an end to that.' The poet, basing his story on the reports of 'ale-drinkers,' looks back to the time when she came over the sea the gold-decked bride of the young hero, and his information is that they lived together in high love without parallel. Offa is commended for his liberality and prowess and wise governance of his people. He was esteemed far and wide. The digression concludes with a reference to Eomer, Offa's son, who was distinguished for his martial qualities, 'skilled in battles.'

Again, if we turn to the names of the Danish princes mentioned in the poem, though the Old English forms do not exactly correspond with those appearing in the sagas, it is, in most cases, not difficult to make out their identity. Scyld answers to Skiöldr, Healfdene to Halfdan, Hrothgar to Hróarr, Halga to Helgi, Hrothulf to Hrólfr Kraki, and Hrethric—less certainly—to Hroerekr. Froda and Ingeld (Froði and Ingialdr) are named by Saxo Grammaticus, who wrote a *Historia Danica* in the twelfth century, relying for his older facts on the evidence of the more ancient sagas. Sarrazin holds that Beowulf himself is identical with the Boðvarr Bjarki of *Hrolfssaga*, but this point cannot be deemed established. Ongentheow is one of the many monarchs of *Widsith*. He is ruler of the Swedes.

Thus an atmosphere of history, or at least of tradition, surrounds the poem. The actuality of Beowulf—not, of course, as the slayer of Grendel, but as a prince and King of the Geats—may be reasonably assumed. It may be, as Professor Sedgefield observes, that 'the names of members of the Geatish royal family do not occur in Scandinavian records,' but the way in which allusions to Beowulf's parentage and connections are introduced, and the character of those allusions, do not differ in any way from references made to other royal descents in the work before us. Striking evidence of this truth is afforded by a comparison of the genealogical tables in Mr. Sedgefield's excellent edition of *Beowulf*. The pedigree of the hero which we there find does not bear the slightest trace of artificiality; it is of such a kind that we are almost of necessity convinced, not, perhaps, of the accuracy, but of the seriousness, of the statements on which it is based. They are discovered in different parts of the poem, and are interwoven with the narrative in the same voluntary or casual manner as the historical digressions before mentioned.

It is to be noted that, apart from the tale of Offa, there is nothing in the poem which in any way certainly connects the epic with England. The one doubt is as to the nationality of the hero and his comrades. Beowulf's exploits, his whole career, are associated with the northern shores of the European continent, but he may have belonged to one of the tribes which made the conquest of Britain. Beowulf was a Geat. Who were the Geats? On this point there is a division of opinion among scholars. It seems to be conceded that the name properly applies to the inhabitants of West Gothland in Sweden. Linguistically it is identical with the Icelandic Gautar and the Swedish Gotar. It has been thought, however, that, owing to some misunderstanding, the name has been borrowed from the Swedish clan and transferred to the Jutes. The theory that the Geats are really Jutes is undoubtedly tempting. It helps to account for the survival of the legend in an Anglo-Saxon poem, in which, according to some authorities, it has been continuously preserved from the days when Jutes, Angles, and Saxons were neighbours on the shores of the Baltic. The weight of the argument is against the explanation that the Jutes are intended, but as Gothland is the most southern of the three old provinces of Sweden, there appears to be no reason why the peoples of the Cimbric Chersonese should not have been acquainted with its traditions.

Turning to the mythical elements of the poem, the hero, in his wonder-working capacity, has been identified with Baldor the Sun-god; and in the match between Beowulf and Breca, the former has been supposed to represent the 'orb of day,' which, in its march from east to west, outstrips the breakers or waves. The monster Grendel typifies, it is said, the horror of the sea bursting its bounds in spring and autumn and swamping the fields and human dwellings, as it has been known to do, in historical times and with disastrous effects, in the Low Countries. This theory, it must be admitted, accords fairly well with the mysteries attaching to Grendel and Grendel's dam, but it is not thus that we are taught to conceive of him in the *Beowulf* poem. There we are reminded that Cain, for the murder of his brother Abel, was banished by the Almighty far from the abodes of men, seemingly to the cold regions of the north, where he begot a race of monsters, ogres, and giants. Grendel then, on this showing, was of the lineage of Cain.

The abode of the monsters is thus described in *Beowulf*:

> They a secret land inhabit, a wolf's hill-side, windy nesses, a perilous fen-path, where a mountain stream under the nesses' gloom down passeth, flood under ground. 'Tis not far thence, in mile-mark, that the mere standeth, over which hang rimy woods, forest fast-rooted, and overtop the water. There every night may one see an evil portent, fire on flood. Of the sons of men liveth not one so wise that he knoweth the bottom. Though the heath-stepper, beset by the hounds, the hart with strong horns, seek the wood, chased from far, first he shall give up his spirit, his life on the bank, ere he will hide head therein. 'Tis not a goodly spot; thence ariseth a mingling of waves dun to the clouds, when wind stirreth hateful storm, till the air darken, the skies weep.

This passage may well be compared with a similar account in one of the Blickling homilies—that on the Mass of St. Michael.

> As St. Paul was looking towards the northern region of the earth, from whence all waters pass down, he saw above the water

a hoary stone; and north of the stone had grown woods very rimy. And there were dark mists; and under the stone was the dwelling place of monsters and execrable creatures. And he saw hanging on the cliff opposite to the woods, many black souls with their hands bound; and the devils in likeness of monsters were seizing them, like greedy wolves; and the water underneath the cliff was black. And between the cliff and the water there were about twelve miles, and when the twigs brake, then down went the souls who hung on the twigs, and the monsters seized them. These were the souls of those who in this world wickedly sinned and would not cease from it before their life's end.[1]

The points of resemblance between the two passages are so many and so striking as to raise the question whether one may not have been copied from the other, or, if not that, whether both may not have had a common original. But the matter that seems of most importance just now is that Grendel, whatever he may have symbolized at an earlier period, is, for the poet and his readers, a demon in likeness of a monster. One of the epithets applied is *helrunan*, and this, it is clear, is not a mere term of abuse. It is plainly stated also that the Danes, to aid whom in their extremity Beowulf took ship, were heathens. They performed sacrifices in heathen temples, and offered up prayers to the Soul-Destroyer, *i.e.*, the Devil. 'Such was their custom, the heathens' hope, 'twas of hell they recked in their imaginations; they knew not the Almighty, the Judge of Deeds, nor wist they the Lord God.' When, therefore, the unholy Grendel carried off the courtiers of Hrothgar, all pagans, all strangers to the blessed rite of baptism, he might be said to claim his own.

But it is quite time that a sketch was given of the plot, especially as *Beowulf* is, before all things, a poem of action. After a prologue referring to the kings of the island Danes, and chiefly remarkable for a description of

[1] Morris's tr.

the passing of Scyld, the founder of the dynasty, we read of the building of a spacious hall called Heorot (hart) by Hrothgar, who then bore rule in Seeland. There he and his vassals live in the greatest happiness day after day, song and harp enlivening them, until from the moors comes a monster named Grendel to wreck everything. Entering the hall by night, he, 'grim and greedy,' steals thirty sleeping thanes and returns to his den. On the morrow there is lamentation and weeping, but this, alas, is only the beginning of evils! The horrible phantom repeats his visit—he comes again and again, and reaves more unhappy thanes from their beds. Twelve winters this continues, and at last Heorot stands desolate. The Danes are at their wits' end what to do.

Then Beowulf, Hygelac's thane, being apprised of Grendel's misdeeds, sets forth in a vessel with thirteen chosen comrades on the chivalrous errand of quelling the oppressor. From the wall the Danish guard, whose duty it is to occupy the sea-cliffs, catches sight of the bright shields in the gangway and marvels who the men can be. Beowulf explains, and he and his company proceed to Heorot. Again he is challenged and made to declare his errand—this time by Wulfgang, a valorous nobleman, Hrothgar's minister and messenger, who, after consultation with the King, ushers Beowulf into his presence. Forthwith King and Prince conclude a fast friendship. The Geats are entertained in the 'beer-hall,' and a clear-toned *scóp* sings to them and the Danes who sit with them. Beowulf recounts his swimming-match with Breca, and then acquaints Wealhtheow, Hrothgar's queen, with his resolve to perform deeds of daring or bide the day of death.

Hrothgar and his men now withdraw, while Beowulf and his party remain and await the coming of Grendel.

In due course the monster arrives and straightway kills one of the Geats. Then he stretches out his hand after Beowulf, but speedily finds that he has met his match. The hero holds him in a way that inspires Grendel with fear, and then rises, still keeping the assailant in his terrible grasp. Thereupon Grendel begins to think of flight and the fens, but can wrest himself free only with the loss of an arm and a shoulder. This mutilation spells death, and Heorot is delivered. As a manifest token of triumph, Grendel's 'grip'—his hand, arm, and shoulder—is deposited by the victor under the wide-spreading roof.

Naturally Hrothgar is full of gratitude. He tells Beowulf that he will cherish him as a son and overwhelms him with presents. At a banquet in the mead-hall the king's minstrel sings of Finn and Hengest and the burning of Hnæf, and Queen Wealhtheow makes a pretty speech to Beowulf, to whom she gives a ring. All seems well once more, but Grendel has a mother, who is constrained to live in dreadful waters and cold streams. To revenge her son's hurt, she comes and seizes Hrothgar's favourite attendant, Æschere. Beowulf, as it chances, is not there, but he is quickly summoned and does his best to console the King. The hero has a wonderful sword called Hrunting, an heirloom, which in battle has never failed any man that has grasped it. With this Beowulf sallies forth to encounter the female monster. He plunges beneath the swirl of waters, but it is a whole day before he can find her. At length a baleful light similar to that which heralded Grendel's approach to the thanes at Heorot proclaims her near. Beowulf is in the clutches of Grendel's dam.

For the first time Hrunting, the flashing falchion, fails the Prince at his need, and it had been a sorry journey for Beowulf but for his corselet—that and holy God, the disposer of victory. On regaining his feet he descries a huge sword with keen edge—an antique weapon forged by giants. Seizing the hilt, the champion cuts the throat of the fury. 'She collapsed on the floor, the sword was bloodstained, the warrior rejoiced in his work.'

Then the lifeless body of Grendel is discovered—maimed just as the conflict at Heorot had left it. Beowulf shears off the head and carries it by the hair to Heorot. There he gives an account of his adventures to Hrothgar, telling him how the protection of God alone saved him from disaster, how Hrunting failed, and how the Ruler of Men showed him the old sword and mighty hanging on a wall. 'Golden-hilt'—for this seems to have been a proper name like Hrunting—is then placed in the hands of the aged warrior-king, who bestows good advice on Beowulf. He is now, Hrothgar says, in the prime of his strength, but soon sickness or the sword, fire or flood, may rob him of it. Beowulf then takes leave of the King of the Danes, who rewards him with twelve treasures and bids him come again quickly.

The hero returns to his home, where King Hygelac and Queen Hygd make much of him and inquire as to his fortunes since he formed the sudden purpose to seek strife over the salt water. Beowulf replies at length and then orders Hrothgar's presents to be borne in—the towering helmet, the figure of the boar's head, the gray corselet, the splendidly decorated sword. The curiously wrought wondrous treasure Wealhtheow gave him—a collar—he presents to Hygd; and Hygelac reciprocates by bestowing on him a relic of Hrethel, Hygd's father, a falchion adorned with gold. 'There was not among the Geats better treasure in the shape of a sword. That laid he in Beowulf's bosom and gave to him seven thousand [pieces of money?] house and throne.' During Hygelac's lifetime Beowulf exercises privileges and enjoys possessions co-ordinately with him, but his uncle retains the sovereignty over the country at large.

At this point occurs a break and we now read of what happened *ufaran dagum*, which, we find, signifies when Beowulf had been fifty years a king. By a sort of parallelism—perhaps intentional—there appears on the scene a dragon stalking by night. The dragon will play an important, and indeed tragic, part in what remains of the poem, but after he has been introduced the writer harks back in order to let us know what has happened in the interval. Hygelac had been laid low and Heardred his son had met with a violent death—that we learn at the outset, but subsequently information comes in richer measure. We are told of the expedition against the Hetware in which Hygelac loses his life and Beowulf greatly distinguishes himself. On his return by swimming the hero cannot be persuaded to take the crown at the expense of the legitimate heir, Heardred, who is a boy, but supports him with friendly counsels in public until he is of age to wield the sceptre. Then Eanmund and Eadgils revolt against their uncle, the Swedish King Onela, and flee to Heardred, who harbours them. For this attention he is attacked by Onela and receives a mortal wound.

Beowulf then ascends the throne. As king, he does not forget the murder of his kinsman, but befriends Eadgils, who, with an army, crosses the sea and slays the King, their common enemy. Thus Beowulf wins through every one of his fights until the day when he has to do battle with the dragon.

For three hundred winters this dragon has guarded a treasure concealed by men of old time in a cairn or cave underground, hard by the sea-surge. One day by accident a poor slave discovers the cave and brings to his lord a vessel of beaten gold. Then the cairn is explored and treasures carried away. When the dragon awakes and perceives the theft, he takes dire vengeance, setting fire to houses far and wide; and amongst others the King's palace, the 'gift-stool' of the Geats, is melted in the whelming flame. Enraged, the lord of that people goes forth with eleven attendants to reconnoitre the dragon. Before a detail is given of the actual struggle, the fatal issue of the fight, Beowulf's predestined end, is foreshadowed for us. We see him seated on the 'ness' or headland—the *goldwine Geata*—and bidding farewell to his retainers. His mind is exceeding sorrowful. The fate is nigh that shall attack the old man, seek the treasures of the soul, and part life and body asunder.

The dragon emerges from his lair; the fight begins. Although Beowulf has armed him with a sword, a relic of ancient days, his weapon belies its fame, and his men prove recreant. The hero is in straits. The fire-breathing dragon is close upon him, and his retainers, instead of forming a circle about him, flee for their lives to a wood—all save Wiglaf, a son of Weohstan, the Swede who slew Eanmund. Wiglaf's shield is burnt by the monster's breath, and the boy then takes shelter behind his kinsman's shield. Beowulf deals a mighty stroke, but Nægling—the name of the sword—breaks in twain. The dragon then rushes upon him and bites him in the neck, but Wiglaf plunges his sword into the 'worm's' belly, and Beowulf administers the *coup de grâce* with a dagger, wherewith he bisects the creature. The hero, himself mortally wounded, does not lose thought of the treasures, which his faithful Wiglaf fetches at his desire, and on which he gazes in his pain, at the same time returning thanks to the Lord of all, the King of Glory. 'Now,' he says to his companion, 'that I have sacrificed my old life for a treasure-hoard, do thou satisfy the people's need.'

Beowulf soon dies, and the spectacle of his dearest friend stretched on the ground dead is a sore trial to the young Wiglaf. The 'assassin' lies dead also—the fearful earth-dragon. It is not long before the poltroons who durst not brandish javelins in defence of their liege lord quit the shelter of the wood and come to the spot where Wiglaf, wearied out, is supporting the hero's shoulder and trying to rouse him with water from his death-swoon. He pours contempt on them, reminding them of Beowulf's gifts, for which they have made such a wretched return.

The main body of retainers is posted in a fort on the summit of a sea-cliff. To them Wiglaf sends a messenger to announce the sad tidings. The messenger does more—he magnifies his office by expatiating at length on a variety of topics, going back upon past times and such ancient history as the slaying of Ongentheow, the old King of Sweden, and uttering dismal prophecies of the future. All then arise, and wend sadly and tearfully to Eagle's Ness to view the strange scene. Wiglaf exhibits the treasure, the hero's body is burnt, and the poem concludes with a description of the funeral ceremonies.

Such, in its main features, is the tale of Beowulf, but, as the reader is already aware, the poem abounds in episodical matter, historical and legendary. Before quitting the topic of its contents, it will be well to advert to one more element, if only because it forms a connecting link between this poem and *Widsith*. To any one who has perused the latter composition at all attentively the name of Hrothgar, the builder of Heorot and Beowulf's host, is necessarily familiar. It is joined with that of Hrothulf or Hrothwulf, the pair being cited as exemplary allies. Now if we turn to ll. 1015-17 of *Beowulf*, we shall meet with a similar conjunction:

> In the high hall were the stout hearted kinsmen,
> Hrothgar and Hrothulf. Heorot within was
> Filled with friends.

Widsith informs us that both took part in repelling the vanguard of Ingeld and annihilating the army of the Heathobards at Heorot.

According to a conjecture of Müllenhoff the Heathobards were a branch of the Heruli, who were originally seated in Seeland, and by whose expulsion the Danes were enabled to erect their island kingdom. Müllenhoff is of opinion that during the period of the truce—the time of the building of Heorot and the Grendel incidents—the princes of the Heathobards and those of the Danes dwelt side by side in Seeland, but Ten Brink holds it more probable that Ingeld's capital lay in some other Danish island or 'somewhere on the East Sea.'

It is from the lips of the aged Beowulf that we learn the motive for the resumption of strife (ll. 2024-66). Freawaru, the daughter of Hrothgar, is plighted to Ingeld, son of Froda, king of the Heathobards, as a means of terminating the feud between the clans. On the occasion of the marriage the bride is escorted to her future home by a retinue of Hrothgar's thanes, when, through carelessness, stupidity, or worse, one of the Danish nobles appears adorned with spoils taken from a slain Heathobard, whose son is present at the feast. An old Heathobard, who had been in the fray, recognizes the treasure and points it out to his young countryman, commenting meanwhile on the extraordinary insolence of the stranger in thus parading his father's triumph.

A fight follows in which the Dane is killed, while his

antagonist escapes—'he knows the land.' The result is that all oaths and pledges are dissolved on both sides; and Ingeld's love for his wife becomes cooler, as wild longings for revenge surge up in his bosom. Beowulf tells us no more, but it is plain from the brief reference in *Widsith* that in the war which was thus provoked the Danes captained by Hrothgar and Hrothulf were victorious.

Ten Brink suggests that the story was the subject of songs that were current in Denmark just prior to the last migration of the Angles, who bore them to England. At some time or other the substance became incorporated with the Beowulf legend, to which were attached other tales connected with the leading narrative, but in no way essential to it. *Beowulf*, therefore, resembles *Widsith* in the sense that it has attracted into its orbit a number of old-world traditions without giving to them that degree of explanation necessary for their comprehension. We shall have occasion to discuss this characteristic more fully hereafter; meanwhile the not unreasonable suggestion that constituents of the poem were derived from folk-songs raises the kindred (and crucial) questions of date and origin.

One fact which stares us in the face and cannot possibly be ignored is that it is difficult to associate the poem with England. It is true that the names Scyld and Beowa are found in the list of West Saxon kings, whose dominions included Wiltshire, that the terms *Grendles mere* and *Beowan hammes hecgan*, relating to places in Wiltshire, occur in a charter of 931, and that the expressions *Grindeles pytt* and *Grindeles bec* are contained in other charters. These coincidences are interesting, but do not carry us very far. The most that can be inferred from them—assuming the identity of Beowa and Beowulf and a monopoly of the name Grendel by the monster—is that the legend was known to the West Saxons in some form, but not necessarily, or naturally, in the form that we have it here.

As the scenes and personages are Scandinavian, it may be deemed an easy solution of the problem to suppose a Scandinavian original, from which the poem in its entirety has been either translated or adapted. But the acceptance of this theory creates a new perplexity. The conjectural date of the poem is the end of the seventh or commencement of the eighth century, at which period the Scandinavian proper names, some of which have been adduced, have only a rough correspondence with those in the text. The latter are undoubtedly more primitive, being derived from older forms of which the saga names are corruptions. To judge from the fact that many of them have been discovered in monastic *libri vitae* and other documents, they are thoroughly English. The inference is that the legends were domesticated along with the names and transmitted as a common heritage of the Anglo-Saxon race. This conclusion involves a broader sense of nationality than might have been expected, but it is by no means impossible that stories of Beowulf were traditional in this country, being included in the repertory of the gleeman order. Some critics, however, seem unable to accommodate themselves to the singularity of a phenomenon violating what is for them a first and fixed principle—that no primitive nation ever borrowed the heroic legends of another. These stories are more likely to have survived in oral accounts of the Geats, whence, it has been argued, the poet—a travelled *scóp*—most probably obtained them,[1] afterwards formulating them in his own fashion. There is much to be said for

[1] The expression 'ic gefrægn,' which occurs several times in the course of the poem, may be thought to indicate actual search for information, but it is probably no more than an epic formula. The phrase 'ealudrincende oðer sædan' may be compared with

this view of the case, which certainly does away with the initial difficulty—the incongruity of the subject with the language.

Whichever version of the circumstances we prefer—whether we hold that, by a sort of natural process, a number of songs and stories have gradually crystallized into a poem of larger dimensions on the soil of England, or that the matter was given in the shape of legends preserved on the reputed scene of the actions—it hardly admits of question that the poem in its present state is the work of a single writer. What that writer accomplished was, perhaps, not a new and original composition, but a revision or redaction of earlier experiments more or less similar. This, however, is open to debate; much depends on our conception of the sources of the narrative.

It is tempting to connect with the finality of the poem the 'Christian colouring' of certain passages. The legends themselves have come down from pre-Christian times, but the writer who last handled them and left his impress on them, was a Christian, possibly a monk, and therefore imbued with sentiments that are sometimes in conflict with the deeds and dispositions he has to record. In such cases he feels impelled to point out and censure the imperfections of pagans, both male and female. There are many acknowledgements of the wisdom and overruling providence of God. Thus when Grendel slays one of the Geats, it is said he would have destroyed more, if God had not hindered him, and the spirit of the hero (Beowulf). Hrothgar, too, in a moralizing vein, remarks how wondrously God distributes gifts among men—talent, courage,

the way romance writers refer to their sources and Minot's artificial rubric prefixed to his pæan on the siege of Calais:

How Edward als þe romance said
Held his sege befor Calais.

dwelling-place. This seems inconsistent with the statement made at the outset of the poem that the Danes are heathen, without knowledge of God. Much stress is laid on this point, and therefore if Hrothgar has been converted to the faith by Beowulf's precepts and example, so important a consequence of his visit would, it might be thought, be triumphantly proclaimed. But the poet has had time to forget—he has unquestionably forgotten.

This suggests that the poem still lacks the master's last touches, his final recension. There are further grounds for this suspicion in a certain inequality of treatment. The epic falls into two main compartments, or, as they are sometimes called, lays—the lay of the Grendel adventures, and that of the duel with the Earth-dragon. The former seems complete, and the second lay appears to bear somewhat the same relation to it as *Paradise Regained* to *Paradise Lost.* It is a sequel or continuation not contemplated in the original design, but certainly presupposing the Grendel lay. The first part is incomparably superior in point of arrangement. Apart from the episodes, the narrative marches straight on to the end, whereas in the second lay, though there is not so much of it, the recital is more confused. It goes forward, then backward, and the digressions are out of all proportion to the story proper. Still, the fight with the dragon and its concomitants are well managed and quite as dramatic as anything in the former part of the poem.

The interest of *Beowulf* is two-fold. It lies partly in the art which is utterly unlike that to which we are accustomed in modern literatures and can only be scientifically appraised in relation to Icelandic poetry, and partly in the tone and contents, which latter reveal a world of ideas and experiences strangely remote from modern life. Style and contents cannot be disjoined, since the courtly style is in keeping with the courtly scenes, and both manner and matter are plainly designed for a courtly audience. The poet has little feeling for external nature, his descriptive powers being confined to weird localities like the abode of Grendel's mother. Strength or beauty in the human form is rather implied than described. But we are never suffered to forget the splendour and etiquette surrounding the existence of princelings, and the pleasures and duties of exalted rank. The poem, in fact, affords an excellent picture of high society in Anglo-Saxon times, and possesses, in a general sense, considerable historical value. At the same time the moralizing tone which runs all through it smacks of ecclesiastical influence, and leads us to imagine that the writer, though versed in court life, was not quite of it. He might have been king's chaplain, or a bishop, if a *scóp* could attain such high office. He has given us much more than a barbaric, bloodthirsty saga, and, though he relates savage encounters and relates them vividly, it is the chivalrous motive rather than mere physical hardihood that engages his sympathy. It may be added that the poet has full command of the resources of his art, and his work has that sustained excellence which marks not only the practised craftsman, but the maturity of his craft, to the perfection of which many minds had contributed. The essence of this art is concentration; on each scene, each fact or trait, the poet focusses his spiritual energy and empties his armoury of words. He is less careful in the matter of transition. Verve rather than delicacy is the distinctive feature, the deliberate aim of this poetry. For the absence of finer effects—and there is little or no gradation of light and shade—there is ample compensation in the salient force and directness of the language and the pulse of a martial rhythm—priceless virtues in an heroic poem.

It may seem hopeless to inquire 'Who was the author of *Beowulf*?' Time was when it was the fashion to credit this, and nearly every work of poetical merit, to Cynewulf, but this wholesale attribution is now recognized to be unwarranted. The late Professor Earle believed that he had identified the poet; and although his conjecture must be received with caution, and full allowance made for scholarly enthusiasm, his remarks are extremely interesting, and no apology is needed for quoting them.

One question remains—who was the poet? My evidence here is of a lighter kind, and if it does not convince the student, it may, nevertheless, amuse him. If the above account of the poem is true, then it is the work of not merely a great poet, but of a person who could speak with weight and authority to the highest personages. If any names beyond those of the Royal family were preserved, we might expect to find the name of such a man written among them. There is one name of such eminence; it is the name of Higeberht, who was chosen by Offa to be Archbishop of Lichfield, and of whom we read in the life of Offa II that he was prime adviser of that King. We have good reason to think that vernacular poetry was in that age cultivated by the greatest persons, and Asser says that it was a favourite study of Alfred. But is there anything like direct evidence of Higeberht's authorship? I have attributed the court of Higelac to the English poet, and therefore here, if anywhere, we should find Higeberht's mark. One thing is plain; the poet, whoever he was, took this King and his disastrous fate out of the *Historia Francorum*, iii, 3, and he changed the form of the name from Chochilaicus to Higelac. Now, though it is not clear what Chochi means, it is pretty safe to say that it does not mean 'hige' = mind, reflection, understanding, and that Higelac is not a true equivalent for Chochilaicus, but an arbitrary adaptation for the poet's purpose. That purpose was to leave in the poem the mark of his own name, Hige-berht, and in the same spirit he gave Higelac's queen the name of Hygd, a word which is one of the same group, an abstract substantive to signify the very qualities with which he has adorned her—namely, good sense and discretion.

The late professor, of course, did not intend, and indeed

plainly discourages, any premature acceptance of a conjecture, confirmation of which is not yet, and may never be, forthcoming. It is a pleasing piece of guesswork, and though worth recording must for the present be dismissed as a half-playful excursus outside the scope of regular study. His method of accounting for the introduction of the Beowulf story into English soil stands on a different footing and calls for more serious attention. At the outset we are under an obligation to him for recalling a fact which, though noticed by historians, is apt to be forgotten—namely, that Offa's proper name was Winferth or Winfrith, and that he became known as Offa only when he developed a likeness to his mythical ancestor, whose virtues are celebrated in the poem. This shows, at least, that the memory of the older Offa was still green in Mercia, and we might therefore be tempted to imagine—a conclusion which Earle does not draw—that other traditions, including that of Beowulf, were similarly diffused.

Earle leans to the belief that ultimately the poem has for its basis a Scandinavian saga—apparently, the Gretti-saga; and he refers to a circumstance, which Vigfusson was the first to point out, that the expression 'hepti-sex,' considered strange in the Icelandic language, has its analogue in 'hæft-mece,' which is found in l. 1458 of *Beowulf*. But the poem, it is said, contains expressions which awaken Latin associations, and, speaking generally, it is remarkable that, while wholly Scandinavian as to its scene, it is devoid of Scandinavian words or phrases. How is this to be explained? Earle is convinced that the original writer was acquainted with the *Historia Francorum* with its account of the disastrous expedition of 'Chochilaicus,' and was himself a Frank. But he goes much farther and holds that the story of Beowulf was a piece of the prehistoric folklore, of which a new edition was made in Merovingian

Gaul, and which was then localized in 'Danish lands.' From Gaul the saga in a Latin dress, for which some Frankish scholar was responsible, passed over into England, and there it was worked up into the epic.

There may seem to be an inconsistency in dwelling upon a common Icelandic and Old English peculiarity in diction, and at the same time tracing the pedigree of the poem to a Frankish saga obscured by a Latin medium, but the difficulty is not real, or not great. Latin writers of the eighth century sometimes stumbled upon native words that were unmanageable. In such instances they escaped from their dilemma by placing the unmanageable word bodily in the Latin text, and this may be a case in point.

Earle has not solved the problem to the satisfaction of all scholars or perhaps many, but we may notice, in support of his theory, the undeniable fact that a number of Old English poems, as well as much Old English prose, are based on Latin originals. He *may* be right.

CHAPTER V

'FINNSBURH' AND 'WALDERE'

WE have now in a sense done with *Beowulf*—that is, as regards the principal topics. But the composition is of use not merely as affording the best example of its kind, but from the aid to be obtained from it in deciphering the fragmentary *Finnsburh* poem. The story told by Hrothgar's *scóp* at Heorot after Beowulf's return from slaying the monster Grendel concerns the vicissitudes of two foes, Finn and Hengest—it treats of a feud. With this is connected by identity of subject a short fragment of some fifty lines descriptive of a fight which took place in Finn's *burh*, which in this context appears to signify 'palace.' Despite its brevity the piece is of considerable poetical merit, and evidently formed part of a much longer composition. On these grounds its elucidation may fitly engage our attention. Curiously enough, an Icelandic fragment—the old lay of Biarki—depicts a similar battle in hall, the object of attack being King Hrolf Kraki—the Hrothulf of *Beowulf*. At dawn of day Biarki, the warder, alarms the inmates, saying: 'The day is up, the cock's feathers flapping; it is time to get to work. Wake and awake, comrades mine, all the noblest kinsmen of Adils. . . . Not to wine do I wake you, nor to woman's spell, but I wake you to the stern play of the war-goddess!' [1]

[1] Ker's *Dark Ages*, p. 297.

The Finn episode in *Beowulf* and the Old English fragment should be studied together, but, even so, the subject will not be free from some obscurity. By way of introduction it will be well to outline the story of Finn. King of the North Frisians and Eotens, the son of Folcwalda distinguishes himself by carrying off the daughter of Hoc, the princess Hildeburh. The indignant father sets out in pursuit and is slain. Years pass, and then Hnæf and Hengest, Hoc's sons, conduct an expedition into Finn's country in the hope of avenging their sire. A battle is fought, in which Hnæf falls, and also a son of Finn. Then a treaty of peace is concluded between Finn and Hengest, and ratified with ceremonial observances, after which the body of Hnæf is burnt on a funeral pyre, every honour being paid him, while Hildeburh laments son and brother, the victims of this unnatural strife. Hengest remains with Finn, by whom or by whose men he is cheated of revenge and killed. Two of his retainers, Guthlaf and Oslaf, escape, and, returning with an army, overcome and slay Finn, whose widow they take back with them over the sea. The Hocings, it should be observed, are Danes.

It is pretty evident that the fight described in the fragment is identical with that of which mention occurs early in the *scóp's* tale, and which results in the deaths of Hnæf and Finn's son—not that which Hengest provokes after the conclusion of the pact. Hengest is a king in the *Finnsburh* poem, whereas his retainers—seemingly in consequence of the fight—are described in the episode as following, lordless, the slayers of their ring-giver. In the fragment Hnæf is still the proud leader of an incomparable band of heroes. 'Never swains gave sweet mead better than to Hnæf gave his young warriors.' Up to that time but one had fallen—Garulf.

The situation seems to have been somewhat as follows.

Hnæf finds himself at Finnsburh, whither he had probably been invited in order to arrange or confirm a treaty of reconciliation. This object is frustrated by the perfidious temper of Finn, who cannot resist the temptation of venting his murderous hatred on his guests now, he thinks, within his power. The latter appears to have been forewarned by looks, words, or deeds, and not only forewarned, but forearmed. At night they retire to rest with their weapons, but certain of the party keep watch. Suddenly a strange light is observed, and suspicious noises are audible. What do these things portend? Hengest answers the question.

'The gables burn never.' Then exclaimed the battle-young King:

'Neither this nor dawneth it from the east, nor fleeth dragon hither, nor burn gables of this hall here, but hither bear [shields?] . . . Birds sing, crickets chirp, battle-wood resounds, shield answers shaft. Now shineth the moon wandering under clouds; now arise deeds of woe, which the spite of this people willeth to perform. But awake now, my gallants, lift up your hands, think on valour, brandish [your arms] in the front, be stout-hearted.'

Then arose many a gold-deck'd thane and girded on his sword. Then to door went the lordly champions, Sigeferth and Eaha, drew their swords; and at other doors [stood] Ordlaf and Guthlaf; and Hengest himself brought up the rear. Then Garulf told Guthere [Gunther, or so impelled his troop?] that as a courteous soul he did not wish to make a set attack on the doors of the hall nor take it by storm, but he asked openly, the bold warrior, who guarded the doors.

'Sigeferth is my name; I am prince of the Secgas, an exile known far and wide; many troubles, many hard fights have I endured. For thee is here appointed whether of the two thou wilt seek at my hands.'

Then on the wall was the din of slaughter; shield and helm brake in sunder in the hands of the bold; the floor of the palace resounded till, first of all earth-dwellers, Garulf, son of Guthlaf, fell in the fray, and about him many a good man and true, reeling corpses. The raven wandered swart and dusky; the gleaming of the swords was as if all Finnsburh were on fire.

Never heard I that sixty fought better in strife of men, and never attendants served sweet mead better than was served to Hnæf by his young warriors. They fought five days without one of the noble companions falling, but held the doors.

Then a wounded warrior went away, saying that his shield was broken, his war-garb ruined, and eke his helm pierced. Him straightway the guardian of the folk[1] questioned, how the warriors recovered from their wounds or which of the lads . . .

At this point the fragment breaks off.

It is singular that Garulf, who challenges Sigeferth, and is the first to fall, should be described as the son of Guthlaf, who both here and in the Beowulf episode is represented as on the side of the Danes. He cannot have joined the defenders of the hall since it is expressly stated that during five days not one of the sixty heroes was slain. We can only infer therefore that for some unexplained reason father and son were opposed to each other in this memorable contest. It is possible that Garulf espoused the cause of Finn for the sake of his countrywoman Hildeburh, but this is the merest conjecture.

Let us now turn to the Finn episode in *Beowulf*, from which we learn something as to the sequel. Hnæf having succumbed, his men under the leadership of Hengest take a sanguinary revenge, and few of Finn's thanes escape. Among the slain is a son of Finn and Hildeburh.[2] Finn arrives at the conclusion that he cannot master his enemies and proposes to Hengest the making of a treaty whereby the Danes are to be received at his court and obtain equal rights and privileges with the Frisians. Hengest assents; a treaty is drawn up and confirmed by both parties, and Finn swears a solemn oath that he will treat the survivors

[1] Probably Hnæf.

[2] Sons? The MS. is inconsistent.

with honour and distinction. No man in word or deed shall violate the treaty, nor shall the Danes, through treacherous attack, ever have cause to lament, though they follow, lordless, the assassins of their ring-giver, the necessity being imposed on them. If any of the Frisians remind the warriors of the murderous hate, the sword shall determine the matter.

Next follows an account of the burning of Hnæf's body with that of Finn's son. The blood-stained arms of the leader, his all-golden boar-image, and the corpses of his retainers, as well as those of the Frisians, heaped up around, are to be seen on the funeral pyre. Hildeburh sings mournful dirges; and at last, the flame having devoured up all, the warriors set out for home—for Frisia. (Hence it may be inferred that Finnsburh was not in the mother-country, but in some colony or domain that Finn had won for himself elsewhere.)

Hengest abides with Finn during the winter. All this time he keeps thinking of home, but may not urge his curved prow through the deep. The sea boils with storm and wages war with the wind. Winter locks the icebound waves. Then comes spring—fair is earth's bosom. Hengest quits the palace abruptly. His thoughts turn to revenge rather than to a sea-voyage, if only he may bring to pass that angry encounter which he contemplates with the children of the Eotens. So he evades not fate when Hun plants in his bosom Lafing, that best of blades, whose edge is well known among the Eotens. Also Finn is assailed by cruel sword-bale in his own home. After a journey by sea Guthlaf and Oslaf lament the grim grip; neither can restrain his restless mood. So the hall is reddened with the corpses of foes. King Finn is slain with a troop of his followers, and his queen captured. The Danish archers carry off to their ships all the monarch's furniture they can find in Finn's house—his brooches and precious stones. The noble lady they convey in a voyage to the Danes—conduct her to her people.

A very obscure passage in this tale is that in which Hengest's failure and death are referred to. In one or two places the reading is in doubt, and Ten Brink's explanation is somewhat different from the version we have adopted, taking Mr. Sedgefield's revised text as basis. Another point which calls for notice is the use of the term 'Eotens,' applied to Finn's people. We mentioned that in the opinion of some scholars the Jutes are intended by the word 'Geats.' The Finn episode almost suffices to refute this theory, since Hrothgar's *scóp* could hardly have blundered so far as to recite, on an occasion of festive harmony, a tale calculated to stir the embers of an old and bitter feud.

The story of the fight at Finnsburh by no means redounds to the credit of the Eotens or Jutes as a nation, and no conclusion can be drawn from their participation in the affair as regards the origin or transmission of the poem. The Anglo-Saxons appear to have forgotten, or to have been indifferent to, the tribal distinctions of their continental kinsfolk and treasured the memory of heroisms like that of Hnæf's warriors in a spirit of large patriotism.

In *Waldere*, yet another epic poem, of which two fragments remain, each consisting of about thirty lines, we get clear away not only from the special interests of the Anglo-Saxons, but from Scandinavian and North German traditions. As in the case of *Finnsburh*, the fragments tell us little, and here we have not the advantage of a *Beowulf* episode to eke out our knowledge of the facts underlying the three speeches, all of which are imperfect. The setting has been supplied by the tenth-century Latin poem of

Ekkehard of St. Gall,[1] aided by allusions in the *Nibelungenlied* and in *Biterolf*. The Anglo-Saxon poem is believed to date from the middle of the eighth century, and is therefore some two hundred years earlier than Ekkehard's version. The title *Waldere* has been bestowed on it from the name of the hero, 'Waldere,' being the Old English equivalent of the Old High German 'Walthari,' and the modern English 'Walter.' He is generally known as Walter of Aquitaine, and figures, despite this German name, as the representative, not of the Visigoths, but of Roman Gaul.

At the court of Attila, the terrible Hun, are three hostages, Hagen, Walter, and a princess, Hildegund. Walter represents Aquitaine, Hildegund Burgundy, and Hagen the Franks. The last-mentioned has been substituted for Gunther (the 'Guthere' of the Old English fragments), the son of Gilbicho, too young to be employed in that capacity. Hagen and Walter grow up together and are fast friends, while Walter and Hildegund from an early age are devoted lovers. After a time Hagen makes his escape. Walter and Hildegund also escape and travel with an abundance of treasure to Worms, on the Rhine, where they are discovered by Gunther. The young prince is indignant at the thought that they are in possession of his father's valuables, and, though Hagen attempts to restrain him, goes in quest of Walter. A fearful fight takes place in the Vosges, in which Hagen refuses to join. Walter kills all his opponents save Gunther, who then urges Hagen, without success, to enter the field against his former companion in exile. During the night Walter and Hildegund keep watch by turns in their fortress, and in the morning the Franks resume the attack. The three

1 The elder (*c.* 937).

chief actors all sustain wounds, after which peace is concluded between them.

Judging from allusions in the first speech, it was uttered after the first fight and before the second. Walter has performed prodigies of valour, and he is exhorted not to let his courage fail. Gunther, it is said, provoked the conflict unjustly, out of covetousness, and it is predicted that he will retire from the fight treasureless or 'sleep here.' As for the speaker, it is natural to suppose that it is Hildegund who thus spurs the brave Walter to fresh achievements. The half line which precedes the opening of the speech, 'hyrde hyne georne' will in that case point back to an intimation by the hero that he has no intention of resigning the struggle, though he seems to have entertained misgivings as to the quality of his weapon—the the sword Mimming. This appears from the reassuring expressions in which he is reminded that 'Weland's work' fails not any man who knows how to handle it, and also from the later injunction:

> ne murn ðu for ði mece; ðe wearð maðma cyst
> gifeðe to geoce unc.
>
> Have no care for thy sword; the best of treasures.
> It was vouchsafed us twain for succour.

Here the use of the dual 'unc' clearly points to Hildegund as the speaker. Of Walter's sword (which, by the way, in the Nibelungenlied is called 'Wasge,' not 'Mimming') we learn from the second speech—obviously Gunther's—that it had been Theudoric's intention to send it, along with much other treasure, to 'Nithhad's kinsman, Weland's son,' Widia, because he had been rescued by that worthy from sore straits. The confusion is extraordinary. In *Widsith* Wudga and Hama are bracketed as champions of Eormanric in the contest with Attila. It is fairly certain that this Wudga is identical with a certain Vidigoia, 'Gothorum fortissimus,' who, says Jordanes, 'Sarmatum dolo occubuit,' and was renowned in the songs of the people. In the legend the Huns took the place of the Sarmatians, and thus Wudga, or Vidigoia, became attached to Eormanric as the adversary of Attila. The name Widia is doubtless a variant of Wudga, and the hero has now been transformed into a vassal or ally of Theudoric, the Frankish monarch. There was an historical Witigis, a King of the Goths, who capitulated at Ravenna in 539; hence it seems probable—especially as in the legend Wudga delivered Ravenna to Eormanric—that the two real personages have been confounded. But what is infinitely more strange is that Widia should be represented as the son of Weland the Smith, a purely mythical being, of whose exploits we have already given some account.

Some, perhaps many, lines are missing before the passage in which the topic of Walter's sword is introduced, and what we have of Gunther's speech yields no very manifest clue as to the nature and purpose of the dialogue. Walter's reply, on the other hand, sheds much light on the point. Although Gunther would appear to have had the worst of the argument in the field of action, he makes a bold demand to his enemy to surrender, and insinuates that Walter owes his salvation to Hagen. The hero replies to this insulting suggestion by defying Gunther to strip him, thus weary of battle, of his gray corselet. Walter has great faith in this armour, which had been worn by his father before him. He is convinced that it will not betray him on the next occasion when he is set upon any more than on the last. But he does not trust in his armour only; if victory comes his way, it will be by reason of his deserts and the favour and justice of God.

The similarity of the names Hilde, Hildeburh, and

Hildegund belonging to the heroines of the legends of which Heoden, Finn, and Walter are the respective heroes is not more marked than the similarity of the legends themselves; and it is highly probable that the Hilde saga is the original or prototype of the other twö. It was partly to illustrate the apparent relationship—not mere coincidence—that the allusion to Hilde found in *Deór's Lament* was expanded on an earlier page. As only fragments survive of *Finnsburh* and *Waldere* the material basis of the poems had, in the same way, to be recovered by the collation of other sources. The effort has not been unrewarded. We are now able to estimate, with something like assurance, the kind of poetry in which our remote ancestors took delight. In its essence it is pagan—a quality which cannot be disguised by a thin veneer of religious sentiment due to the patronage of Christian editors. There is a relentlessness in the lust of blood that even the closest ties, the most solemn oaths do not avail to mitigate, but when this passion lies dormant, courtesy and kindness have ample scope. The rough morality, however, is rather chivalrous than Christian. The centre of the social system in each petty community or tribe is the hereditary chief or king; and reverence for his person, submission to his commands, is the first and almost the last duty of his attendant thanes. He, in turn, is expected to be the father of his country, and to set an example of rectitude, liberality, and courage.

Beowulf is the ideal monarch. As a prince with no expectation of succeeding to the sceptre and thus at liberty for adventure, he confronts and destroys noxious beings, the enemies not of his native land, but of humanity. As king, he lays down his life for his people, for whose welfare he is solicitous with his latest breath. Walter of Aquitaine is on a lower plane, but he typifies, in a remarkable degree, the splendid virtue of unyielding fortitude, of unquenchable heroism. Hnæf and Hengest are less admirable, because dominated by revenge; still, they and their men are paragons of valour and fidelity. War is a game to such intrepid spirits—indeed, we often encounter expressions like 'hildeplega' ('battle-play') in these poems—and the only, or principal, lesson high-born youth has to learn is that laid down in the words of Hildegund:

ðu scealt aninga oðer twega
lif forleosan oððe lange dom
agan mid eldum.

Thou must choose one of two things simply,
either to lose thy life or lasting fame
own among men.

Here, one can hardly doubt, the allusion is to the service of minstrelsy. Tacitus informs us that among the Germans old songs were the only kind of history, while Eginhard, in his Life of Charlemagne, refers to 'barbarous and very old songs, wherein were chanted the deeds and wars of ancient kings.'

The Finn episode in *Beowulf* has been rendered into English by Thorpe. He made use of a somewhat defective text, and in places his interpretation admits of a doubt. On the whole, however, the version is at once faithful and elegant, and, as such, appears worthy of reproduction at the close of this necessarily brief chapter.

There was song and sound
At once together
Before Healfdene's
Warlike chiefs,
The wood of joy was greeted,
The lay oft recited,
When the joy of hall,
Hrothgar's bard,
After the mead-bench,
Should recount
Concerning Fin's offspring,
When them peril overwhelm'd;
When Healfdene's hero,
The Scyldings' Hnæf,
In Frisian slaughter
Was doom'd to fall.

Not Hildeburh at least
Had need to praise
The faith of the Jutes:
She was of her innocent
Beloved ones deprived
At the linden-play,
Of her children and brothers:
They in succession fell,
By the dart wounded.
That was a mournful woman:
Not without cause.
Hoces daughter
The Lord's decree bemourn'd
After morning came,
When she under heaven
Might see
The slaughter of her kinsmen,
Where she ere had most possessed
Of worldly joy.
War destroy'd all
Fin's thanes,
Save a few only:
So that he might not
On the battle-place
Against Hengest
At all contend,
Nor the sad remnant
By war protect
From the king's thane;
But they to him conditions offer'd,
That they to him another dwelling
Would wholly yield,
A hall and high seat;
That they half power
With the sons of the Jutes
Might possess,
And at the money-gifts
Folcwalda's son
Every day
The Danes should honour,
Hengest's band
With rings should serve,
Even as much
With costly treasures
Of rich gold,
As he the Frisian
In the beer-hall
Would adorn.
Then they confirm'd,
On the two sides,
A fast peaceful compact,
Fin to Hengest
Earnestly, without dispute,
That he the sad remnant,
By his witan's doom,
Piously should hold,
That there no man
By words or works,
Should break the compact,
Nor through guileful craft
Should they ever complain,
Though they their ring-giver's
Murderer followed,
Lordless.
Since they were so compell'd;
But if of the Frisians any one,
By audacious speech
This deadly feud
Should call to mind,
Then it the edge of his sword
Should appease.
The oath was completed
And moreover gold
Rais'd from the hoard
Of the martial Scyldings
The best of warriors
On the pile was ready:
At the heap was
Easy to be seen

The blood-stain'd tunic,
The swine all golden,
The boar iron-hard,
Many an ætheling
With wounds afflicted
(Some had in the slaughter
fall'n).
Bade then Hildeburh
At Hnæf's pile,
Her own sons[1]
Be to the fire committed
Their carcases be burnt,
And on the pile be reduced
The miserable ones to ashes.
The woman mourn'd,
Bewail'd in songs;
The warrior ascended,
Wended to the clouds;
The greatest of death-fires
Roar'd before the mound;
Their heads were consum'd,
Their wound-gates burst;
Then out sprang the blood
From the corpse's hostile bite:
Flame swallow'd all
(Greediest of guests)
Those whom war had there of
life bereft.
Of both people was
Their flower departed.

The warriors then departed
Their villages to visit,
Of their friends deprived,
Friesland to see,
Its dwellings and high burgh.
Hengest yet
The death-hued winter
Remain'd with Fin,
Without strife,
His home remember'd
Although he might not
On the sea drive
The ringed prow.
Ocean boil'd with storm,
Warr'd against the wind,
Winter lock'd the wave
With icy band
Till that came the second
Year to the courts.
So now yet do
Those who constantly
Watch a happy moment,
Gloriously bright weather.
When winter was departed,
Earth's bosom fair,
The stranger hasten'd,
The guest from the courts.
He on wily vengeance
Was more intent
Than on a sea-voyage,
If he a conflict
Could bring to pass;
For he the sons of the Jutes
Inwardly remember'd,
So he refus'd not
Worldly intercourse,
When he Hunlafing,
The flame of war,
The best of falchions,
In his bosom placed;
For with the Jutes there were
Men fam'd for sword play,
Also of spirit bold.
Fin afterwards o'erwhelm'd
Cruel misery from the sword,
At his own dwelling,

[1] MS. 'son.'

When the grim one with gripe
Guthlaf and Oslaf
After a sea-journey
Grievously upbraided.
Reproach'd for his part in their
woes:
He might not his wavering soul
In his breast retain.
Then was the hall beset
With foemen,
Also Fin slain;
The king amid his people,
And the queen taken.
The Scyldings' warriors
To their ships bore
All the house chattels
Of the earth-king,
Such as at Fin's dwelling
They could find,
Of jewels and curious gems.
They on the sea-road
The princely woman
To the Danes bore,
To their people led.

CHAPTER VI

EARLY BALLADS

IN his introduction to the *Oxford Book of Ballads,* Sir A. Quiller-Couch whimsically discusses the question, 'What is a ballad?' If we understand him aright and may venture to state his conclusion in our own words, it is shortly this—that a ballad is a ballad, a thing to be felt, recognized intuitively, enjoyed *per se* rather than defined and analysed. For our present purpose it will be enough to quote the definition given in a well-known dictionary, while admitting its inadequacy—'A popular semi-epic or patriotic tale of adventure or daring, originally sung to the harp.' This account exactly matches the two poems of which we are now to treat.

One feature in the epic poems before reviewed—a feature on which we have been at some pains to insist—is their courtly or aristocratic tone. The heroes, Beowulf, Finn, Walter, all belong to the highest circles of society, and the interest of the narratives turns on the personal history and achievements of kings and princes, who, it may be added, are sufficiently remote in point of time as well as place. Even when the subjects are of less exalted position, and the *scóp* puts in a word for himself, the figure of the patron is necessarily prominent, the minstrel being almost inconceivable without the lord and the fortune of the former hingeing entirely, or nearly so, on the liberality or meanness, prosperity or adversity, of his superior.

In a certain loose and vague sense, those poems are patriotic—that is, they must be deemed to respond to the sentiment of a common race—but they are decidedly not popular in the ordinary and accepted sense. They are not founded on local incidents nor on the exploits of neighbours, in which the auditors might feel that they had a share, and of which, accordingly, they might be proud. The presence of one or other of these elements—preferably, of both—was necessary in order that a tale might be really popular: and to these conditions the ballads we are about to consider strictly conform. They are not properly epic, because the topics are historical and recent, not ancient and mythical, but those topics are unfolded in the epic measure, and in the words, phrases, and methods there are many echoes of the traditional heroic verse.

We have noted that, according to the evidence of Tacitus, history existed for the Germans only in the form of songs or poems. His exact words are 'carminibus antiquis, quod unum apud illos memoriae et annalium genus est' (*De Moribus Germanorum*, c. i). It is a singular circumstance that in the *Anglo-Saxon Chronicle* for the years 937, 941, 973, and 975, poetry is used instead of prose. Thorpe is inclined to regard these pieces as later insertions for which the original compilers are in no sense responsible, but it is open to us to interpret the phenomenon as an instance of reversion to type. Either the writer of the section found the poems ready to his hand or he felt moved to attempt versification as a relief from dry annalistic composition. Whatever the explanation, the poems are there—four out of the five which are the subjects of the present chapter.

The earliest of the ballads is *The Battle of Brunanburh*. The poem has been re-inspired and, so to speak, regained for the benefit of future generations by Tennyson's admirable verse rendering based, as he tells us, more or less on his son's translation in the *Contemporary Review* (November 1876). As the writings of Tennyson are more generally accessible than the *Anglo-Saxon Chronicle,* and his version may be studied by many in preference to the Old English text, it is of interest to learn how nearly the translation approaches the original in form and meaning. For the sake of comparison, therefore, we adduce parallel citations of a passage chosen at random, merely observing that several Old English copies of the poem have been preserved in different MSS., between which there are occasional variations, seldom of any importance.

Feld ðænnede
secgas hwate, siþðan sunne up
on morgen tíd mære tungol
glad ofer grundas, Godes condel beorht,
eces Drihtnes, oð sio aþele gesceaft
sah to setle. Ðær læg secg monig
garum ageted guma norþerna
ofer scild scoten. Swilce Scyttisc eác
werig wiges sæd.

All the field with blood of the fighters
Flowed, from when first the great
Sun-star of morning-tide,
Lamp of the Lord God
Lord everlasting
Glode over earth till the glorious creature
Sunk to his setting.

There lay many a man,
Marr'd by the javelin,
Men of the Northland,
Shot over shield.
There was the Scotsman
Weary of war.

This specimen shows that the late laureate's rendering is actually what it professes to be—a translation. It is seldom that it partakes of the nature of paraphrase, and then only in a very small measure. By an occasional happy touch Tennyson has known how to accentuate the poetical effect, but he has been careful to conserve to the poem all that he found there, adding at the same time little or nothing. We shall therefore assume a knowledge of the ballad in all essentials, and proceed to deal with some of the topics connected therewith.

Tennyson's prefatory note furnishes a brief epitome of the circumstances. He says:

> Constantinus, King of the Scots, after having sworn allegiance to Athelstan, allied himself with the Danes of Ireland under Anlaf, and invading England, was defeated by Athelstan and his brother Edmund with great slaughter at Brunanburh in the year 937.

The battle of Brunanburh, one of the most famous conflicts of the age which preceded the Norman Conquest, was due to the determination of the Danes to secure a footing in the island. Similar attempts had been made repeatedly and not, as we shall presently see, without success. The English, having dispossessed the old British inhabitants of most of the country, had to defend themselves against the attacks of kindred peoples eager for a share of the soil. The Northmen were not particular in their choice of allies, and associated with themselves, in their systematic aggressions, the 'harried Welshman,' the perfidious Scot. The Battle of Brunanburh was, in fact, a kind of Armageddon, in which the English won a decisive victory over a combination of hostile forces. The leaders of the expedition were Anlaf (Olaf), a Danish prince who bore sway in Ireland, and his father-in-law, Constantine III, King of Scots, who were supported by Owen of Cumberland, and a number of British chiefs. Dr. Weymouth propounded the theory that 'by Scots here is probably meant Irish,' on the ground that 'three out of the four MSS. of the *Anglo-*

Saxon Chronicle edited by Thorpe mention Ireland—all four mention Dublin—as the place of retreat of the defeated invaders.' The Scots, at their first appearance in authentic history, were no doubt the people of Ireland; nevertheless, Dr. Weymouth is demonstrably in error. That the Scots of Britain are intended is proved by the lines:

> Also the crafty one,
> Constantinus,
> Crept to his North again,
> Hoar-headed hero.

The details of the expedition, however, are somewhat confused, and the site of the battle, especially, is an almost insoluble problem. It is not that the records are at all scanty. Accounts of the affair appear in the *Anglo-Saxon Chronicle*, in Egil's saga, in the works of Simeon of Durham, William of Malmesbury, Florence of Worcester, Ingulf—not to mention later historians. What is so troublesome is that these different versions, where they are not mere copies or abstracts, not only contain discrepancies, but are hard to reconcile with the probabilities of the case. Thus Simeon states that Anlaf set sail from Ireland with six hundred and fifteen ships, and landed in the Humber. This is confirmed by Florence of Worcester and the Chronicle of Melrose. But it has been represented as incredible that Anlaf should have undertaken the long, toilsome and dangerous voyage round Scotland, and having reached Northumbria, should have proceeded to the most southerly part of it before disembarking.

Simeon states also that the battle took place at 'Wendune,' and here he has certainly some support from the Icelandic saga, where the site is described as 'à Vinheidi vid Vinuskóda.' But the name 'Brunanburh' is that found in the ballad and most other versions, and if we accept the account that the Danes landed in the Mersey, it seems quite feasible that the subsequent engagement occurred at the village of Barnborough, on the Dearne, a stream which falls into the Don a short distance above Doncaster. William of Malmesbury gives no hint as to the place of landing, but he declares that Anlaf was beguiled by Athelstan to advance into the interior. On the assumption that Anlaf entered not the Humber, but the Mersey, it has been argued that Bromborough, near Birkenhead, was the scene of the conflict, but the extreme uncertainty of the matter may be gauged from the fact that while some scholars favour Dumfriesshire others espouse the cause of Devonshire!

It would occupy too many pages to compare the various narratives point by point, but peculiar interest attaches to the report in Egil's saga, which contains a long account of the battle and its preliminaries, followed by the song. Northumbria is described as the northernmost part of England, having York for its capital. Olafr (Anlaf), 'King of the Scots,' with a large army crosses over to England 'towards the south,' and arriving in Northumbria, makes a hostile advance. He is at first victorious, and defeats the eorls appointed by Athelstan to defend the province. Then Athelstan assembles his forces, and a parley ensues between the chieftains. It is agreed that the place of battle shall be defined by a fence of hazel, and that there shall be no harrying of the neighbouring country. The field was for the most part a plain, having on one side a river, on the other a vast wood. After fruitless negotiation with a view of buying off the invader on the terms of his becoming a tributary of Athelstan, the fight begins, and is described at great length, ending in the defeat and flight of Anlaf and the triumph of Athelstan.[1]

This version—the version accepted by the kinsfolk of the vanquished—has no higher authority than those that have

[1] J. B. Davidson, *Athenæum*, 9th October 1885.

come down in English or Latin, and the task of evolving from this tangled skein an orderly, consistent, and trustworthy narrative of events is plainly one that does not fall to the merely literary historian. In Lappenberg's *History of England under the Anglo-Saxon Kings* the story is told as well, perhaps, as in any other chronicle. At any rate, Lappenberg will serve.

The opportunity of profiting by Æthelstan's participation in the affairs of Europe was not neglected by his conquered, but not humbled enemies in the north of England. Anlaf (Olaf) a son of Guthfrith, had married a daughter of Constantine, King of Scotland. Through this union the plan may necessarily have suggested itself of a Dano-Northumbrian kingdom, which might serve as a wall of defence for the independence both of Scotland and Cumberland. An extensive combination of the Danes in England and Ireland with the Scots and the kindred states was consequently formed against Æthelstan. With six hundred and fifteen ships Anlaf arrived in the Humber from Ireland, and united his forces with those of his father-in-law, Constantine, Owen of Cumberland and many princes of British race. Æthelstan, who was well skilled in the art of deceiving by negotiation, made use of the time thereby gained to place himself in a condition to oppose them with a well-appointed army. The courage and craft of Anlaf are acknowledged by his enemies. In the guise of a harper, he gained admission into the camp of Æthelstan, where he played before the King and his guests during their repast, and was enabled during his stay to gather the information he sought. Disdaining the hireling's reward that had been bestowed on him by Æthelstan, he buried it in the earth. Whilst engaged in the operation, he was observed and recognized by a soldier who had formerly served under him. The man instantly communicated his discovery to the King, who on upbraiding him for not having betrayed the Dane the instant that he recognized him, received for answer, "King! the same oath that I have taken to you I took to Anlaf; had I violated it, you might have expected similar perfidy towards yourself; but deign to listen to your servant's advice; move your tent to some other spot, and there await in patience the arrival of your reinforcements." The King followed the soldier's counsel. In the evening Werstan, bishop of Shireburne, arrived with a body of forces, and established his quarters in the place previously occupied by the King. During the night Anlaf entered the camp, where his first victims were the bishop and all his attendants. Following up his success Anlaf next attacked the quarters of the King, who, being awakened by the tumult, succeeded after a severe conflict in repelling the assailants.

Two days after the above-mentioned event was fought the great and memorable battle of Brunanburh, in Northumberland, one of the most celebrated conflicts of the Middle Age, in which was manifested to the utmost all the intenseness of hate existing between the contending nations. The Saxon chronicler, disdaining the simple language of prose in recounting the glorious achievements of his heroes, Æthelstan and his brother Eadmund, has recourse to song, and from his verses later annalists have chiefly drawn their accounts of this famous battle. Five kings, among whom Eligenius, an under-King of Deira, is named, seven earls of the Danes and their allies, a son of the Scottish King Constantine, who fell by the hand of the valiant chancellor Thurcytel, by whom the citizens of London and a body of Mercians under Singin were led to the conflict, besides an almost countless number of warriors, are said to have fallen. Constantine and Anlaf fled to their ships. Among the slain on the English side were Ælfwine and Æthelwine, brothers of Thurcytel and cousins of Æthelstan. No greater carnage, says the poet, had ever taken place in the island since those proud warsmiths the Angles and the Saxons from the east first came over the broad sea to Britain. According to the Scandinavian accounts of the battle of Brunanburh, on which, however, no implicit reliance can be placed, some Northern mercenaries, led by Egil and Thorolf, were in the pay of Æthelstan, who, by annihilating the Irish auxiliaries, had mainly contributed to the victory; and, if credit may be given to Egil's saga, Eric Blodöx, the son of Harald Harfagr, by the fair Hewa, had, some time before the battle of Brunanburh, been invested by Æthelstan with the kingdom of Northumbria, on condition of defending it against Scots and Irish and receiving baptism. But on this point not only are all the English chroniclers silent, but an event hereafter to be mentioned, which took place ten years later, under the second successor of Æthelstan, appears to have occasioned the cession to him of that country [1]

[1] Thorpe's translation, vol. ii, pp. 114-17.

The ballad states that the Norsemen, 'shamed in their souls,' fled over the breakers in their nailed prows to Dyflen (Dublin).

Also the brethren
King and Atheling,
Each in his glory
Went to his own in his own West-Saxonland,
Glad of the war.

In these lines we seem to have a clue to the tradition that the battle of Brunanburh was fought in the neighbourhood of Axminster, Devon. Leland quotes a Norman-French chronicle to that effect. A cartulary of Newenham Abbey (near Axminster), A.D. 1340, asserts that King Athelstan gave the church of Axminster to seven priests, who should for ever serve God for the souls of seven earls and many others slain in a battle that raged from Calixdown to Colecroft in 937. In the British Museum there is a chart of the south coast of Devon and Cornwall, *temp.* Henry VIII, which speaks of 'v Kings, viii erles' as slain at Axminster in the time of King Athelstan. Lastly, Camden in his *Britannia* describes Axminster as 'a town famous only in ancient histories for the tombs of those Saxon princes who were slain in the bloody battle of Brunenberg and brought hither.'

On comparing these accounts with the Song—universally regarded as most authentic—it will be seen that the seven (or eight) earls are supposed to have fought and fallen in the army of Athelstan, whereas they were really Anlaf's supporters. This discrepancy proves that the memory of events had become dim, the precise circumstances forgotten, but there must have been some reason for connecting Axminster with the great battle, and this may be found in Camden's statement that the bodies of the Saxon princes were buried there. Assuming this to be true, the inhabitants may in time have come to believe—not unnaturally—that the battlefield itself was not far off. Guesses as to the locality would gradually harden into positive assertions in the absence of evidence to the contrary, and even in the teeth of such evidence. But the Battle of Brunanburh, wherever else it befel, did not take place anywhere in Wessex, otherwise there would be no point in the words—

Went to his own in his own West-Saxon-land.

We have now to say something of the ballad on its poetical side. It is, first and foremost, a lyrical effusion, the few facts which it mentions being no more than are needed for the historical definition of the subject. The poet refers to those facts not in the style of a chronicler, but as a patriot exalting over the discomfiture of his country's foes, and the glory reaped by the royal brothers on the momentous occasion of which he treats. Professor Ker rather depreciates the poem by calling it a 'conventional panegyric.' True, it has none of those intimate touches that suggest personal participation in the event in question; not a syllable would lead to the conclusion that the writer knew more of the battle than he might have learned by hearsay. But the excellence of the paean is the fruit not of a cold study of models and precedents, but of the glowing passion, the intense realization with which the writer enters into every phase of his theme. Poetry conceived in the womb of real feeling shapes itself after its kind, and seldom fails of fit and adequate expression, the gift of eloquence and some preliminary cultivation of versification being always supposed. This is an instance in which a born poet has 'let himself go' with an almost unconscious employment of the means, having already acquired sufficient practice in the difficult art of alliteration to move freely in the shackles of technical obligations. His own instincts guide him in the culling of epithets, the forging of sentences, and the marshalling of his matter. Phrases like 'the *fallow* flood' are to be met with, but we ought, perhaps, to look upon them as consecrated rather than trite. In any case, the poet has succeeded in clothing his composition with a freshness and originality, a power and incisiveness sustained to the triumphant close, which testify alike to a strong personality and the profound impression left on his imagination, and the imagination of his age, by the glory and carnage of the Battle of Brunanburh.

Great as was the victory of Athelstan and Edmund, the political effects were somewhat meagre. Anlaf escaped alive—destined, ere his death, to cause more trouble; and, as for the Danes, there had long been permanent bodies of them in Mercia and Northumbria—particularly in the Five Towns (Derby, Lincoln, Nottingham, Stamford, and Leicester). It may be observed in passing that the Danish name 'Deora-by' (Derby) had supplanted the Saxon Northweorthig, just as, further north, Whitby had lost the name Streoneshealh, by which it had been known to the early Saxon inhabitants.

Athelstan's death tempted the Danes to new enterprises, and Anlaf was summoned from Ireland to be their King and leader. Owing to this revolt Edmund, Athelstan's son and successor, experienced great difficulty in establishing his authority, but in the end he prevailed. One of his first achievements was the reduction of the Five Towns before mentioned; and this is the subject of the second of the patriotic songs, which takes the place of a prose entry for the year 941. As poetry, it has no special distinction, and a similar remark applies to the rhyming records of 973 and 975, save that they strike a chord of human interest, which bids us pause.

The former describes, in exuberant strain, Edgar's coronation at Bath.

> Her Eadgar wæs Engla waldend
> corðre micelre to cyninge gehalgod
> on ðære ealdan byrig Acemannes ceastre.

(At this time was Edgar, lord of the English, with great pomp consecrated as king in the ancient burgh, the city of Akeman.)

The latter, doubtless by the same hand, commences with the mention of Edgar's death—the inevitable end of all that state.

> Her geendode earðan dreamas
> Eadgar Engla cyning, oðer leoht ceas him,
> wlitig, wynsum, þis wace forlet lîf þis læne.

(At this time Edgar, king of the English, ended earth's joys, chose him another light, beauteous, winsome—left this frail, this transient life.)

The periphrastic expression 'ceas him oðer leoht' reminds us of *Beowulf* (l. 2469) 'godes leoht geceas,' and the yet commoner circumlocution 'geceas ecne ræd,' which may be translated 'chose the eternal course.' Phrases like 'wace' and 'læne lîf' are frequent in Cynewulf's writings, as applied to mortal existence, but these are less singular.

Edgar's son Edward was a 'cyld unweaxen,' and the miseries of his reign are directly attributable to the King's immaturity. Part of the song is taken up with an account of these troubles, but space is found for narrating the appearance of a comet—a celestial portent on which the writer, with evident complacence, bestows the correct name.

There are other metrical entries in the *Anglo-Saxon Chronicle*, some of them quite short, but, ignoring these little canticles, let us turn to a ballad of very great interest and importance—the *Lay of Maldon*. Although differing from the *Battle of Brunanburh* in certain features, it cannot be reckoned in any sense inferior to it—many, indeed, will be of opinion that of the two the *Brunanburh* ballad could be better spared. The main distinction between them is that the *Battle of Brunanburh* conserves the memory of a national event, and is marked by a breadth of treatment suited to the grandeur of the theme and the momentous nature of the occasion. The *Lay of Maldon* deals with a similar incident, but one of a local or provincial significance, a parallel to which may be found in 'an unlawful entry' into Devon and Cornwall in the reign of Edward III. In the year 1339, Stow tells us, 'certaine pirates of Normandy and Geneva,' did much injury on the coast of Devon and Cornwall, and at last entering Plymouth Haven, burnt certain great ships, and most of the town. They were met, however, by Hugh Courtenay, Earl of Devon, a knight of eighty, who slew or drowned about five hundred of the said pirates! In each instance there is a recognition of the principle *noblesse oblige*. The author of the lay must either have been present at the combat or in close touch with eye-witnesses, since he is able to furnish a consecutive version of the affair illustrated with manifold details which compose a vivid picture of valiant resistance and heroic self-sacrifice.

The *Lay of Maldon* is not one of the series in the *Anglo-Saxon Chronicle*, and it is almost by a miracle that it has been saved to us. The only known manuscript of the fragment—for, despite its comparative fullness, the poem is obviously incomplete—was destroyed in the fire at the Cottonian library in 1731. Fortunately Hearne, whose appetite for everything Old English was insatiable, had made a copy of the ballad, which he published as prose at the end of his edition of John Glaston's *Chronicle of*

Glastonbury Abbey. The title of the ballad is, of course, of modern origin, some editors and historians preferring the alternative description the *Death of Byrhtnoth*, which suggests more the character of the piece. The poem is a tragedy in the sense that the splendid courage which it celebrates was entirely wasted. The ransom demanded from, and refused by, the proud ealdorman and his gallant East-Saxons was paid, and for generations continued to be paid, by the English people in the form of Danegeld thanks to the pusillanimity of King and council, who, instead of taking example by the noble spirit of the patriot, allowed themselves to be cowed by his fate. For the setting of the ballad we may glance once more at the pages of Lappenberg.[1]

Æthelred's joy at this treaty must have been the greater, as the intelligence had without doubt reached him of an attack made by the Northmen upon Ipswich; Justin (Jóstein) and Guthmund, probably in the service of the Norwegian King Anlaf or Olaf Tryggvason (who either accompanied them or arrived soon after) ravaged the country thereabout the more cruelly in revenge for a defeat they had suffered a few years before. The brave ealdorman Byrhtnoth, on being contumeliously challenged by the Northmen, encountered them at Maldon, where he died the hapless death of the vanquished. So great was the panic caused by this deplorable event among the chief counsellers of Æthelred, that, yielding to the advice of the Archbishop of Canterbury, Sigeric, of the ealdorman Æthelweard, and of Ælfric the ealdorman of Mercia, he allowed them to purchase a peace for the provinces in which their respective possessions chiefly lay, for the sum of ten thousand pounds, in consideration of which the two chieftains above-mentioned engaged to cease their ravages in England, and to maintain firm peace. This is apparently the treaty alluded to in the preamble to another between the three Norwegian leaders Anlaf (Olaf), Justin, and Guthmund, wherein it was said that a sum of twenty-two thousand pounds had been given for the peace, from

[1] Vol. ii, p. 154-6 (Thorpe's translation).

the conditions of which, viz., those attaching to homicide, to breach of the peace, to the attaching of stolen goods, etc., it is evident that no immediate departure of the hostile army was contemplated. The precise date of the treaty cannot be ascertained, as no mention occurs in the chronicles of a payment of twenty-two thousand pounds; though it may be presumed to have taken place very shortly after that between the archbishop and the two ealdormen [*sic*]. By this treaty it appears the Danes or Northmen were admitted as guests, like the old German warriors (*hospites*) into provinces of England, where till then they were unknown, and, as in many similar cases, out of an apparently temporary state of things, a burden arose not to be shaken off by peaceable means. At the same time the levying of the tribute on the people gave rise to an impost, which under the name of Danegeld continued as an odious and oppressive tax, on the laity long after the object of its imposition ceased to exist. The clergy were exempted from the payment of Danegeld, a benefit for which they are probably indebted to its original propounder, the archbishop Sigeric.

The name 'Maldon' does not occur in the poem, but the locality of the engagement is roughly indicated by the mention, twice made, of the River Pante, on whose banks the battle took place. The present name of the stream is the Blackwater, which it has borne at any rate from Drayton's time, since the 19th song of his *Polyolbion* has the quaint lines:

> When *Chelmer* scarce arrives in her most wishèd bay,
> But *Blackwater* comes in through many a crooked way,
> Which Pant was call'd of yore, but that by Time exil'd
> She *Froshwell* after hight, then *Blackwater* instil'd.

The course of the Pante, it will be noted, is described as 'crooked'; and what happened apparently was this. The vikings sailed upstream until they arrived at a point where the river takes a north-easterly direction. It then makes a westward bend. The vikings, having moored their vessels, took possession of the wedge or enclave thus formed. In the meantime Byrhtnoth with his armed array descended from the north and drew up his force on the left bank of the Pante before it quite reaches the apex of the angle. Hence the Northmen, when they attack, are said to advance

west ofer Pantan,

'west' being tantamount to 'westan' (from the west) just as we speak of the west wind.

The poem commences with an indication of the temper of the English on the eve of the conflict—death before dishonour. Joined to this is a personal and chivalrous devotion to the doughty eorl. Bryhtnoth instructs and encourages his men, having done which he alights from his horse in their midst, for it had been resolved from the first that all should fight on foot.

The quick seamen have sent me to thee, bidding me tell thee speedily to send rings. Better for you is it to requite this spear-rush with tribute than we should inflict so hard a battle.

Appealing to Byrhtnoth as the richest of those present, he informs him that if it is his purpose and desire to ransom his people, he has only to pay money to the seamen according to their assessment, and they will repair to their ships with the treasures and maintain peace. The English leader disdains the proposal. Raising his shield and brandishing his slender spear, he answers angrily and with determination that the tribute his people consents to pay consists solely of javelins, poisoned shafts, and old swords. The messenger is to carry back the news that the eorl with his host stands there undaunted, and that he will defend that heritage, the territory of his master Ethelred, land and people; the heathen shall fall in the fray. Too shameful it seems to him that they should embark with English treasures without a blow being struck; now that they have penetrated so far inland, they are not to obtain treasure so softly. 'Rather point and edge become us—grim warplay.'

The herald having been thus dismissed, Byrhtnoth commanded his men to advance and station themselves, one and all, along the bank of the stream. Owing to the flowing tide, neither army could deliver an attack, and the opposing forces, drawn up in line, stood confronting each other, no damage being done except by arrow-flight. Then the 'shield of the warriors'—'hælaþa hleo'; observe this echo of old heroic poetry[1]—bade a veteran fighter, whose name was Wulfstan, the son of Ceola, defend the bridge with his family; and the first man who ventured to set foot on it was transfixed by Wulfstan's javelin. Beside him stood the fearless warriors, Ælfere and Maccus, and staunchly they defended themselves against the foe the while that they could wield weapons. The odious guests found this reception so little to their liking that they now resorted to cunning and sent a request that they might cross the ford and ascend the opposite bank. Byrhtnoth, in his pride, granted the desired leave to large numbers of the enemy. Then began the son of Byrhthelm to call over the cold water, whilst his men listened: 'Now room is made for you, come quickly to us, ye men, to battle. God alone knoweth who may possess the battle-field.' Then waded the wolves of slaughter—for water they recked not—across the Pante, across the shining water, bearing their shields and bucklers, even to the land. There stood Byrhtnoth and his men in readiness, facing the cruel foe. He commanded them to form the battle-hedge with shields and maintain the array firmly against the enemy. Then was the conflict nigh and the glory accompanying it. Then

[1] See p. 53.

was the time come wherein doomed men were to fall. Then was a cry raised, ravens flew around, the eagle greedy for carrion, while on earth was tumult. They (the warriors) made file-hard spears, sharpened javelins fly from their hands, bows were busy; shield received point; bitter was the shock of battle. Men fell; on each side were prostrate young soldiers. Wulfmær was wounded, Byrhtnoth's kinsman, his sister's son, and 'chose a bed of slaughter'; he was sorely hacked with falchions. Vengeance soon overtook the vikings, since Eadweard struck one so sorely that he fell at his feet a doomed champion. For this the leader gave thanks to his chamberlain that he had such a son.

So the fight went on. The lads strove who should be the first to 'win life' among doomed men in the war, Byrhtnoth encouraging them and bidding each lad throw himself heart and soul into the conflict if he wished to achieve glory among the Danes. The lord of the combatants was now himself wounded by a 'southern' javelin —that is, one that had been hurled from the English side, and was returned by a sea-warrior. The eorl thrust with his shield so that the shaft brake in sunder and the spear sprang back. In a rage he stabbed the proud viking who had given him the wound, and drove his weapon through the lad's neck, and with another penetrated his heart. The eorl was the blither; he laughed, proud man, and spake thanks to his Maker for the day's work the Lord had granted him.

Then out of the hand of some soldier flew a spear that transfixed 'Ethelred's thane.' Beside him was standing an immature lad, his attendant in the field, Wulfmær the Young, the son of Wulfstan, who full quickly drew the bloody javelin from the warrior's body and sent it flying back. The point entered the person of the man who had struck the lad's master, and he too was levelled with the ground. Then strode an armed man to the eorl, intent on carrying off his rings and armour and ornamented sword. But Byrhtnoth was not yet dead. Drawing from its sheath his broad and brown-edged blade, he struck at the corselet, but a certain mariner maimed his arm, and prevented him from doing more. The yellow-hilted sword fell to the ground; the hero could hold the hard weapon no more. Still, he bade the bold lads, the good comrades go forward, though he himself could no longer stand firm afoot.

The hoary warrior, conscious of his approaching end, now looked up to heaven, and said: 'I thank thee, Ruler of the peoples, for all the pleasures I have enjoyed in the world. Now, merciful Creator, I have most need that Thou grant to my spirit this measure of good that my soul may pass to Thee, may journey to Thy domain, Lord of the angels, in peace. I beseech Thee that the miscreants of hell may not dishonour me.' Thereupon heathen common soldiers hewed him in pieces, and the two heroes Ælfnoth and Wulfmær, who stood beside him, were stretched even with their lord and gave up the ghost. Some of the Englishmen now lost heart and fled from the battle. The first to desert were the sons of Odda—Godric and Godrig. The former leapt on his master's steed, forsaking the good man who had given him many a horse; and he and his brother and many more sought the fastness of a wood. Here it is recalled that Offa had once said to brave and generous Byrhtnoth in a public assembly that there many spoke proudly who would not afterwards show constancy on the field of battle.

Thus then the leader of the folk, Ethelred's eorl, was fallen; all his comrades saw that their lord lay slain. Then hastened to the spot the proud thanes, men who would not fly, all of them resolved on one of two things, either to lose their lives, or avenge their beloved commander. Ælfric's son, the young warrior Ælfwine, exhorted them, saying: 'Remember the valorous speech, the talks we often had at the mead, when we, heroes in hall, raised threat concerning hard conflict. Now may it be proved who is brave. I will now demonstrate to all my noble birth, that I was of high descent in Mercia. My old father was called Ealhhelm, a wise ealdorman, blest with worldly possessions. Never shall thanes make it a reproach to me among the people that I am willing to depart from this army, seek home, now that my leader lies hewn in pieces on the battlefield. To me it is the greatest of calamities; he was both my kinsman and my lord.'

Then he strode forward, thinking of revenge, and one of the sailors was overthrown by his weapon. Offa then spake, brandishing his ashen spear, and saying: 'Now that our prince is fallen, need is there that each of us others fight like heroes, so long as we can have and hold our weapons. Godric, the coward son of Odda, hath betrayed us, split our forces, shivered the shield-fence.' Leofsunu, raising aloft his buckler, addressed the warrior: 'I promise I will not flee hence a foot's breadth, but will go further and avenge my dear lord in battle. They shall have no need round Sturmere[1] to reproach me, a steadfast warrior, for journeying home lordless and turning away from the battle.' Then Dunhere took up his parable: 'Never may he fear nor have a care for his life, whoso thinketh to avenge his lord among the people.'

The retainers, the grim javelin-bearers, obeyed. They fought hard, and as they fought, prayed God that they might avenge their lord and friend, and work havoc among

[1] 'On the south, the river Stour at its rise, stagnates in a great fen, called Stourmeer' (Gough's *Camden*, vol. ii, p. 43, 1st ed.).

their enemies. The hostage gladly lent his aid. He was of a stern kindred in Northumbria, the son of Ecglaf; and his name was Æscferth. He sent forth showers of arrows. Standing in the forefront Eadward the Tall boasted that he would never flee a foot's breadth, and he made good this boast, breaking the shield-wall and fighting with the warriors. Ere he sank in the slaughter, he worthily revenged his treasure-giver on the seamen. Ætheric, brother of Sibyrht, did the like, and many another, cleaving the keeled shield. Then Offa slew the seaman, the kinsman of Gadd, but was soon cut down. He had, however, fulfilled the promise he had made to his lord, for they had mutually sworn that they would both ride to the burgh, return home safe and sound, or both fall in the army and perish of their wounds on the field of battle. Like a true thane he lay next to his lord. Then was there a breaking of shields; the seamen pressed, maddened with fighting; often javelin penetrated the life-house of the doomed. Wistan, the son of Thurstan, threw himself into the *mêlée*, and slew three of the enemy before the son of Wigelin fell to his spear. A few words of general description follow, ending with a half-line previously used, which has something of the effect of a refrain:

wæl feol on eorþan.

The earth was drenched with gore.

Oswald and Ealdwald, brothers, urged the warriors to hold out and ply their weapons vigorously; and then out and spake the old vassal, Byrhtwold, grasping his shield and brandishing his spear: 'The mind should be the harder, the heart the bolder, the courage greater, as our strength diminishes. Here lies our leader, all cut to pieces, a good man in the dust. For ever may he grieve, whoso now thinketh to turn from this battle-play. I am old and stricken in years; hence I will never stir, but think to lie beside my lord, by so dear a man.' Likewise Æthelgar's son Godric emboldened them all to conflict; often he sent javelin, slaughter-spear, spinning among the vikings. Foremost went he among the people, hacking and havocking until he fell in the fray. That was not the Godric that flinched from the fight.

Here the fragment ends. Following Ten Brink's example, we have given what is practically a literal translation of the piece. Some passages have been omitted, others curtailed, but the version as a whole is much fuller than that supplied by the illustrious German scholar. One reason for adopting this course is the undefinable charm of balladry. In this instance it is a contemporary history permeated by the spirit and illumined with the art of heroic poetry, but the lyrical element is at least equally prominent. The writer does not mention himself, but his personality is none the less felt. The narrative is charged with emotion—there is passion, there is pathos—and it is this undercurrent of irrepressible sentiment, of keen sympathy, which, more than any other feature, constitutes the poem a ballad. It is not a mere tale to amuse, but a trumpet-call to the courage and patriotism of the nation, which, in some quarters, were evidently beginning to flag. The contrast between the conduct of Ethelred and that of 'Ethelred's thane,' as set forth in Lappenberg's account and the anonymous poem, is deplorable, and must have caused the monarch to blush for shame, if ever he heard or read this obituary of the noble Byrhtnoth. It is possible that the ballad was never finished, the composition having been interrupted and, so to speak, stultified by the news of the national surrender. On this supposition there is twofold reproach in the abrupt conclusion:

Næs þæt na se Godric þe ða guðe forbeah.

That was not the Godric who forbore the fray.

Finally it may be observed that the ejaculatory style, the half-inconsequent manner, due to the want or neglect of connective particles, which is native to Old English heroic poetry, better accords with ballads than with set epic poems. A ballad is irresponsible, a law unto itself; it contains as much or as little logic as the fancy or feeling of the writer will tolerate, whereas order, regularity, sequence, belong to the essence of narrative poems properly so called. One is meteoric; the other has, or should have, something of the formality and precision of a planetary system.

PART II. RELIGIOUS POETRY

CHAPTER I

CÆDMON

When we turn from the Old English epic to the religious poetry of the Anglo-Saxons, it surprises us to find that, while the subjects are different, the diction, style, and temper to which we have become accustomed remain, to a great extent, unchanged. In truth, the two classes interlock. The war-poems embrace passages that are almost obtrusively religious; nothing, for instance, can be more edifying than Byrhtnoth's valediction to the delights of life—the faith and submission with which he commends his spirit into the hands of his Maker. The heathen gods have no part in these narratives, except dimly as devils, but the frequent occurrence of the term 'fæge' ('doomed') testifies to a species of fatalism more pagan than Christian. This word survives in the curious Scots expression 'fey,' signifying a strange alteration in a person's habits or demeanour on the approach of death, the same notion being conveyed by the English provincialism 'against his end.'

In most Old English religious poems will be observed a strong infusion of martial metaphor; sometimes, indeed, the symbolism is so consistent as to raise the question whether the writer has rightly apprehended the humble character and humble status of the first disciples, or has consciously idealized them conformably with his own ideas of what was befitting the princes and protagonists of the early church. Peaceful Oriental fishermen are transformed into Anglo-Saxon eorls or thanes, the breath of whose nostrils was war. We are reminded of the astounding exaggerations of the *Boke of Saint Albans*: 'Christ was a gentleman and bare coat-armour.' 'The iiii. Evangelists were Jews and of gentlemen come by the right line of that worthy conqueror Judas Machabeus, but that by succession of time the kindred fell to poverty after the destruction of Judas Machabeus, and then they fell to labours and were called no gentlemen; and the iiii. doctors of holy Church Saint Jerome, Ambrose, Augustine, and Gregory were gentlemen of blood and of coat-armour.' In a society in which the highest virtue was military courage and nobility was a hereditary attribute, it was found difficult to assimilate the simplicity of the Gospel. Christianity, on the part of many, was official and only skin-deep. The worship of Odin had been prohibited, but kings were still proud to trace their descent from the northern divinity. Thus the *Anglo-Saxon Chronicle*, under the year 626: 'Pybba begat Penda; Cryda begat Pybba; Cynewald begat Cryda; Cnebba begat Cynewald; Icel begat Cnebba, Eomær begat Icel; Angeltheow begat Offa; Wærmund begat Offa; Wihtlæg begat Wærmund, and Odin begat Wihtlæg. Penda, of course, was a pagan, but his successors were Christian, as was also the chronicler, to whom we are indebted for the pedigree.

It was necessary, then, that Christianity should be naturalized in order that it might take its place in the scheme of Old English life. Parts of the Old Testament could undergo this process with far less incongruity than the New; and it may be remarked that the author or editor of *Beowulf* seems to have possessed a better acquaintance with the earlier than with the later books of Scripture. It so happens that the Cottonian MS. (Vitellius A 15) which contains *Beowulf* contains also a fragment of *Judith*, a poem relating to the heroine of the Apocrypha, which has always been in high esteem with the critics. It has not only been preserved in the same codex, but it is instinct with the same warlike ardour; and, apart from a few proper names, we might have imagined that we were perusing a northern saga, every feature to which we have drawn attention being faithfully reproduced. We even meet with the phrase 'fæge frumgaras' ('doomed chieftains'). Accounts of Old English religious poetry usually commence with Cædmon. For the reasons assigned we will venture on an innovation and begin with—Higeberht?[1]

The tale on which the poem is founded is supposed to date from the second century B.C. By some it has been believed to be an allegory, but, more probably, it is legend with a substratum of truth, although no incident in any way akin to it is recorded by Josephus. The following are the main outlines: Judith is a beautiful Jewess, who attempts to save her native town, Bethulia, from Holofernes, the general of Nebuchadnezzar, by gaining admission to the tent of the Assyrian commander at the imminent risk of life and chastity. Her errand succeeds. She cuts off Holofernes' head and escapes with it to Bethulia, where the townsmen are so fired by her example that they sally forth and rout the besiegers.

The subject is exactly suited to the genius of Old English poetry, turning, as it does, on the antithesis between justice and fortitude, on the one hand, and cruelty, oppres-

[1] See p. 76.

sion, and brute force on the other. It would be hardly apposite to compare Holofernes with Grendel—Grendel is unique—but we shall not be far out if we term the monster, as he is presented to us in the poem, another Eormanric. Among the many injurious epithets with which the author belards the tyrant is 'wær-logan' ('treaty-breaker'). The same expression is applied to Eormanric in the opening lines of *Widsith*, and is full of suggestion. Destitute of honour, indifferent to their word, such tyrants seem capable of any crime; and being armed with the power to give effect to their inhuman instincts, are naturally objects of terror. Holofernes is described as 'the dreadful lord of eorls'; and he appears to have, and misuse, the attributes of sovereignty. But the poet does not depict him solely as the quintessence of malice; he makes him odious by the imputation of other vices. Holofernes is libidinous and coarse; and he keeps fit company. Four days after Judith's arrival in the camp he makes a feast to which the principal thanes, his companions in wickedness, are bidden. This banquet is an orgy of inebriety, in which Holofernes plies his nobles with so much liquor they one and all become 'dead drunk' ('swylce hie wæron deaðe geslegen'). Neither the feasters nor their host have any foreboding of calamity, but the poet casts a shadow of impending destruction over the unconscious revellers.

> Doom'd they partook of it,
> Renown'd shield-fighters, tho' he ween'd it not, the rich,
> The terrible lord of eorls.

Holofernes laughed and laughed again, and was so noisy that the sons of men might hear him afar off. At length dark night drew near, and he commanded the bright maid to be brought to his lofty pavilion. There, we are told, was a fair fly-net, all golden, hung round the chieftain's bed, through which he could look and observe any one who came in, while none could see him, save such of his soldiers as he ordered to approach.

Up to this point Holofernes has retained his senses, but it was not the Lord's pleasure that he should pollute His servant. His wine-bibbing now took effect, and he fell in a drunken swoon. The attendants having withdrawn, Judith considered how she might most easily deprive the monster of life before he awoke. First, she breathed a prayer to the Persons of the Trinity, craving the boons of victory and true faith. Then she seized Holofernes by the hair, and with a sharp sword cut half through his neck, afterwards repeating the stroke, with the result that the head of the heathen hound rolled on the floor. The foul and mangled corpse lay on the bed, while the ghost of Holofernes set out on a journey to the nether regions, the hall of dragons, there to suffer torments and abide in darkness for ever and ever.

With this concludes what may be termed the first 'fytte.' Judith had come with a 'foregoer,' a pale-faced lady, who had brought provisions for them both in a sack. In this sack the heroine placed the bloody head, and gave it into the hand of her young attendant to carry home. Setting out from the camp together, the ladies presently descry the shining walls of the beautiful city of Bethulia. At the gate were watchers keeping ward, Judith herself having enjoined this course on her dejected fellow-countrymen. She was now ceremoniously received within the gates, and made a pious speech to the burghers, giving God the glory. Men and women, young and old, rushed pell-mell to the gate in their thousands, and the victorious maid delivered a second oration, in which she urged all capable of bearing arms to march out and attack the foe.

Her exhortation bore fruit. The Hebrews, under their war-banners, bore down on the Assyrians, and engaged them in stern fight. The chief captains of the enemy, realizing the gravity of the case, wished to apprise Holofernes, whom they supposed to be occupying the beauteous pavilion in company with the lovely maid. No one, however, durst awaken him until, the peril growing more and more acute, at last one of the warriors entered the tent to find his gold-giver extended on the bed—a pale and lifeless corpse. Chilled to the core, he fell to the ground, and in his grief of mind began to tear his hair and rend his clothes. Finally, he went forth and told his comrades of his discovery, which he represented as ominous of the fate about to overtake them all.

Thereupon the Assyrians threw down their arms and took to flight, the Hebrews following in close pursuit. Most of the Assyrian leaders were laid low in the fight or flight; and then for the space of one month the victors were engaged in conveying to the bright burgh, Bethulia, the spoils—helms, corselets, war-harness decked with gold—more treasures than any man might tell. Judith having been the Joan of Arc of the occasion, to her the eorls brought for reward the sword of Holofernes, his bloody helm, his ample corselet adorned with red gold, and whatever else of value had been owned by the commander, bracelets and bright treasures. All this Judith offered to the Lord of Hosts, in whom she had true faith. The poem concludes with a doxology:

> Therefore unto the dear Lord
> Be glory for ever, Who made wind and air,
> The heavens and the wide world; also, the raging sea,
> And celestial joys, through His own mercy.

In this rapid summary it is possible that we have failed

to show the close analogy between *Judith* and the epic poems dealt with in our opening section, but reminiscences abound, more particularly in the second 'fytte,' which describes the battle and its sequel. Thus the phrase

laðan cynnes lythwon becom
cwicera to cyððe

Of the race of foemen came there few
Home alive,

is very similar to ll. 2365-6 of *Beowulf*:

lyt eft becwom
fram þam hildefrecan hames niosan.

Few from among
Those heroes came again to visit home.

'On ðam dæge-weorce' (in that day's work) reminds us of 'ðæs dægweorces' (for that day's work) in the *Lay of Maldon*, while the expression 'earn æses georn' (eagle greedy of carrion) occurs in both poems. One of the most striking passages in the *Battle of Brunanburh* is thus rendered by the late Poet Laureate.

Many a carcase they left to the carrion
Many a livid one—many a sallow skin—
Left to the white-tail'd eagle to tear it, and
Left to the horny-nibb'd raven to rend it, and
Gave to the garbaging war-hawk to gorge it, and
That gray beast, the wolf of the wold.

Commenting on this translation, Mr. Morton Luce remarks:[1] 'with fine effect the poet adheres closely to the form of his original. But not to the form alone; for the prose rendering of Hallam Tennyson, "the raven with the horny beak," becomes in his father's poem "the horny-*nibb'd* raven"; and thus with the aid of verse, the Laureate

[1] *Handbook to Tennyson's Works*, p. 374 (G. Bell and Sons, Ltd.).

could retain the graphic *nebban* of the *Chronicle*.' Now if we turn to *Judith* we shall find this identical epithet applied, not indeed to the raven, but to the eagle. It has often been remarked that, just as a shark will follow for days a vessel in which lies one sick unto death, so on the eve of an engagement birds of ill omen will hover above an army, ready to swoop on the bodies of the fallen. The author of *Judith* refers to this instinct in lines which obviously resemble the passage above quoted.

> Therefore rejoiced the
> Lean wolf in the weald and the dark raven,
> Bird greedy of slaughter, from the west both,
> In that the country-men thought to deliver
> Attack on the doom'd. But on their track flew
> Eagle for food eager, with dank plumage;
> The sallow coat sang war-charm,
> Horny-nibb'd.[1]

It would be a simple matter to multiply evidences of the affinity between *Judith* and the series of epics—notably, the hammering insistence on the utterly depraved and pernicious nature of the reprobate Holofernes. In three successive half-lines he is dubbed 'diabolical,' 'lecherous'

[1] Cp. *Elene*, ll. 27-30:

> fyrdleoð agol
> wulf on wealde, wælrune ne mað;
> urigfeðera earn sang ahof
> laðum on laste.

> warsong sang
> Wolf in the weald, nor blood-counsel shunned;
> Eagle with dewy feathers chant upraised
> On the foes' track.

Ibid., l. 52:

> hrefen uppe gol
> wan wælfel.

> raven sang aloft
> Dusky, cruel fell.

and 'baleful.' There is rather a tendency in Old English poetry to dwell preferably on the uglier, the more uncanny side of things; and when such a topic occurs, the writer has at command an inexhaustible vocabulary of which he makes full use. Beauty, on the other hand, is depicted somewhat perfunctorily. In this poem the term 'beorht' is certainly overworked. Taken as a whole, however, *Judith* reveals high qualities of imagination, and the unknown author is an adept in the art of narration leading us on from point to point by the easiest of transitions, while every fresh development is carefully motived. He has succeeded also—where it would have been fatal to fail—in limning a charming portrait of his heroine. We cannot think of Judith as a murderess, nor even as more masculine than her work demands. Throughout she is a simple, courageous girl, who conceives of herself as an instrument in the hands of Providence in liberating her country from a grievous incubus. At the same time she has a share of the spirit of adventure which prompts Beowulf to seek and assail Grendel's mother in her den. In that and other ways she may be considered the female counterpart of the Geatish hero.

Judith is only one of several books of Scripture that have appealed to Anglo-Saxon poets. Before, however, more is said on this subject it is desirable to make some reference to Cædmon, who has been credited with the authorship of certain extant compositions. So many Old English poems are anonymous that it is refreshing to be able to give *any* account of *any* writer of verse. A sketch of this father, as much saga as biography in the strict sense of the term, is contained in the Venerable Bede's *Historia Ecclesiastica Gentis Anglorum* (*l.* iv, *c.* 24), and also in the translation of that work attributed to King Alfred, in which it may be read with equal, if not greater, pleasure.

The tale is very charming. The historian has been descanting on the virtues of St. Hild, the famous abbess of the minster of Streoneshealh, which, as we have noted, was the ancient name of Whitby. Mention is then made of a certain gifted brother, resident in the minster, who composes edifying songs. After him many others of the English race essayed the sacred muse, but without attaining the same degree of merit, the reason being that he was instructed by no human teacher, but directly inspired from above. Hence he might apply his talents to no fictitious subjects, but to those alone which conduced to devotion.

This man abode in a secular condition until he arrived at a mature age, and during all that time he was a stranger to minstrelsy. This ignorance was a source of inconvenience to him. It was his wont to attend convivial meetings, in which all present were expected to contribute songs, accompanying them on the harp. When he saw the harp approaching, he must needs for shame steal forth and return to his house. On one such occasion he had left the festal scene and gone out to tend the oxen of which he had charge for the night. Lying down to rest, he fell asleep, when in a vision a man stood by his side, saluted him by name, and said, 'Cædmon, sing me something.' He answered, 'I can nothing sing, and therefore I departed from the beer-drinking and came hither.' But the spiritual visitant would not be denied, so Cædmon inquired 'What shall I sing?' The reply was 'Sing me the Creation.' Thereupon in verse and language he had never heard, the layman began to laud and magnify God, the Maker of the Universe.

On awakening from sleep, Cædmon recollected the song, and repaired to the town-reeve, his ealdorman, to whom he related the miracle. The magistrate conducted him to the Abbess, who summoned all the most learned men and masters, and in their presence bade him rehearse the vision and sing the song. Their judgement was that the Lord Himself had bestowed upon him a heavenly gift, but, that no doubt might remain, the wise men appointed him a task—that of turning into metre a sacred theme and words of divine doctrine. The following morning Cædmon came again and sang the composition to them.

The Abbess, delighted, urged him to abandon his secular condition and become a monk. To this he was well inclined, so she received him into the minster and joined him to the congregation of God's servants.

Next she commanded him to be taught sacred history; and, being apparently unable to read, he was constrained to learn it by word of mouth. He stored it up in his memory, and, like clean animals ruminating converted it into the sweetest song. So winsome were words and melody that his teachers themselves wrote them down at his dictation and learned them. First he sang of the creation of the middle-earth, the origin of mankind, and all that is related in Genesis, the first book of Moses; then of the departure of the Children of Israel from Egypt and their entrance into the Promised Land, and many similar subjects; of the Incarnation of Christ, His Passion, and Ascension into Heaven, the coming of the Holy Ghost, and the teaching of the Apostles; also of the awfulness of the future Judgement, the horrors of infernal punishment, and the sweetness of the heavenly kingdom, together with many other religious and devout compositions.

As a monk, Cædmon was remarkable for his observance of rule and discipline, and always highly incensed at signs of laxity in others. And so his life had a fair close. Particulars of his departure are given, but with these we need not trouble the reader.

A poem of supernatural origin bespeaks unusual attention. Bede in the text of his *Historia* imparts only a Latin translation, on which he passes the just remark: 'Neque enim possunt carmina, quamvis optime composita, ex alia in aliam linguam ad verbum sine detrimento sui decoris ac dignitatis transferri.' That is true of all versions, whether metrical or in prose. We are not, however, without the means of forming an estimate ourselves, since the original has been preserved at the conclusion of an ancient MS. A comparison of the two—the original and the translation—establishes that the latter is very nearly, as Bede says, *ad verbum*, word by word. It is interesting also to note that the Alfredian or West-Saxon copy corresponds with the Northumbrian text with two exceptions, one of which is manifestly a corruption.

The poem, although it seems almost blasphemous to say so, is not at all out of the common, but it certainly loses in the Latin rendering in which it has necessarily to forgo not only the advantages of rhythm and alliteration, but the incommunicable aroma of words and phrases which would have composed half its charm to the poet and his fellows. As the song is so brief, it may not be amiss to cite it in all three forms in which it has descended to us.

NORTHUMBRIAN

Nu scylun hergan hefænricæs uard,
Metudæs mæcti, end his modgidanc,
Werc uuldurfadur; sue he uundra gihuæs,
Eci dryctin, or astelidæ.
He ærist scop ælda barnum
Heben til hrofe, haleg scepen:
Tha middungeard moncynnæs uard,
Eci dryctin, æfter tiadæ
Firum, foldu, frea allmectig.

WEST-SAXON

Nu we sceolan herian heofon-rices weard,
Metodes mihte, and his mod-geþonc,
Wera Wuldor-Fæder: swa he wundra gehwæs,
Ece Dryhten, oord onstealde.
He ærest gesceop eorðan bearnum
Heofon to hrofe, halig Scyppend;
þa middangeard moncynnes weard
Ece Dryhten æfter teode
Firum, foldan, Frea Ælmihtig.

BEDE'S VERSION

Nunc laudare debemus auctorem regni coelestis, potentiam Creatoris et consilium illius, facta Patris gloriae. Quomodo ille, cum sit aeternus Deus, omnium miraculorum auctor exstitit, qui primo filiis hominum coelum pro culmine tecti, dehinc terram custos humani generis omnipotens creavit.

Although 'auctor' is sometimes used in the sense of 'guardian,' this is not the signification that would naturally occur to us, and it is conceivable that Bede understood the word 'uard' in the first line as meaning the same as 'ord' or 'oord.' It is more probable, however, that 'ord' or 'or' was his reading, although the evidence of the West-Saxon copy is against the supposition. Again, 'astelidæ' may possibly have been employed in a neuter or reflexive sense, but this interpretation appears forced, and it seems a fair conjecture that Bede read 'astod,' especially as the shorter word would help to preserve the balance of the two half-lines.

Taking the song as it stands in the Northumbrian dialect, it may be thus rendered in modern English:

Now ought we to praise the Guardian of the Kingdom of Heaven, the might of the Maker, and the thought of His heart, the work of the Father of Glory, inasmuch as He, Eternal Lord, instituted the rise of every wonder. He first fashioned the heaven as roof for the children of men, the Holy Creator; then, Guardian of mankind, Eternal Lord, he afterwards formed for mortals the middle-earth, the ground, the Lord Almighty.

We shall not be accused of bestowing disproportionate attention on this short poem—remarkable enough, if it was indeed the production and first-fruits of an unlettered peasant—when it is stated that this is the only composition that may be assigned, with any degree of assurance, to Cædmon, the one name familiar to the generality of people in connection with Old English literature, save always Alfred the Great. Most students, however, are aware that extant poems of considerable length and sufficient note are traditionally associated with this early bard, who is supposed to have died about A.D. 680. We have learnt from Bede that Cædmon tried his hand on the historical Scriptures, and, amongst the rest, the first two books of the Pentateuch. Now it so happens that we possess Anglo-Saxon poems dealing with the matter of Genesis and Exodus (which, by the way, should not be confused with Middle English poems bearing the same titles and analogous in subject); and thus it is easily comprehensible that these remains, otherwise unfathered, should be given to Cædmon, whose works, many and excellent, must otherwise be held to have perished.

Another, more sentimental, reason for wishing to believe that the Old English poetical version of Genesis is by Cædmon is that such a circumstance would constitute a link between the founder of Christian poetry in England, as Bede evidently conceived him, and its greatest representative—John Milton. It was Francis Junius who first attributed the paraphrase to Cædmon, and Junius' edition, published in 1655 at Amsterdam, may have been known to Milton. Be that as it may, it has been well observed that Satan's speech in Hell, as set forth by the author of *Genesis*, is characterized by a simple yet solemn greatness of imagination which may possibly have influenced at some period of his life the magnificent genius of his Puritan successor.

Instead of 'the author of *Genesis*,' we ought, it would seem, to have spoken of '*one* of the authors,'—almost certainly not Cædmon. A fact which has been brought out with absolute clearness by modern criticism is that the poem is not the production of a single mind; and that portion of it which may be termed the Anglo-Saxon *Paradise Lost*, and is conspicuously superior to the residue—being, indeed, a superb composition—is beyond question a later interpolation. Ten Brink had already divined this on the evidence of style alone, and refused to be moved from his conclusion by the argument that the revolt of the Angels is described twice over in other mediaeval elaborations of Genesis, when Dr. Eduard Sievers threw a new and valuable light on the problem. Intuitively he had recognized it as forming part of a poem in the manner of the Old Saxon *Heliand*, and that poem he was convinced was not originally Old English. As long as this explanation remained a mere theory, scholars were, of course, free to pass any opinion they chose upon it. Some accepted it; by others it was rejected. By a lucky accident, however, Sievers discovered in the Vatican a book that had come from Heidelberg, on the blank spaces of which some ninth-century scribe had copied passages of Old Saxon poetry. One of these passages was found to tally with ll. 790-817 of the Anglo-Saxon *Genesis*. It is thus no longer a matter of conjecture that the part of the poem which displays the richest imagination and the highest gift of expression has been borrowed from a Continental rendering.

The poem opens with a tribute to the Divine Creator, particularly with reference to the heavenly mansions. It goes on to describe the bliss of the angels, the fall of

Lucifer and his companions, and the vacant seats, the spectacle of which induced the Almighty to undertake the creation of the world. From this point the account of canonical Scripture is followed with considerable fidelity as far as the sacrifice of Isaac, at which point the poem ends. Leaving out of the question the section which we now know to have been interpolated, it may be said of *Genesis*—what has been said of Cædmon's song—that it is not at all out of the common. Bede's verdict on Cædmon's genius for religious poetry is hard to reconcile with the tameness of the paraphrase, but his principles of criticism may have been different from ours, and he may have found more merit in scrupulous adherence to the sacred text than in free flights of fancy. These remarks apply mainly to the larger aspects—the treatment of the incidents, characterization, motive, and so forth; in minor matters, whether he desired it or not, a poet was bound to allow himself some liberty. If as Thorpe held and Ten Brink is inclined to grant, Cædmon supplied the groundwork—much modified by later versifiers—it is patent that, at the outset, the only literary traditions behind the monk, at any rate in his own language, were those of epic poetry. He was therefore almost bound to observe its conventions, including the use of stock epithets and appositional phrases. In point of fact, Old English poetry never outgrew the swaddling-clothes of epic usage for the simple reason that it never renounced the alliterative form of verse, which could hardly dispense with such artifices. For us, redundancy and the grouping of words in stereotyped combinations are obvious defects, and it is worthy of note that the best passage of the poem—that which has been designated as *Paradise Lost*—is less affected by these constitutional taints. In a higher sphere also it bears traces of an admirable independence. We may take as an example the account of the temptation of our first parents. We are told in Scripture that the serpent was more subtle than all the beasts of the field, and, by virtue of this quality he succeeds in persuading his victims that the Tree of Knowledge may be robbed of its mystic and divine secret without risk of detection. Here another touch is added. Satan pretends that the irksome interdict has been removed. But there was more than one tempter on this occasion, and, as proof of the poet's eloquence and resource, we cannot better than adduce Eve's speech to her partner after she has partaken of the forbidden fruit.

> Adam, my lord! this fruit is so sweet, so glad to my breast, and this messenger so bright, God's good angel; in his garb I see that he is our sovran's envoy, from the King of Heaven. Better his favour for us twain than his anger against us. If to-day thou spake aught grievous against him, yet he will forgive it, if we render him homage. Why this vexing strife against the servant of thy Lord? We have need of his grace; he can bear our errand to the King of Heaven. From this place I can see Him where He sits to the South and East, in His goodliness enfolded, who was the Maker of this world. I see in compass round about Him His angels flying with their wings, a mighty host, a gladsome company. Who could give me this knowledge, but if God sent it straight to me? I hear unhindered, and far and wide over the broad creation I look upon all the world; I hear the mirth of Heaven. Light is my thought without and within me, since I ate of the fruit.[1]

As we have observed, the art of *Genesis* is epic, but the general tone is rather elegiac than heroic. Old English poetry oscillates between two extremes—battle fury and almost womanish repining. There is something of the latter element in *Beowulf*; in the *Wanderer* it is absolute; while in *Judith* and the *Lay of Maldon* it asserts itself only in the significant term 'fæge' (doomed). In *Genesis* there is more of pathos than of passion, but the fourteenth chapter

[1] Prof. Ker's tr.

of the first canonical book, with its suggestive record of the pitched battle between the kings, four against five, awakens the dormant spirit of slaughter, and so we are treated to a sympathetic description of the mighty conflict with all the familiar notes. Cædmon is represented as deriving his inspiration from no common source, but here at least the poet, whoever he may have been, is of the earth earthy. The reader may hardly credit it, but even the swart and expectant raven, the bird with the dewy feathers, comes upon the scene and sings his hateful song. On the other hand, there are plentiful traits that recall the song to which Bede alludes, and of which a full account has been given. Expressions like 'moncynnes weard' (Guardian of mankind), and the poet's consistent attitude of ecstatic adoration towards the world's Creator, beget the conclusion that, though he may have been drawn for a moment into another humour, the pure, serene atmosphere of his earliest effort is still his choice, prompting him to the use of identical language.

It is not difficult to conceive that Cædmon, assisted by men of learning, may have had something, and perhaps a great deal, to do with the composition of *Genesis*, but it is, we must confess, much less easy to imagine that he was in any degree accountable for *Exodus*, which has for its text the departure of the children of Israel, the passage of the Red Sea, and the destruction of Pharaoh's host. The dramatic events preceding and paving the way for the manumission of the oppressed people are left unnoticed, while Moses, a great historical figure, assumes no extraordinary prominence. The subject being a popular migration, the writer seems to have been transported, in spite of himself, to a region of experience with which the English had become only too familiar. He has, in a way, lost his bearings, since he applies to the Israelites the wholly inapposite phrase 'sæ-wicingas' (sea-robbers). This circumstance helps to explain the marked freedom with which the episodes are handled. But for the moralizings at the commencement and towards the close of the poem we might have supposed that the intention was simply to relate a stirring martial tale. Even as it is, such is the wealth of military details, so unmistakable the zest for warlike incident and adventure, that we are still of the belief that this was the chief aim and motive. It is true there is no actual battle—the Scriptural narrative did not allow of that—but carnage is, so to speak, in the programme, and every preparation is made for it. Bird and beast are on the alert, for the wolf and raven are here no less surely than at the battle of Brunanburh and the battle of Maldon. Only the Red Sea prevents the onset of the Egyptians; and, like old Byrhtnoth, Moses raises his shield in addressing his countrymen ere they essay the crossing.

The interest and merit of the poem are incontestable. To a complete mastery of technique it joins fine power of imagination and an enthusiastic temper which make for a vivid realization of the actions. As Ten Brink remarks, the strength of the writer lies above all in an intuitive grasp of situations. Who that writer was is a mystery. He may have been a *scóp* turned monk, who on entering the cloister had been loth to resign his beloved art, but this is a mere conjecture. It is to be regretted that the poem has not come down to us entire. An hiatus occurs immediately before the account of the destruction of the pursuing army. It seems possible also that the passage in which mention is made of the sacrifice of Isaac, and other ancestral topics, has been interpolated, but it is not unworthy of the context, and there are similar retrospective allusions in *Beowulf*.

The last of the paraphrases—that of the Book of Daniel

—is likewise imperfect, breaking off about the middle. This composition by no means attains the excellence of *Exodus*, but it is superior to the general level of *Genesis*. The writer adheres to the narrative of the Bible, except that he selects from it certain elements as best suited to his purpose, which is to draw out the contrast between the virtues of humility, patience, and submission to the Divine Will, as exemplified by Daniel and his fellows, and the opposite qualities of overweening arrogance, rashness, and presumption exhibited by their persecutors. Like the author of *Exodus*, this writer fastens by choice on the critical points of the story; and he bestows his greatest labour on the miracle of the burning fiery furnace into which the angel of the Lord descends to comfort His martyrs. This portion of the poem includes a good rendering of the Song of the Three Children. The Exeter codex contains, under the title of *Azarias*, a much longer and more prolix version. The title of this latter poem is derived from the name of the first speaker, which occurs indeed in the opening line.

Old English poetry is generally not rich in similes, but the advent of the angel is figuratively described in lines that demand quotation:

> . . . wæs in þam ofne þa se engel cwom
> windig and wynsum wedere onlicust
> þonne on sumeres tid sended weorþeð
> dropena dreorung mid dæges hwile
> swa wæs in þam fire for frean meahtum
> halgum to helpe.

> . . . it was in the furnace, when the angel came,
> windy and winsome, to the air most like,
> when in the summer-tide a fall of drops
> chances to be sent some time of day;
> so was it in the fire, by the power of the Lord,
> to help those holy men.[1]

[1] Gollancz' tr.

CHAPTER II

CYNEWULF AND HIS SCHOOL

THE *Azarias* poem is in the Exeter Book, and the Exeter Book, though it contains things now disassociated from him, cannot be named without recalling to us Cynewulf. His life-story is really unknown, but a study of one of the poems which may not unreasonably be attributed to him is fruitful in suggestion of spiritual experiences, enabling us to comprehend the mysticism which envelops them all. By a steady process of evolution we pass from the literalness of *Genesis* to the bolder conceptions of *Exodus*, and thence to the complete emancipation from the tyranny of material, and almost from matter itself, that characterizes the prophesyings of Cynewulf. For in Cynewulf the contemplative faculty is raised to the highest power. He has the strength of the eagle's flight, the keenness of the eagle's vision; and, poised in a supersensual atmosphere, he views the whole realm of being from a standpoint in which the common term 'middangeard' has a singular appropriateness. He sees all round the orb of the earth—above and beneath; and for him whatever happens on its surface is significant only as it regards eternity.

Until the nineteenth century, when, rather strangely, an Anglo-Saxon MS. was discovered at Vercelli in Lombardy and edited for the Ælfric Society by that well-known scholar and writer, J. M. Kemble (1847-56), Cynewulf's compositions were comprised within the four corners of the Exeter Book. We may therefore well pause to make a brief allusion to this priceless treasure of the Western see. It was one of some sixty books bequeathed to the library of the cathedral by the first Bishop of Exeter, Leofric, who strove to ensure their safe keeping by a formal curse, which, alas, proved ineffectual save in this single instance! 'Si quis,' he wrote, 'illum inde abstulerit eterne subiaceat maledictioni.' But the Reformation, salutary as it may have been on the whole, had the unfortunate result of relaxing men's consciences in various ways, for which literature and art both owe it a grudge. The present learned and accomplished Chancellor—Canon Edmonds—pronounces just condemnation on a wretched betrayal of trust: 'The Dean and Chapter of 1602 were not afraid, nor rent their clothes, but gave up their treasures with prodigal economy, and illustrated one of the vicissitudes which befall a cathedral library, the danger of which has come when the question is provoked, "quis custodiet ipsos custodes?"'

In the middle of the eleventh century Leofric, who had been chaplain to Edward the Confessor, transferred his see from the small town of Crediton to Exeter for security against the Danes. His library, as appears from the inventory printed in the Rev. F. E. Warren's edition of Leofric's Missal, consisted of English and Latin books in about equal proportions, though some of the former seem to have been 'di-glots'—that is, in English and Latin. Others must have been in English only.

A perusal of this list intensifies, if that be possible, the disgust and indignation with which we look back on the folly of those dignitaries who parted so lightly with the ancient MSS. If we have not to lament the disappearance of many, if any, original writings—even that is not certain—every student of Old English literature would have welcomed the opportunity of examining works, of which only the titles now remain. The 'englisc cristes boc' probably means the Gospels, but we cannot be sure of that. The 'full spel boc wintres and sumeres,' we fancy, was not, as Mr. Warren would lead us to suppose, 'a complete *spell* book for summer and winter'—of course, the Anglo-Saxons had their spells—but a history book, a book of homilies, or a combination of both kinds. The 'sumer ræding bec,' of which there were two, and the 'winter ræding boc,' of which there was one, were probably of a similar character to that which has just been mentioned.

The last on the list is a 'mycel englise boc be gehwilcum þingum on leoðwisan geworht' ('a great English Book concerning sundry things in song wise wrought'). This is the precious document which is sometimes styled on classical analogy the Codex Exoniensis. It is of all the Exeter books the most important, being absolutely unique. Its loss would have been irreparable, but a kind Providence has preserved it to us. Chronological questions here require careful discrimination. The date of the benefaction is not necessarily or probably the date of the MS.; and neither the date nor the dialect of the MS. is likely to be that of the original composition—at any rate, in the case of those poems with which we are principally concerned. The MS. appears to belong to the tenth or early part of the eleventh century, but this is no clue to the age of the writer. Earle places his *floruit* in the eleventh century; Ten Brink holds that he was born between 720 and 730, and that may be considered the most probable, as well as the most widely accepted, view. Opinion is not quite unanimous, either, as to Cynewulf's native province. Most critics are agreed that he was a Northumbrian, but not all.

One distinguished scholar, whose argument is cited by Professor Ker, but by no means endorsed by him, puts the matter thus:

> Poetry will not flourish in the middle of raids and plunderings; poetry needs quiet. Now in the eighth century there were many more kings of Northumbria than of Mercia; which proves the comparative unrest and insecurity of Northumbria; therefore Cynewulf was a Mercian.

Nothing is farther from the truth than that 'poetry needs quiet.' It is with periods of popular tension, movement, and excitement that the greatest poetry is associated, not with those of lethargy, stagnation, and fat contentment. And Cynewulf, in his way, is a great poet, since he inaugurated a new tradition which bore the stamp of his own masterful personality.

Advocates of the Baconian theory of the authorship of Shakespeare's works lay much stress on supposed clues which their opponents dismiss as fanciful. There is nothing fanciful—nothing, that is to say, imaginary—in the clues with which Cynewulf, evidently of set purpose, has 'earmarked' certain of his poems. The fact that only four are thus authenticated does not involve the inference that these alone are genuine, for the incorporation of the poet's name in the text of his writings is a device to which he would not resort very often. It might be done ingeniously, or it might be done awkwardly, but at the time the precaution must have appeared superfluous, as the MSS. would no doubt have been bound up together and duly docketed. Those MSS., however, have perished—lost, as we may well believe, in the confusion—the 'raids and plunderings'—which afflicted Northumbria in the days of its decadence. The consequence is that Cynewulf's poems have been transmitted only in West-Saxon versions—those of Exeter and Vercelli.

The four poems bearing Cynewulf's signature are his *Crist*, *Juliana*, *Elene*, and the *Fates of the Apostles.* It is thought by some that the last-mentioned is not a distinct poem, but the conclusion of *Andreas*, which, in that case, must be definitely assigned to Cynewulf, although Sievers impugns his authorship.[1] By what was perhaps a mere caprice the poet has not only redeemed his name from oblivion, but afforded grounds for surmising—mainly from internal evidence—the paternity of poems not so signed.

Let us now turn to the methods, which are of two kinds —simple and complex. In the legend of St. Juliana, the letters that compose the name Cynewulf are found in three lines, two of which contain three letters each, and the third two. These are in every instance runes, which are employed as capital letters in the Scandinavian 'futhorc' (or alphabet). The persons for whom the letters stand bear the names of the runes. Thus ᚳ or C would be 'cæn,' and so throughout the series; ᛚ or L being fully pronounced 'lagu,' and ᚠ or F 'feoh.' But the explanation will be better understood if the passage in which the acrostic occurs is given entire, viz.:

geomor hweorfeð
C. Y. and N. cyning biþ reþe
sigora sylland þonne synnum fah
E. W. and U. acle bidað
hwæt him æfter dædum deman wille
lifes to læne. L. F. beofað
scomad sorg-cearig.

Sad shall depart
C. Y. N. The king, the giver of victory
shall then be wroth, when sin-stain'd

[1] *Anglia*, xiii.

E. W. and U. trembling shall await,
what he will adjudge to them, after their deeds,
as life's reward; L. F. shall quake,
and linger sorrowful.[1]

The system on which runes are introduced in *Crist* is somewhat different. There also dispersed capitals make up the poet's name, but in that case the words represented by the letters are interwoven with the texture of the passage. It should be explained that the name of each rune signifies an idea or object. Thus 'lagu' ('lake') means water; 'feoh' ('fee') means property. These terms, in *Crist*, are worked into the fabric of the sense as well as of the verse; in *Juliana*, into the fabric of the verse only. It may have been noticed that in each of the lines above quoted, in which runes occur, one is alliterated, according to rule, with a word beginning with the same letter or with a vowel.

The use of runes in England seems to have been peculiar, or nearly so, to the Angles; in all three kingdoms, Northumbria, Mercia, and East Anglia, traces of runic writing have been discovered, ranging from the seventh to the tenth century. From our present point of view incomparably the most interesting is the inscription on Ruthwell Cross, which was indeed long a *crux* to antiquaries.[2] In 1838 it was deciphered by J. M. Kemble, who found it to consist of a fragment of a poem on the cross carved alternately down one side of the stone and up another. When, a few years later, the Codex Vercellensis was brought to light, Mr. Kemble was in the happy posi-

[1] Gollancz' tr.

[2] Professor G. Stephens, who devoted a special treatise to the subject, did not hesitate to attribute the runic verses on the Ruthwell Cross to Cædmon, whose name he deciphered on the monument. Dr. Bradley thinks the verses older than *Elene*, the author of which (probably not Cynewulf) incorporated them in his poem.

tion of being able to confirm his solution by means of a more complete copy of the poem—the *Dream of the Rood.* That poem has been adjudged to Cynewulf on internal grounds, and the attribution may be deemed to be strengthened by the poet's acquaintance with, and predilection for, runes, as shown in the spelling of his own name. Indeed, it seems possible that the whole of his poetry was written originally in runic characters, like the Dumfriesshire inscription. The use of this alphabet, the invention of which was traditionally assigned to Odin, was in general discountenanced by the Church, but it has been pointed out that, after the death of Edwin and the flight of St. Paulinus, the restoration of Christianity in Northumbria was effected by missionaries of the Irish school, whose policy, differing from that of St. Augustine and his brethren, was to tolerate such remains of heathendom.

However that may be, it appears as certain as any conclusion can be that is based on inference only, that the West-Saxon versions were derived from North Country originals. As Gollancz expresses it, 'Wessex merely preserved the poems; Northumbria produced them.' Northumbria not only loved runes, but was the stronghold of alliterative poetry, whereas Wessex, from the time of Alfred onwards, preferred prose. This distinction obtained as late as the days of Chaucer, whose Parson is made to say:

> Trusteth well, I am a Sotherne man,
> I cannot geste *rom, ram, ruf*, by my letter,
> And God wote rime hold I but litel better,
> And therefore, if you list, I will not glose,
> I wol tell you a litel tale in prose.

It has been supposed that Cynewulf began life as a professional *scóp.* His mastery of form is sure to suggest this conjecture, and we are far from condemning it as altogether unwarrantable, although the fact that he knew

Latin, and even composed an occasional Latin verse, points to a degree of education that could hardly have been acquired elsewhere than in a monastery. It would be safer, perhaps, to infer that the cultivation of native poetry was a permissible recreation for clerks. Bede's testimony is positive as to the practice of vernacular composition in one Northumbrian convent; and it would be contrary to reason, as also to the tenour of his evidence, to assume that this was an exceptional instance. Ten Brink admits that Cynewulf has bequeathed nothing in harmony with the *rôle* of wandering minstrel except the riddles of the Exeter Book. It used to be believed that the first of these riddles was an 'allegorical device' for the poet's name, but more recent and better instructed criticism has invalidated this explanation, and now it is a matter of the gravest doubt whether not only the first, but any of the riddles can be properly claimed for Cynewulf. We must, therefore, discard all the hypotheses deduced from this source with respect to Cynewulf's youthful tastes and character—his fondness for festivity, appreciation of the pomp and circumstance of war, etc.

On the other hand we have in the *Dream of the Rood* and *Elene* plain evidence of a spiritual metamorphosis, or what is termed conversion. St. Paul, St. Augustine, and many another example of the transforming influence of Divine Grace might have been known to Cynewulf, and even Cædmon's vision might have counted in suggesting a supernatural motive, but, despite these precedents, the conviction forces itself upon us that Cynewulf underwent personal experiences analogous to those which he describes —that the ecstasies were real rather than imagined or invented for poetical purposes. It is to this circumstance that much of the excellence and most of the interest of these compositions are due. To Cynewulf the Holy Cross is an obsession; and whether he treats of it directly or not, he writes evermore in its shadow.

The poems are, of course, not dated, and accordingly it is within our discretion in what order we elect to treat of them. The *Dream of the Rood* may not have followed immediately on the event—it may have been preceded by other writings less intimate, but, in a psychological sense, it is too significant, too essential to be kept in the background. The theme, broadly speaking, was not new. It was the subject of one of the grandest and best known of Church hymns—that beginning

> Pange lingua gloriosi proelium certaminis,

which was written in the sixth century by Venantius Fortunatus, Bishop of Poitiers, and a translation of which may be found in a very accessible work, *Hymns Ancient and Modern.*[1] The original is given in Mone's *Hymni Latini Medii Aevi,*[2] with annotations; and, in a mangled form, in the Roman Breviary. The eighth stanza, of which the English version is

> Faithful Cross, above all other
>   One and only noble Tree,
> None in foliage, none in blossom,
>   None in fruit thy peer may be;
> Sweetest wood and sweetest iron,
>   Sweetest weight is hung on thee.

was used after each of the others as a refrain or chorus.

The great renown of this hymn would lead us to believe that Cynewulf knew it, and, as a Latin scholar, he would have known also some of the legends of the Cross, many of which were to be made into verse by the author of the Middle-English *Cursor Mundi.* But whatever Cynewulf

[1] No. 97.   [2] Tom. i, p. 131.

knew, or did not know, he appropriated and individualized the theme by an original style of approach. Like all poets worthy of the name, he was so far enamoured of his subject as to allow no distraction—no thought of audience, or fame, or pecuniary recompense—to interpose between it and him.

It is night, and the poet is plunged in meditation. His reflections are not cheerful, for he sees himself 'contaminated by his deeds, bound by his sins, broken by grief, rudely manacled, encompassed by a host of sorrows.' Suddenly there appears to him in the profundity of heaven, encircled by angels, the Cross glittering with gold and jewels, and dashed with blood. The Tree of Victory becomes a sentient, a living thing, and, through the stillness, accosts the visionary. 'Vast time has elapsed, but I recollect it still. I was asleep on the border of the forest when I was cut down. I was planted on the mount.'

The wood speaks of the Passion and its own subsequent fortunes. After the entombment it was buried deep in the earth, but afterwards raised out and adorned by the servants of God with silver and gold. The time has arrived when heroes—a favourite expression of Cynewulf's, who uses it synonymously with 'confessors'—far and wide pay reverence, and address prayers, to the Sign. The Son of God has suffered on it, wherefore it shoots up triumphant under heaven and is efficacious for the healing of the nations. The Tree concludes with a charge to the poet. He is to tell men of the vision, and warn them of a future day of doom when all will be judged according as they have deserved in this transitory life. Full of joy, Cynewulf prays to the Tree; his peace of mind has been restored.

In *Elene* the poet again treats of the Cross—this time, the Invention of the Cross by the Empress Helena, mother of Constantine the Great. Again he strikes a personal note. If, as seems likely, the *Dream of the Rood* was the earliest of Cynewulf's extant poems, so it is probable that *Elene* was the last—his swan-song. In the epilogue he writes as one who has fought a good fight and finished his course. He recalls his vision, and praises God for having vouchsafed him the gift of song and abundance of knowledge, but there is not wanting a strain of sadness and solemnity. The ideas of the transitoriness of life and of coming judgement inspire this tone of melancholy.

Cynewulf then is the very type and model of extreme 'otherworldliness'; that this earth is capable of yielding one grain of real satisfaction or lasting happiness, is in his eyes the greatest of heresies. Just as he has signed his poems, four of them, with his name in runes, so in these passages he has given us what musicians term the key-signature of his poetry, which indicates always the prevailing key. Cynewulf writes, on the whole, in a minor key with an occasional modulation to its relative major—that is to say, the secondary or Christian significance of words like 'cempa' passes insensibly into primary and pagan meaning. The main substance of *Elene* is more akin to *Andreas* than the *Dream of the Rood*, both being more epic in quality than the generality of Cynewulf's productions. We must look for the explanation of this circumstance to the subject-matter, for St. Helena, unless she is belied by her legend, was an imperious, as well as an imperial, lady, and her methods of dealing with the Jews, in her endeavour to wrest the desired secret, were none of the gentlest.[1] As regards St. Andrew, we do not

[1] The E. E. T. S. volume on the *Legends of the Holy Rood* contains an Anglo-Saxon prose version of the Invention of the Cross, the substance of which is identical with that of *Elene*, and depicts the empress with the same fierce characteristics.

learn much of his character and achievements from the Bible, in which he figures as a less distinguished brother of the Apostle, St. Peter—'Simon Peter and Andrew his brother.' St. Peter gives clear proof of warlike readiness, and so there is no breach of probability—though brothers do not always resemble each other—in depicting St. Andrew in similar colours. It has been conjectured that Cynewulf obtained his knowledge of St. Helena's expedition to the Holy City from a Greek source—not directly, of course, because Greek was unknown in the West, but through some Latin medium. What is mere conjecture in the case of *Elene* amounts to certainty with regard to *Andreas*, since the Greek text of the story—Πράξεις 'Ανδρέου καὶ Ματθαίου—is to be found in the Bibliothèque Nationale at Paris. The Latin version, through which it filtered, remains yet to be discovered. The author of the *Blickling Homilies* may have had access to it; he certainly knew of Mermedonia and the miracles wrought in that country.

Although the Bible preserves complete silence on the life of the first disciple after the crucifixion of his Divine Master, certain of the early Fathers—*e.g.*, Origen—have left statements regarding him, on the strength of which the Russians maintain that he carried the torch of the Gospel into Muscovy. Not one of these statements, however, lends support to the wild legend here presented to us. Having graduated on the Sea of Galilee, St. Andrew sets out on a voyage—presumably to the distant north. Being not only a mariner, but a 'warrior,' he sustains the part of a spiritual viking.

The whole apparatus of epic convention is requisitioned for the description of the barque and its course over the whale-road or swan-road. The ship's crew comprises our Saviour and two angels; and the motive of the voyage is the deliverance of St. Matthew, whom the Mermedonians have imprisoned and purpose to put to death. Arrived in the country, St. Andrew successfully achieves his mission. His fellow disciple is released from bonds, and greatly cheered, but alas! St. Andrew himself is seized, imprisoned, and subjected to most cruel tortures. These, however, he survives, and inflicts signal punishment on the fierce and barbarous people. He beholds nigh at hand walls, mighty pillars set up in the midst of the plain, weather-beaten columns—'the old work of giants.' He adjures the marble in the name of God, before whom all tremble, to cause a whirl of waters, a seething ocean, to rise from its foundation and swallow the men up. Straightway the stone is cloven asunder, streams gush forth and pour over the soil. At break of day the land is covered with foaming waves. Awakened by this overflow of bitter drink, the warriors would fain fly the yellow billows, but the way is barred by an angel with a flaming sword. The deluge grows, the torrents roar; on all sides are heard cries of lamentation and woe. Terrified by this portent, the Mermedonians submit, acknowledge the power of God, and turn to the true faith.

The *Fates of the Apostles* is a brief poem of less than a hundred lines, in which the martyrdoms of the twelve disciples are rapidly sketched. Couched in a strain of high enthusiasm, it concludes with an appeal to the lovers of the song to implore the aid of the holy troop for the sorrowful writer. The last verses are like an echo of the *Soul's Address to the Body*, but elsewhere, and generally, the poem is permeated with the martial spirit and martial metaphors recalling the more ambitious *Andreas*.

If *Elene* and *Andreas* are more epic, *Juliana* is more dramatic than the bulk of Cynewulf's poems. It comprises a large element of dialogue, and very striking dialogue. It is doubtful whether the heroine is historical, but there is no question as to the reality of Galerius' and Maximian's persecution, of which Nicomedia—the scene of the story—was the centre. Juliana has a pagan lover—one Heliseus, a 'rica gerefa,' or powerful count. She will not comply with his desires or renounce her belief, so she is compelled to undergo horrible sufferings and is finally beheaded. Withal Juliana triumphs; her victory in the interview with the son of Satan is most pronounced and prepares us for her show of constancy in the last dread ordeal. The confessions of this thwarted and humbled emissary make him appear to have been the active minister in every misfortune that has overtaken humanity since the Creation and Fall. Amongst other mischiefs promoted by him were broils between friends or half-reconciled foes—probably by no means uncommon incidents in those days of unrestrained indulgence.

Sume ic larum geteah
to geflite fremede þæt hy færinga
eald-æfþoncan edniwedan
beore druncne ic hym byrlade
wroht of wege þæt hi in winsele
þurh sweord-gripe sawle forletan
of flæsc-homan, fæge scyndan
sarum gesohte.

Some have I led on by my teachings,
Have urged to strife, so that full suddenly
Have they renewed old grudges,
Drunken with beer; for them have I poured forth
Strife from the cup, that in the guest-hall,
Through clutch of sword, have they let forth the soul
From fleshly-sark; death-doom'd they hastened forth,
Beset with wounds.[1]

Heliseus and four-and-thirty ruffians, after the martyrdom of Juliana, take to ship and are drowned. 'Helle

[1] Gollancz' tr.

sohton' is the phrase. The poet gloats over their fate in terms strongly reflecting northern life and manners:

ne þorftan þa þegnas in þam þystran ham
seo geneat scolu in þam nyðran scræfe
to þam frumgare feoh gestealda
witreda wenan þæt hy in winsele
ofer beor-setle beagas þegon
æpplede gold.

(The thanes, the retinue, had no need there in that dark home, in that nether cave, to expect from their chief rich possessions promised, that they in hall across the beer-bench should receive rings, embossed gold.)

Hitherto we have said little of what is universally accounted Cynewulf's masterpiece—his *Crist*, but the study of some of his minor poems forms no unsuitable preparation for it. The narratives bridge over the chasm between *Beowulf* and *Crist*, since a portion of the interest belonging to them resides in the plot and its unfolding. On the other hand, they are much too spiritual in scope, much too didactic in manner, to be classed with the productions of the courtly *scóp*. Cynewulf's writings are one and all distinguished by a fatal facility of expression, a rich luxuriance of language, which exaggerates a tendency already noted as inherent in alliterative verse. Where, however, a definite story has to be told, there is obviously a limit even to the most graceful verbiage. Progress must be made, or the very notion of a story is belied.

In *Crist* and *Guthlac* the stimulus may be said not to exist or to be superseded by a more powerful motive, recitation of familiar facts, or facts impracticably few, being felt as incomparably less important than the tremendous lessons, the vast issues depending on their full and complete realization. This, then, is Cynewulf's task. He sets himself to paint in the broadest colours transcendent interests—the supreme drama of human salvation. To this lofty aim all other considerations are subordinated, and canons of art, where they do not subserve his purpose, are brushed aside as impertinences. The governing principle is line upon line, line upon line, precept upon precept, precept upon precept! And yet it would be inexcusable to represent *Crist* or *Guthlac* as if it were mere tautological instruction in righteousness. Poets like Isaiah and Cynewulf, when bent on edifying a nation, do not teach—they prophesy. The Old English poet had sufficient practice in the apt choice of words, the structure of the period, and the mechanical exigences of verse to give free rein to his imagination, and his apocalyptic visions are the natural fruit of a severe morality wedded to a genius that no enterprise can daunt, and neither time nor space can confine.

At first we may be inclined to regard the poem as a species of religious rhapsody in which we find ourselves transported from the mystery of the Incarnation to the miracle of the Ascension, and thence to the convulsions of the Last Judgement by a whirlwind of ecstatic emotion, spiritual fervour, and rhetorical declamation. Cynewulf's command of language impresses us from the outset, but he appears to labour from a common besetment of preachers —that of eddying round a thought or theme instead of making a steady and logical advance. And yet he reaches his goal, masking his transitions in a way which may have been intentional, but, for reasons that will be stated presently, seems rather to have been the consequence of an afflatus carrying him away and altering and shortening his projected course. Saturated with the spirit of his subject, full of the 'new wine' of profound and moving conviction, the poet passes insensibly from one topic to another, but not until he has discharged his conscience by a profuse eloquence illumining every phase.

Crist, like some other famous compositions, is not easy to classify. The term 'epic' is manifestly out of place in relation to a work in which there is rightly speaking no backbone of narrative, which is a poem of sentiment rather than of action. Lyrical and subjective, it is more like an ode, or series of odes, though the metre is simple—the ordinary staff verse. The whole effusion may be summed up in the expressive Old English word *dream*. It is a kind of exalted revelry, a *dreama dream*, as far as this can be represented in human speech. In this paean, this hymn of triumph, Christian joy reaches its apogee. It may strike the reader as a somewhat curious description of a poem, much of which is taken up with scenes of horror and suffering, but Cynewulf evidently contemplates the sight of the torments of the damned as adding to, not detracting from, the bliss of the redeemed.

> The third [sign] shall then be—the blessed bard
> Shall see the lost ones in the baleful gloom
> Suffering, in penance for their sins, sore pain,—
> The surging flame and luring serpents there
> With bitter jaws—a shoal of burning things;
> And thence shall winsome joy ensue for them,
> When other men they see dreeing the ill
> They have escaped through mercy of the Lord.[1]

The subject is really the Kingship of Christ. He is called not only 'cyning,' but also and repeatedly 'helm,' which, as we have had occasion to point out, is the epic equivalent of that term. Hrothgar, for instance, is 'helm

[1] Gollancz' tr. This passage may perhaps have been modelled on the well-known lines of Lucretius (ii, 1-4):

> Suave mari magno turbantibus aequora ventis
> E terra magnum alterius spectare laborem;
> Non quia vexari quemquam est iucunda voluptas
> Sed quibus ipse malis careas, quia cernere suave est.

Scyldinga.' The apostles are his bodyguard of retainers. They are styled 'hæleð hyge-rofe' ('valiant warriors') and 'þegnas þrymfulle' ('glorious thanes'). 'Hyge-rofe' is an epithet applied to Beowulf, and Jusserand well observes that, when the Anglo-Saxon poets describe the saints of the Gospel, we might fancy that we beheld the companions of that hero. We have seen what Cynewulf has made of St. Andrew; in his *Crist* though the disciples are naturally less prominent, the point of view is substantially unchanged. Christ is a conqueror, too. The idea of conquest comes out more particularly in connection with the harrowing of hell, but to the Christian imagination martyrdom has always the signification of victory, and thus the whole train of events succeeding the Crucifixion bears the seal of triumph. The majesty of Christ is revealed, most of all, in the portrayal of the Doom:

halig scineth
wuldorlic ofer weredum waldende God
ond hine ymb-utan æþel-duguð betast
halge here-feðan hlutre blicað
eadig engla gedryht.

glorious o'er the hosts
The sovereign God shall shine in holiness;
And Him around, the goodliest chivalry,
The holy warrior band, the blessed angel-troop,
Shall brightly gleam.[1]

What was in Cynewulf's mind when he entered upon the composition is indicated perhaps in that passage in which he refers to our Lord's six 'leaps.' These are the Conception, the Nativity, the Crucifixion, the Burial, the Harrowing of Hell, and the Ascension. The poem as it stands consists of three sections descriptive of the

[1] Gollancz' tr

Nativity, the Ascension, and the Last Judgement. The text is defective at the commencement, and apparently in one or two other places, but there is no reason to suspect any considerable *lacunae,* or interferences and additions by later editors. The third section—that on the Doom—is by far the longest and contains some remarkable lines. For compressed power the following would be hard to excel:

> ðeoþeð swearta leg synne on fordonum
> and gold-frætwe gleda forswelgað
> eall ær-gestreon eþel-cyninga.
>
> Swart flame shall seethe on those fordone by sin,
> And gledes shall gorge the golden ornaments—
> All ancient treasures of the kings of earth.[1]

Speeches are frequent, and there is one dialogue, very piquant and dramatic, between Joseph and Mary, in which the former sets forth his awkward predicament—the public scandal, the contempt showered upon him—as the consequence of his bride's condition. Several apostrophes occur, one being addressed to the Blessed Virgin, and another to her Divine Son. Cynewulf's exuberant eloquence has ample play in these digressions, which include a panegyric on the heavenly Jerusalem, the home of the redeemed. This it will be sufficient to quote in translation:

> O sight of peace! holy Jerusalem
> Choicest of royal thrones! citadel of Christ!
> The native seat of angels and of the just,
> The souls of whom alone rest in thee ever,
> Exulting in glory. No sign of aught unclean
> Shall ever be beheld in that abode,
> But every sin shall flee afar from thee,
> All curse and conflict. . . .
> The King of Heaven

[1] Gollancz' tr.

Seeketh thee in His course, and cometh Himself,
And taketh His dwelling in thee, as in days of yore
Soothsayers so wise declared in words;
They made known Christ's birth, and told it for thy comfort,
Thou best of cities! Now the Child is come,
Awakened to transform the Hebrews' works;
He bringeth thee joy; He looseneth thy bonds.[1]

On a previous page we have commented on the close resemblance between certain descriptive passages in *Beowulf* and one of the Blickling Homilies. The conclusion of *Crist* is strikingly like the peroration of another of the Blickling Homilies—that on the Communion of Saints. Although the ultimate source and model is the same—Rev. vii, 6; xxi, 4—it is evident from the antithetical construction and almost identical wording of some of the sentences that one Old English writer copied from the other—which signifies, if Cynewulf flourished in the eighth century, that the homilist imitated the poet.

CRIST

There is love of beloved ones, life without end-death, glad host of men, youth without age, splendour of the heavenly hosts; health without pain, for right-doers, rest without conflict of the blest with power, day without darkness, brightness full of glory, bliss without sorrow, peace between friends evermore without malice; for the happy in heaven concord without strife, in the holy multitude; there is there neither hunger nor thirst, sleep nor sore disease, nor scorching sun, nor cold, nor care.

B. H.

There is that eternal light without darkness; there is youth without age; there is that noble life without ending; there is joy without sadness; there is neither hunger nor thirst, nor wind, nor storm, nor sound of water, nor severance of beloved ones, nor

---

[1] Gollancz' tr.

gathering of foes, but there is everlasting rest, and there the festivity of saints shall be perpetual. There is that ineffable Kingdom which God giveth unto all them that will love Him.

We have spoken of the conclusion of *Crist*, but, strange as it may appear, Grein and Gollancz are at issue as to the dividing line between that poem and *Guthlac*. If internal evidence is ever of any value in determining questions of authorship, this ought to be decisive in favour of Cynewulf's right to *Guthlac*, although it is not one of his 'signed' compositions. The hero does not belong to that wide category of Anglo-Saxon saints, whose names are known, if known at all, through the dedications of churches or to readers of such compilations as Alban Butler's *Lives of the Saints*. His legend has found its way into J. R. Green's *Short History of the English People*, where the following account is given of him:

Wilder even than the western woodland was the desolate fen-country on the eastern border of the Kingdom [of Mercia] stretching from the "Holland," the sunk, hollow land of Lincolnshire, to the channel of the Ouse, a wilderness of shallow waters and reedy islets wrapped in its own dark mist-veil and tenanted only by flocks of screaming wild-fowl. Here through the liberality of King Wulfhere rose the abbey of Peterborough. Here, too, Guthlac, a youth of the royal race of Mercia, sought a refuge from the world in the solitudes of Crowland, and so great was the reverence he won, that only two years had passed since his death when the stately Abbey of Crowland rose over his tomb. Earth was brought in boats to form a site; the buildings rested on oaken piles driven into the marsh; a great stone church replaced the hermit's cell; and the toil of the new brotherhood changed the pools around them into fertile meadow-land (pp. 31-2).

The anarchy which had driven Ini from the throne broke out on his departure in civil strife, which left Wessex an easy prey to the successor of Ceolred. Among those who sought Guthlac's retirement at Crowland came Æthelbald, a Mercian of royal blood flying from Ceolred's hate. Driven off again and again by the King's pursuit, Æthelbald still returned to the little hut built beside the hermitage, comforting himself in hours of despair with his companion's words. 'Know how to wait,' said Guthlac, 'and the kingdom will come to thee; not by violence or rapine, but by the hand of God.' In 716 Ceolred fell frenzy-smitten at his board, and Mercia chose Æthelbald for its king (pp. 35-6).

Relatively, then, to the national history Guthlac is distinctly a 'red-letter' saint; and it will be hardly necessary to remind the reader that the foundation with which his name is inseparably linked, the fen-country so long his abode, were the scene of the final struggles of the English to maintain their independence, as pictured in the last of the sagas—Kingsley's *Hereward the Wake*. Guthlac is said to have died in 714; and for the few details of his biography included in the main division of the poem, Cynewulf was probably indebted to well-established tradition. The continuation is based on a Latin *Vita Sancti Guthlaci* by the monk Felix of Croyland. It contains a description of the good hermit's last commission to his faithful companion and his burial, and concludes with his servant's mournful errand to the saint's sister. This portion of the work is incomplete. To suppose any close dependence on the original would be inconsistent with Cynewulf's characteristics as a writer, especially as manifested in this poem, which bears the impress of his strong personality. The Latin narrative merely furnishes the occasion; the pathos, the delineation, are Cynewulf's own.

The composition is so transcendental, so elevated above earthly interests and ordinary concerns that its perusal must be somewhat tedious for those who do not share the poet's enthusiasm for the mystic forms of religion. The fundamental idea is the extrusion of a regiment of demons from their domain—the fen-country—by Guthlac's erection therein of a cell, which serves the purpose of a Christian stronghold. The notion that devils inhabit waste places is a very old one. Our Lord's temptation took place in the wilderness, as did also St. Anthony's. There is, indeed, a great deal in the account of that worthy's struggles and sufferings that may have been appropriated by Cynewulf, and worked into his version of Guthlac's spiritual combats and experiences. Grendel, the adversary of Beowulf, hailed from the moors; and this conception of the waste, as peculiarly the abode of fiends, was thoroughly ingrained in the minds of Northern converts to Christianity. As the term 'heathen' was applied to their unbelieving neighbours, it would almost seem as if the demons, haunting and infesting the moors, were typical of the lingering remnants of paganism. If so, Guthlac's crusade may actually have been a missionary enterprise, a scheme for the suppression of the few heathen customs that still disfigured the land.

That, however, is not the way in which Cynewulf represents it to us. Guthlac is shown as a Lenten hero, engaged in a desperate warfare with evil spirits, whom he has dispossessed of their resting-place. Cynewulf is an artist in devils. He paints their misery, their weakness, their malice, their persistence, their homelessness with a master hand, and his conceptions may safely challenge comparison with those of Dante and Milton. The Florentine's devils are so grotesque as to be preposterous and unreal, while Milton's Lucifer is too noble to excite that horror, loathing, and contempt which should ever be the portion of vice. Cynewulf succeeds in making his demons ugly and repulsive, and formidable only for their number. It is a pack of famished hell-hounds that the noble Guthlac keeps so strenuously at bay.

The *Phoenix* is a poem of quite another description. It is attributed to Cynewulf on internal grounds, and has for its subject the congenial topic of the Resurrection. The work on which it is based is unquestionably the *Carmen de Phoenice* ascribed by ancient tradition to Lactantius, but it has been doubted whether it is really Christian in intention, though it lends itself readily enough to Christian symbolism, and it is so interpreted here. Cynewulf's poem is not a translation, but a paraphrase in which the Anglo-Saxon poet permits himself full liberty of thought and expression. It may be considered less elegant than its prototype, but, in revenge, it escapes some of its conceits and affectations. We may take as an illustration the following example. The Latin has a passage which abounds in paradoxes, viz.:

> Mors illi Venus est; sola est in morte voluptas:
> Ut possit nasci, haec appetit ante mori.
> Ipsa sibi proles, suus est pater et suus haeres;
> Nutrix ipsa sui, semper alumna sibi;
> Ipsa quidem, sed non eadem, quae est ipsa nec ipsa est.

In Cynewulf's rendering all this torturing of sense and language simply disappears. We have instead:

> forþon he drusende deað ne bisorgað,
> sare swylt-cwale, þe him symle wat
> æfter lig-þræce lif edniwe,
> feorh æfter fylle, þonne fromlice
> þurh briddes hád gebræded weorðeð
> eft of ascan edgeong weseð
> under swegles hleo: biþ him self gehwæðer
> sunu and swæs fæder and symle eac
> eft yrfe-weard ealdre lafe.

(Therefore, though drooping, it careth not for death, for the sore pangs of dissolution, for always it knoweth after the flame's violence life renewed, animation after destruction, when effectually in bird's form it becometh roasted, and thereafter out of its ashes it waxeth young again under the protection of heaven. It is to itself both son and sweet father, and ever also in turn heir of its ancient relics.)

Not only has Cynewulf changed the sex of the bird—therein agreeing with Tacitus, who, in his *Annals* (vi, 28) certainly makes it a male—but he has incorporated one or two Old English touches—notably the phrase 'ealdre lafe.' 'Laf' is a term with all the tender associations of our modern heir-loom, while 'eald' reinforces the suggestions of intimacy and attachment. The addition 'swæs' is due, of course, partly to the need of alliteration, but it is happily selected and aids in transforming the passage from an exhibition of dry acrobatic ingenuity into a semblance of real poetry. Cynewulf makes no specific acknowledgements, but repeats the epic formula, so frequent in *Beowulf*, 'mine gefrægе.' In one place, indeed, there is an intimation that the poet composed in detachment from any particular model. After comparing the renewal of the Phoenix to the restoration of lost humanity through the coming of the King of Glory, he continues:

Is þon gelicost þæs þe us leorneras
Wordum secgað and writu cyþað.

Most like thereto is this bird's course,
As doctors tell to us and books reveal.[1]

'Job's song' is quoted in support of the statement 'Let none of human kind imagine that I of lying words compose my lay'—the reference being doubtless to the well-known saying, 'though after my flesh worms destroy this body, yet in my flesh shall I see God'—but this is an isolated instance. It may be as well to point out that the Phoenix signifies primarily the rising again of our Lord on the third day after His crucifixion, and only secondarily, the general resurrection of mankind on

[1] Gollancz' tr.

the last day. This is plainly intimated in the text of the poem.

swa fenix beacnað
geong in geardum god-bearnes meaht.

The Phoenix thus, young in its home,
The power betokeneth of the Child Divine.[1]

The conclusion of the *Phoenix* is macaronic, and it is noticeable that the alliteration is maintained throughout both sections of each line—English and Latin.

Hafað us alyfed lucis auctor,
þæt we motun hér merueri
gód-dædum begietan gaudia in celo,
þær we motun maxima regna
secan and gesittan sedibus altis,
lifgan in lisse lucis et pacis
agan eardinga, alma letitiæ
brucan blæd-daga, blandem et mitem
geseon sigora fréan sine fine;
and him lof singan laude perenne,
eadge mid englum, alleluia.

To us hath vouchsafed the Author of Light that we mayh ere deserve by good deeds to obtain joys in heaven, where we may visit kingdoms the greatest and sit in high places, live in favour, own dwellings of light and peace, enjoy genial and delightsome prosperous days, behold the Lord of Victory, gracious and merciful, world without end, and to Him sing praise in laud unceasing, blessed with the angels. Alleluia.

Amongst the contents of the Exeter Book is a poem on the 'Varied Gifts of Men,' which may have been written by Cynewulf, or, if not, was almost certainly due to his inspiration. It appears to be an expansion of ll. 664-85 of *Crist*, and treats of all sorts and conditions of men in relation to this world's affairs. On the whole, perhaps, it is

[1] Gollancz' tr.

more likely to be the work of a disciple and imitator, who had been tempted to borrow the theme. No one pretends that the whole of the poems in the Exeter codex are Cynewulf's handiwork, and several of the pieces assigned to him on the score of merit and similarity may actually have been the effusions of men of talent, who had inherited a portion of his spirit, Cynewulf having founded a school of prophets, or, in other words, established a vogue in religious poetry which stirred the emulation of whatever there was of culture, imagination, and literary ambition and aptitude in his own and succeeding generations.

The Exeter Book and the Vercelli MS. between them provide an interesting series of elegies. In speaking of the typical *scóp*, we took occasion to mention the *Wanderer* and its pendant, the *Seafarer*, but relatively to their genus or dominating quality, their place is here. Goethe, in his autobiography, comments at length on the profound melancholy that pervades English poetry. This malady manifested itself quite early. In *Beowulf* there are symptoms of it; in the elegies it arrives at efflorescence. Disillusionment, despair, finds poignant expression as the poet looks around on a world that seemed so fair, but has now lost its charm and become a veritable charnel house. There is indeed a silver lining to the cloud—a bright gleam of hope in the realized gloom of earthly existence. It is the Christian faith. Even this, however, does not avail to produce buoyancy of spirits. The Wanderer is a confirmed pessimist. The Seafarer, if he feels the call of the sea, has a lively sense of the discomforts of a lonely voyage, and likens them to the trials which are the avenue to eternal joy. The *Ruin* is a picture of a desolate city—Balclutha—and the poet bestows lavish pains on the details of that appropriate and congenial symbol of the fate which he and his compeers behold as awaiting all human achievement. This poem has been preserved in fragmentary form, but is one of the most precious of the series on account of the high gifts of imagination that have gone to its making.

These compositions are lugubrious, but a Vercelli and Exon poem is more than mournful—it is morbid, *macabre*. In the *Departed Soul's Address to the Body*,[1] the writer broods over the process of decomposition, the sickening labour of the worm. The dead man is apostrophized thus: 'Better had it been if God had created thee a bird, a fish of the sea, or that, a brute without understanding, thou hadst cropped thy food in the fields, or that in the wilderness He had made thee the worst of wild beasts, or even better had it been for thee to be, by God's grace, a serpent, the cruellest of all.' With this language Jusserand aptly compares a passage of Marlowe's *Dr. Faustus*:

> . . . this soul should fly from me
> And I be changed into some brutish beast;
> And beasts are happy when they die;
> Their souls are soon dissolv'd in elements.
> O soul! be changed into small water-drops,
> And fall into the ocean, ne'er be found.

Other parts of the poem may be paralleled by Claudio's words in *Measure for Measure*:

> Ay, but to die, and go we know not where:
> To lie in cold obstruction, and to rot;
> This sensible warm motion to become
> A kneaded clod . . .

---

[1] The soul sent from heaven chides the body as a guilty associate—which is not the same thing as an associate in guilt.

> I dwelt in thee; nor might I from thee go,
> With the flesh cumber'd. Me thy sinful pleasures
> Oppressed, so that it seem'd to me full oft
> That 'twere not less than thirty thousand winters
> Unto thy death-day.

The hypochondria of English poetry may thus be considered established without bringing in Young's *Night Thoughts*, Cowper's *Castaway*, and Johnson bodily with his inherited 'vile melancholy.' What Johnson was to his age, that Bede was to Anglo-Saxon letters, with the necessary distinction that Bede wrote in Latin. His image looms like a gigantic shadow in the background of many productions to which his name cannot be attached as that of the author, but it is surprising how often, and in what various contexts, we are obliged to recognize his example or authority. It is not at all certain that the fashion of writing elegies—which, by the way, is a characteristic of Anglo-Saxon literature not shared with kindred languages, Norse, Old High German, etc.—may not be traced to admiration for Bede, in whose *Ecclesiastical History* is a passage in which an Anglo-Saxon chieftain urges on King Edwin the acceptance of Christianity as a solution of the supreme mystery. 'Often as it has been repeated,' says Professor Ker, 'the story of the conversion of Edwin, the Parable of the Swallow, remains unspoilt, as sincere as the Anglo-Saxon poetry to which it is so closely related, elegies over the vanity of earthly glory.'

Treating the language as an accident—it could have been no more to the learned poets whose compositions fill out the Exeter Book—it is worth while to see how far Bede's 'Swallow' was capable of serving as a prototype. For the convenience of the reader we will essay to translate the passage:

The present life of man on the earth as compared with that portion of time which to us is obscure, is like as when thou hast sat down to supper with thy chiefs and thanes in the winter season, the hearth has been kindled in the midst, the chamber heated, whilst without hurricanes of wintry rain or snow are raging, a sparrow hath come and flown very swiftly through the house.

Entering at one door she hath speedily departed by another. The while she is within, she is not touched by the winter's storm, but when the brief interval of calm is past, speedily returning from the storm into the storm, she glides away from thy sight. Even so the life of man appears for a little space, and of what shall follow or what hath gone before, we are utterly ignorant. Therefore, if this new teaching hath brought more certainty, it seemeth good to follow it.

Writing to a friend after the saint's decease, Cuthbert describes him as *doctus in nostris carminibus* ('skilled in English poetry,') and declares that on his deathbed he murmured in 'our tongue' the following lines on the awful parting between soul and body:

Fore there neidfæræ nænig uiurthit
thoncsnotturra than him thar[f] sie,
to ymbhycggannæ, ær his hiniong[a]e,
huæt his gæstæ, godæs æththa yflæs
æfter deothdæge doemid uuorth[a]e.

Before the necessary journey nobody waxes more wise than need be to comprehend, ere his going hence, what shall be decreed for his spirit, of good or evil, after death-day.

This death-song is the only native verse that can be definitely connected with Bede, and he may not have composed it. Cuthbert's statement cannot be deemed to involve the conclusion that Bede practised English versification, although in the case of so diligent a writer, interest in native poetry might be expected to fructify in original compositions. Knowing as we do so little of the chronology of the period, speculation is dangerous; but it is tempting to regard Bede as a link between Cædmon and Cynewulf. This might well be the case if we accepted Trautmann's theory, which identifies Cynewulf the poet with the Cynewulf who became Bishop of Lindisfarne in 737, and died in 782. Bede had died in 735.

We have seen that Cynewulf in his *Crist* expatiates on

the terrors of Doomsday. Now there is a Latin poem, *De Die Judicii*, which has been variously ascribed to Bede and Alcuin. It may be found in an appendix to the works of the former published in Migne's *Patrologia*, but, curiously enough, a large part of it is assigned to Alcuin, *e.g.*, in Frobenius's edition of his writings (1777). The authorship of the poem may therefore be considered a little uncertain, although the probability is that Bede has the better claim. We possess not only the Latin poem, but an Old English version of the same, which is, of course, much later, and exhibits a considerable degree of freedom, such as might be anticipated from a disciple of Cynewulf, who had studied not only his subjects, but his methods. The exordium is a charming vignette, a delightful little picture of rustic peace and seclusion; and most of it belongs to the Anglo-Saxon writer, for the Latin foundation consists of but two verses:

> Inter florigeras fecundi caespitis herbas
> Flamine ventorum resonantibus undique ramis.

The Old English translation is open to the charge of prolixity, but, on the whole, the added touches heighten the poetical effect. The language is carefully chosen, and some of the expressions are gems of imagery.

> Hwæt ic ana sæt innan bearwe
> mid helme beþeht holte tomiddes
> þær þa wæterburnan swegdon and urnon
> on middan gehæge, eal swa ic secge;
> eac þær wynwyrta weoxon and bleowon
> innon þam gemonge on ænlicum wonge
> and þa wudu-beamas wagedon and swegdon.

> Lo! I lonely sat within a bower
> With shade bedecked amidst a wood,
> Where the water-burns murmured and ran,
> Amid an enclosure, all as I say.

There also pleasant plants waxed and bloomed
Amid the gathering in a peerless meadow,
And the trees of the wood waved and rustled.[1]

The term 'sweg,' as has been pointed out, connotes, if it does not denote, music, being especially appropriated to the sound of the harp. 'Swegdon' is therefore singularly suggestive as used in the last line, leading us to think of an Æolian harp. But a change comes over the spirit of the dream.

Through warring of the winds the welkin was desolated,
And I suddenly, fearful and sad,
This gloomy verse began to sing.[2]

In the description of hell we meet with the lines:

One while there the eyes without measure will weep,
For the scorching of the furnace, he is full of misery;
One while too the teeth of men for great cold will gnash.[3]

This represents what was understood by our Lord's words of warning 'There shall be weeping and gnashing of teeth.' The same interpretation occurs in the Saxon *Genesis*, and more or less pervades literature. There is intense cold in Dante's hell as well as intense heat; and Claudio's dread of death in *Measure for Measure* has as one of its elements the thought that the 'delighted spirit' may be condemned

To bathe in fiery floods or to reside
In thrilling regions of thick-ribbed ice.

The eschatologist, too, does not forget that other saying 'There the worm dieth not'; and there are grim accounts of the operations of those ministers of torture.

The Bodleian MS. containing *Genesis*, *Exodus*, and *Daniel*

[1] Lumby's tr. [2] *Ibid.* [3] *Ibid.*

has an appendix consisting of three fragments which appear to have been regarded as portions of one and the same composition. The subjects are certainly near enough akin to warrant the belief that the fragments may have belonged to a poem on the scale of *Crist*, but this is purely a matter of conjecture. The first has been christened the *Fall of the Angels*, and is one of the best specimens of Old English poetry remaining to us. The writer makes it his aim to depict the mental anguish of the lost angels at the recollection of the joys that they have forfeited. They are crushed with a sense of their dire misery, and there are passages in which regret almost takes the form of contrition.

The second treats of Christ's descent into hell, His Resurrection and Ascension, and the Last Judgement. These were subjects dear to Cynewulf's heart, although, as has been pointed out, *Crist*, in the form in which we have received it, includes no description of the Harrowing of Hell. The defect is here remedied, the consternation of the devils on Christ's coming amongst them being portrayed with peculiar vividness. The evidence of style rather militates against any assumption that the poem is the handiwork of a disciple of Cynewulf, since it bears traces of the influence of other and older models; but Cynewulf's exploitation of the same or similar themes may have been known to the writer and prompted his experiments.

The third fragment, which is much shorter, concerns our Lord's Temptation. The account of the incident is marked by some departures from the Biblical narrative—none of any great moment—and at its close the Devil proceeds, on our Lord's injunction, to measure hell. He finds that from the floor to hell-gate the distance is 100,000 miles. The object of this errand is that Satan may be duly impressed with the power of the Creator, or, in other words, Christ himself. It is worthy of note that in the first fragment Christ is regularly represented in this character, and also as the victorious adversary of the revolting angels. It will be recollected that in *Juliana* it is not Satan, but Satan's son who comes in direct and malevolent contact with mankind. In the first fragment we again hear of this being, whom his father sets up as a sort of pretender to the Divine office and functions, and for that reason and treason is sentenced to heavier chastisement.

> Segdest us to soðe, þæt þîn sunu wære
> meotud moncynnes: hafastu nu mare susel.
>
> Saidest thou forsooth that thy son was
> Lord of mankind; now hast thou greater torment.

Cynewulf's Crist { Nativity, Ascension, Judgment.

Christ & Satan (Caedmonic) { Fall of Angels, Harrowing of Hell, Temptation of Christ.

CHAPTER III

RIDDLE AND RUNE

AMONG the contents of the Exeter Book are a number of poetical riddles. At one period the author of these little things was thought to have been Cynewulf, but satisfactory reasons have been advanced for questioning this belief. The interest of the compositions, however, does not vanish with the personality of the supposed writer, since they possess abundant charms of their own, and, as a class, harmonize better with the genius of the Anglo-Saxons than, perhaps, any other form of literature. We have already remarked that Old English is exceptionally rich in figurative and periphrastic expressions. The riddle is an illustration of this tendency carried one stage farther, and may be described as an allegory in miniature.

The North—Scandinavia—appears to have been the home of this species of enigma, but at an early date English scholars, like Aldhelm, Tatwine, Boniface, and Alcuin, betook themselves to the writing of Latin riddles as a mental pastime, modelling their compositions on those attributed to Symphosius. The collection in the Exeter Book contains several translated from Aldhelm, while others may have been traditional, at any rate as regards the substance.

Riddles were sometimes turned to pious account, but that was by no means their sole or chief purpose. In general, they are a mild form of pleasantry and extend to a great variety of topics, which embrace the most homely experiences and articles of common use. The principle on which they are constructed is that of defining the object without giving to it a name. Enumeration of the attributes is supposed to lead to the discovery of the hidden theme, the solution of the mystery. This method is sometimes accompanied by the play of fancy, and necessarily calls into exercise the descriptive faculty, which draws upon the accumulated store of epic metaphor and verbal convention. The poet will take, for instance, a bullock's horn and make it recount its experiences. In its time it has played many parts. Once a doughty warrior, it is overlaid by a proud young hero with gold and silver and twisted wire. These kiss it; it summons to the field of battle willing comrades. At times it it borne by a steed over the border; at times a 'sea-stallion'—'mere-' or 'brim-hengest' is frequent synonym for 'ship'—transports it over the billows. Now a gold-decked maiden fills its bosom; now, stripped of its trappings, it must needs lie neglected. Once more, in glorious adorning it is suspended on the wall, where warriors drink. At times it bids proud heroes to the wine-feast; at times it has to wrest from adversaries stolen goods and chase hostile rievers.

One of the riddles commences:

> Mec se wæta wong wundrum freorig
> Of his innaþe ærist cende.
>
> Me the wet meadow wondrous frozen
> Out of its womb first brought forth.

One suspects a sheep, but the idea is quickly dissipated, for the speaker in the next line disclaims all connection with fleeces of wool, and then, with much particularity, all connection with the weaver's art. He (or she) is equally independent of the decorative silkworm. For all that it is said:

> Wile mec (mon) þwæþre seþeah wide ofer eorþan
> hatan for hæleþum hyhtlic gewæde.
>
> Natheless will one far and wide o'er the earth
> Call me for mortals a garment of hope.

The reader is challenged to state 'Hwæt þis gewæde sy.' The answer is a coat of mail.

Apart from the intrinsic merits of the riddle—its ingenuity and poetical charm—special interest attaches to it, because it has been preserved not only in the West-Saxon version of the Exeter Book, but in what may be its primitive Northumbrian form. This has been discovered at the end of the MS. Voss 106 in the library of the University of Leyden, where it follows immediately the Latin riddles of Symphosius and Aldhelm, and printed in *The Oldest English Documents* [E.E.T.S.].

The tales of the horn and the rainbow remind us of a class of poems known in the later Middle Ages as bestiaries, but in earlier times as *physiologi*. The explanation of the term *physiologus* is that in these works animals are made to symbolize certain properties or 'natures' (φύσεις). Not only the languages of Europe, but Syriac, Coptic, and Arabic can boast of such repertories. All of them, it would appear, are traceable to a Greek original composed at Alexandria in the second century of our era. The Exeter Book contains a portion of a *physiologus* in the shape of two complete tales—the 'Panther' and the 'Whale'—and some few lines of a third, which is concerned with a wondrous bird. The recitals are really allegories. Of the panther we are told that, having gorged himself, he withdraws to his secret lair in a mountain glen, and sleeps for three days. He then wakes, utters loud and melodious notes, and therewith discharges a delicious fragrance. The animal signifies Christ—His death, burial, and resurrection.

As for the whale, when it is in repose, its enormous bulk deceives mariners, who take it for an island, and, having mounted it, are suddenly plunged into the deep. Another feature of the whale is that it has a sweet breath, with which it allures other fish and quickly gobbles them up. The monster is emblematical of hell. In the Anglo-Saxon poem the whale has a name—Fastitocalon. This is doubtless a corruption of ἀσπιδοχελώνη, the fish which performed these disagreeable feats having been originally the sea-turtle. When in the process of time the whale, as more familiar to northern nations, was substituted for the turtle, the former inherited, in a distorted form, its predecessor's name.

In the preceding chapter reference was made to a poem in which a father addresses sundry admonitions to his son. Somewhat similar reflections on men and manners occur in a quartette of poems, one of which is a singular medley of comments on seasonal changes, the way kings should woo, the ideal of a lady, social etiquette, marital concord, etc., winding up with a charming lyrical outburst.

To the Frisian wife
Comes a dear welcome guest;
The keel is at rest;
His vessel is come;
Her husband is home;
Her own cherished lord
She leads to the board;
His wet weeds she wrings;
Dry garments she brings.
Ah! happy is he,
Whom safe from the sea,
His true love awaits.[1]

[1] Gollancz' tr.

A series of affecting lyrics is dedicated to the tender relationship between man and wife. The first of the riddles in the Exeter Book is a longing lament on the part of a wife for her absent 'wolf.' In another poem, some of which is decidedly obscure, a woman, banished to a dim wood, gives expression to her grief and desire for the husband from whom she is parted. In yet another poem the husband sends his partner a staff inscribed with runes, which conveys his message. Driven into exile by a feud, he charges his wife to rejoin him across the sea, soon as she hears the cuckoo's cry in the wood. She is to permit no one to deter her from the voyage, since he awaits her longingly. Of gold he has enough, and a goodly estate in the foreign land. Many proud warriors wait upon him, though he left home a lonely fugitive. The man has now conquered melancholy. He covets neither horses nor gems, nor joy of mead, nor king's daughter, if he be without her, contrary to the ancient vow of them both.

This brings us to the Runic Song, in which twenty-nine of those characters receive a poetical interpretation. To each is assigned a short strophe of from two to five lines, the usual number being three. Despite the admixture of Christian ideas, glimpses of the old pagan beliefs peep out. Thus the name of one rune is 'ing,' the letter representing 'ng' or 'ing'; and this was also the name of an old Scandinavian divinity. Its meaning in this context seems to be 'stranger' or 'newcomer,' and the term was applied to the god who was likewise known as 'Frea' ('Lord'). He was apparently a sun-god, and the notion underlying the name 'Ing' is that it was not known whence he came nor whither he went. Ing, it is supposed, was regarded at one time as the son of Nerthus, the goddess of the earth, a wain being the symbol of both. 'Ing,' says the Runic Song, 'was first seen among the East Danes,

Banished Wife's Lament
Husband's Message

until he thereon went over the sea, the wain rolled after.' The description 'East Danes' probably does no more than signify the eastern horizon from the point of view of the old home of the Angles.

In his *Analecta Anglo-Saxonica* Thorpe cites from a Cottonian MS. (Calig. A 7) a spell for restoring fertility to land rendered sterile by witchcraft. Full directions are given with regard to the ceremonies and incantations to be used, and most of the latter are entirely of a Christian character. Here again, however, in two of the poems, appear traces of heathen mythology. After certain rites, in which an almsman takes a prominent share, the injured farmer is to recite the formula:

Erce, erce, erce, eorþan modor,
geunne ðe se Alwalda, ece Drihten
æcera wexendra, etc.

Erce, erce, erce, Mother of earth,
May He grant thee, the Almighty, Eternal Lord,
Waxing fields, etc.

Then, the plough having been driven forward and the first furrow cut, the farmer has to repeat:

Hal wes þu, folde! fira modor,
beo ðu growende on Godes fæðme
fodre gefylled, firum to nytte.

Hail to thee, earth! Mother of men,
Be thou growing under God's protection,
Filled with food for the use of men.

The name or word 'erce' has perplexed scholars, but it may be identical with 'Nerthus.' Instances of the initial n being dropped are not unknown. The Old English form of 'adder' is 'næddre.' In Middle English 'nowche' and 'owche' (meaning a 'clasp' or 'buckle') are used interchangeably, but perhaps the most familiar example is 'apron,' of which the Middle English form is 'napron.' The disappearance of the final *s* is a philological possibility, many proofs of which might be adduced, and careless pronunciation may account for the rest of the transformation.

PART III. PROSE

CHAPTER I

ALFRED

THE greatest Englishman, perhaps, of all time—the greatest, beyond question, of the period before the Norman Conquest—Alfred excelled in the arts of peace no less than in those of war. The devastations of the Danes had been terribly destructive of learning and civilization. In the preface to his translation of St. Gregory's *Regula Pastoralis* Alfred tells us that at his accession there were very few south of the Humber, and not one south of the Thames, capable of translating a Latin work. Before the time of ravage and fires he had seen the churches and the whole of England filled with treasures and books and a multitude of God's servants, but all this had been changed. With a view to the restoration of the older and better state of things, he had determined to endow his native language with versions of Latin works of which this was one. His plan is to translate 'sometimes word for word and sometimes sense for sense, as I learned from Plegmund my Archbishop and Asser my Bishop, and Grimbold my mass-priest and John my mass-priest.'

Asser has an interesting story which shows that in Alfred's case the boy was father of the man. One day his mother[1] drew the attention of the prince and his brothers to a volume of English poetry which she held in her hand. 'Whichever of you,' she said to them, 'can first learn this book, shall have it for a gift.' Charmed with the beautiful illumination, Alfred inquired whether she really intended to bestow the book on the one who first understood and could repeat it. She assured him she did. Thereupon he carried it off, learned to read it with the help of his master, and, returning to his mother, recited it.

To us nothing is more surprising than the fame of the Spanish priest Orosius as the chief historical authority of the Middle Ages. In two lines Dante at once testifies to his importance and accounts for it. He calls him

> Quell' avvocato dei tempi cristiani,
> Del cui latino Augustin si provvide.

which Longfellow renders:

> That advocate of the Christian centuries,
> Out of whose rhetoric Augustine was furnished.

Orosius was the author of a universal history, of which St. Augustine made use in his *City of God*, and the object of which was to confute those gainsayers who maintained that Christianity had been the cause of more harm than good to the world.

Alfred does not merely translate—he expounds Orosius. On glancing at Mr. Sweet's edition, in which the Latin original and the Old English version are printed in parallel columns, we are immediately struck with the fact that the translation usually occupies a much larger space than the corresponding text. Closer observation reveals that this disproportion does not arise solely from the difference in the genius of the languages, or from the King's colloquial

[1] Really stepmother; Queen Judith.

manner of addressing the reader, but from the inclusion also of explanatory matter, which must have been culled from written commentaries, or possibly from the oral communications of those distinguished clerks who aided Alfred in the elucidation of obscure passages. The King was thirty-nine years old before he began the study of Latin; and as the burdens of state would have militated against proficiency in that difficult tongue, it is nothing but reasonable to suppose that the collaboration of professed scholars was vital to the performance of the monarch's cherished enterprise. The erudition of all of them together was not always equal to emergencies; and it would be easy to enumerate cases in which the sense has been entirely misunderstood.

The object the King had in view was to provide an education in the history of past ages, through an orthodox medium, for the noble youth of his nation—an object for which he showed himself solicitous in other ways, such as the institution of schools and seminaries, and the invitation to his court and country of foreigners famous for their accomplishments in learning, like his friend and biographer, Asser. At the present time it is not too much to say that Orosius is esteemed not so much for his intrinsic merits as a writer and historian as for his industry in amassing useful knowledge. By a fortunate accident his name has been linked with those of St. Augustine, Alfred the Great, and Dante, each of whom was signally indebted to him; and, in addition to those lights in the intellectual firmament, generations of humbler students had to thank him for most of their information concerning the course of events down to the fifth century of our era. By unlocking the treasures of Greek and Latin literature, the Renaissance deposed Orosius from his seat of authority, and now if we turn to Alfred's translation of his work, we are attracted less to his own pages than to certain passages in which he had no share at all. The King has enriched the book with personal contributions in the shape of authentic accounts of expeditions to the North and East taken down apparently from the lips of the two adventurers. The extraordinary interest of these recitals, whether they are considered as specimens of the royal author's composition or only from the point of view of their age and contents, will justify reproduction of these obviously honest narratives at some length:

Ohthere said to his lord, King Alfred, that of all the Northmen he dwelt most to the north. He said that he dwelt in the land northward over against the Western Sea; he said, however, that the land extends thence a very long way to the north, but it is all waste, save that in a few places the Finns have scattered habitations, being engaged in hunting in the winter, and in the summer in fishing by the sea. He said that he at one time wished to find out how far that land lay direct north, or whether any man dwelt to the north of that waste, wherefore he journeyed direct north of the land, leaving the whole way the waste land on the starboard and the wide sea on the larboard, for three days. He was then as far north as whale-hunters journey at the farthest. Nevertheless he journeyed direct north as far as he might sail in the next three days. Then the land inclined direct east, or the sea bore in upon the land, he knew not whether, only he knew that he waited there for a west wind, or one a little northerly, and sailed thence east along the land, as far as he might sail in four days. Then he was obliged to wait for a direct north wind, for the land inclined direct south, or the sea bore in upon the land, he knew not whether. Then he sailed direct south along the land as far as he might sail in five days. There lay there a great river [the Dwina] reaching up into the interior of the land; they turned in upon the river, for they durst not sail forward past the river by reason of hostility, for the land was all cultivated on the other side of the river. He had not before met with any cultivated land since he journeyed from his own home, but it was all waste on the starboard, save for fishers and fowlers and hunters; and they were all Finns, and on the larboard was always the wide sea.

The Beormas had their land very well cultivated, but they durst not set foot upon it; but the Terfinns' land was all waste, save where hunters encamped, or fishers, or fowlers. Many tales the Beormas told him both of their own land and the lands that were round about, but he knew not what truth there was in it, for he did not see it himself. The Finns, it seemed to him, and the Beormas spoke nearly one tongue.

The Dwina, then, was as far as Ohthere, a rich inhabitant of Halgoland in Norway, could penetrate. He makes no concealment of the fact that his object was not purely exploration, but search for the tusks of 'horse-whales,' or walruses—very noble ivory. He then proceeds to describe his own domestic economy and that of the wealthiest Beormas, who levied tribute on the Finns, always in kind. He gives some account of the nature and extent of the country of the Beormas and the border raids between them and their neighbours, the Amazons! Ohthere's narrative concludes with more geographical details relating to the coasts of Scandinavia, and given with much exactitude.

The other traveller, Wulfstan, takes up his parable nearly at the point where Ohthere breaks off. He sets out from a port called Hæthum, or æt Hæthum, in Sleswig, and sails to the mouth of the Vistula. To the east of that great river, and on the shores of the Baltic, dwelt the Estas or Osterlings; and most of Wulfstan's report has to do with the very interesting funeral customs of that people.

And there is a custom among the Estas, when a man is there dead, that he lieth within unburned, with his kinsmen and friends, a month, sometimes twain; and kings and other men of high estate as long a space as they have more wealth, sometimes half a year that they be unburned, and lie above the earth in their houses. And all the while the corpse is within, there must be drinking and play until the day they burn him. On the same day they will bear him to the funeral pyre they divide his property which is there remaining, after the drinking and play, into five or six parts, sometimes more, according to the value of the property. Then the largest part they lay one mile from the town, then the second, then the third, until it be all laid in the one mile; and the last part must be nighest the town wherein the dead man lieth. Then shall be gathered together all the men that have the swiftest horses in the land, five miles or six miles from the property. Then they all run towards the property; then cometh the man that hath the swiftest horse to the first part and the largest, and so each one after the other, till it be all taken: and he taketh the last part who gaineth the property nighest the town. And then each rideth on his way with the property, and all may have it; and therefore swift horses there are inconceivably precious. And when his treasure is thus all spent, then he is borne forth and burned with his weapons and clothes; and for the most part they expend all his wealth what with the long lying of the dead man within and their laying in the way for strangers to run up and take it.

As an explanation of the circumstance that dead bodies could remain so long without decomposing, it is stated, in conclusion, that among the Estas was a tribe skilled in the art of refrigeration.

The insertion of these narratives in a translation of Orosius is an extreme instance of Alfred's attitude of independence towards those authors whom he took under his patronage. In his version of Boethius this boldness is displayed in other ways. We do not refer to the fact that the *De Consolatione Philosophiae* is partly in metre, while Alfred's translation is in prose, but to differences not involved in this process of simplification. Living when he did, writing in the Latin language, and addressing himself to a learned constituency, Boethius was under the spell of centuries of literary precedent and tradition, and his work is a model of elegance. The King's rendering, on the other hand, is evidently designed for babes and sucklings in learning, and the freshness of the style suggests a certain innocence in the translator. His *naïveté* betrays itself also in reference to religion. Probably he never harboured any suspicion on the subject of his author's orthodoxy, although this is by no means a matter to be taken for granted. Usener has cleared up all doubts as to the personal Christianity of the poet, but his faith has not been shown in his work, which is inspired throughout by Plato and Aristotle. The element which is entirely or almost lacking in the original, Alfred, himself a sincere and devout believer, supplies in ample measure. Where Boethius fails to rise to the occasion, there Alfred steps in with the requisite application of Christian doctrine. The story of Orpheus provides good illustrations of the King's artless yet charming manner, and his inclination to moralize is a Christian direction.

It happened formerly that there was a harper, in that province that was called Thracia, which was in the kingdom of Greece. The harper was extraordinarily good, and his name was Orfeus. He had a very excellent wife, who was called Eurydice. It began to be said of the harper that he could harp so that the wood shook and the stones they stirred for the noise, and wild deer there would run up and stand, as if they were tame, so still, though men or hounds chased them, that they did not shun them. Then said they that the harper's wife died and her soul was conducted to hell. Then was the harper so grieved that he might not remain in the company of other men, but took to the woods, and sat on the mountains, weeping and harping, so that the woods trembled, and the rivers stood still, and no hart shunned any lion, nor any of them any hound, nor any beast felt any hatred or malice against any other, for joy of that sound. Then it seemed to the harper that he had no pleasure in anything in this world, and he resolved that he would visit the gates of hell, and begin to flatter them with his harp, and pray them to give him his wife again. When he came thither, there came to meet him the hound of hell, whose name was Cerverus, who had three heads, and began to fawn with his tail and play with him because of his harpings. There was there also a very terrible porter, whose name was Caron, who had also three heads, and who was of a very great age. . . .

After he had harped for a long, long while, the King of the inhabitants of hell called and said Let us give the man his wife, for he hath earned her with his harpings. Then he commanded him that he should well understand, that he should never look behind him, after he was gone thence, and said, that if he looked behind him, he should lose his wife. But, alas! it is with very great difficulty that love is forbidden. Lo, Orfeus led his wife with him until he came to the border of light and darkness; then his wife followed after him. When he had come forth into the light, he looked behind him towards his wife; then was she lost to him immediately.

This lying tale teacheth every man, who hath a desire to flee the darkness of hell, and to come to the light of the true God, that he look not to his old evil deeds, in such wise as he may perform them as fully as he did aforetime; for whosoever, with full intent, turneth his mind to the evil deeds that he erewhile forsook, and then performeth them, and taketh full pleasure in them, and never thinketh to forsake them, loseth all his former good, save he amend it.

In Chapter XVII Alfred makes a personal confession of the greatest interest, in which he discloses the ruling principle of his life and the most notable lesson he has deduced from experience. There is perhaps some admixture of ambition—'that last infirmity of noble minds'—in his reluctance to accept oblivion, but he at least recognizes that mere skill and ability are not sufficient passports to immortality. They must be attended by wisdom, without which there can be no achievement. To Alfred wisdom was not what it is to many—enlightened selfishness—but the practice of virtue. 'I have striven,' he says, 'to live worthily as long as I live, and, my life ended, to bequeath my memory to them that come after me, in good works.'

The King's endeavours were so far crowned with success that for generations he was regarded as the embodiment of all that is truly great and kingly; and the Norman Conquest, far from obscuring or obliterating his renown, rendered his memory, if possible, more dear and precious.

Subsequently to that event there appeared an anonymous work entitled the *Proverbs of Alfred* (printed by Kemble in an appendix to his edition of *Salomon and Saturnus*), and here he is styled 'Englene derling'—'England's darling.'[1]

We have remarked above that in instituting a comparison between the original verse and the translation it will be wise not to lay undue stress on the fact that the latter is in prose. Obviously so, for where metre is employed, and especially where a strange and difficult versification is imitated, the tendency is to produce a work continuously departing from the style of that which it purports to represent. Alfred, however, seems to have been touched by a feeling to which all lovers of literature are more or less subject, that poetry implies regular forms—that it is based upon song as much as upon beauty of language and imagination; and that, consequently, the translator's task is only half accomplished when he reproduces the sense of his author without offering any equivalent in the matter of verse. In the preface of each of the two manuscripts, in which the translation has been preserved, it is stated that Alfred afterwards recast it in a poetical mould. The earlier presents us with this *rifacimento* in the national alliterative verse; from the later it is absent. It may be added that the intimation regarding the King's second experiment does not emanate from Alfred himself; and it is almost inevitable that some scepticism should be expressed as to the genuineness of the composition. Ten Brink evidently looks upon such questioning as gratuitous, but if Alfred's authorship be granted, the work is not of such a kind as greatly to enhance the monarch's literary reputation. Prose and verse renderings resemble

[1] For the *Proverbs of Alfred* see *An Old English Miscellany* [E.E.T.S.].

each other as closely as the necessities of rhythm and alliteration admit; and no attempt has been made to improve the occasion by consulting the *Metra* anew and engrafting some of their graces. Under any circumstances, this would have been a difficult undertaking, as the peculiar excellences of the Latin poetry were foreign to Anglo-Saxon culture in its traditional aspects.

The *Pastoral Care* of St. Gregory the Great was one of those works that attained such celebrity in the Dark Ages as almost to mark itself out for translation. It was one of a select company, in which the writings of Orosius and Boethius were also found, that travelled to the uttermost confines of Christendom.

The story in the Icelandic *Bishops' Lives* of the death-bed of Thorlak, the third Bishop of Skálholt († 1133), is a testimony, in addition to King Alfred's translation, showing what efficacy the *Pastoral Care* had, and in what honour it was held. He asked to have it read to him as he lay sick, 'and men thought that he looked forward to his death with a better courage than before the reading began.' That a manual of directions for the practical work of a clergyman among his people should have been available in this way for the comfort of the dying is some proof of a human virtue in it, besides its ecclesiastical merits.[1]

Nevertheless, it must have been its ecclesiastical merits that commended it, most of all, to Alfred's loving care and industry. The King was anxious for the welfare of all classes of his subjects, and we know from his own testimony that learning had declined to so low an ebb among the clergy that it may be doubted whether many of them, without some such provision, would ever have made the acquaintance of this valuable enchiridion. Through the agency of the pastors Alfred was ministering to the spiritual needs of the entire nation; and therefore

[1] W. P. Ker.

it is easily understood that he attached particular importance to this version. He sent a copy of it to every one of the bishops. It is worthy of note that the example preserved in the Bodleian once belonged to Werferth, Bishop of Worcester, who may be described as Alfred's colleague in the work of translation, for to him was due an Anglo-Saxon version of Gregory's *Dialogues* with Peter the Deacon, which he undertook at the King's instance. For a long time this remained unprinted, but it is now obtainable in Grein's invaluable *Bibliothek der angelsächsischen Prosa*, vol. v. The *Dialogues* might have had for sub-title *Recreations of a Holy Father*, for they are compounded, to a large extent, of a mass of legends and visions, many of them sufficiently wonderful.

The facts already referred to afford ample explanation of the popularity of Gregory's writings, but, as regards England, there is an element in the case of which Alfred and his collaborators could not be unaware, and that was bound to attract them to the literary remains of the great pope. It was through Gregory, in the first instance, that the conversion of the English to the faith of Christ was brought about. The story is told in Bede's *Ecclesiastical History*, but nowhere so charmingly as in one of Ælfric's homilies,[1] which commemorates the anniversary of the saint's death, and in the opening sentence of which he is designated as 'the Apostle of the English People.'

It happened at a certain time, even as it often does still, that English merchants brought their wares to the city of Rome, and Gregory went along the street to the Englishmen, viewing their goods. He then saw set among the wares, slave-boys, who were of a beautiful figure and fair countenance, and noble locks. Gregory remarked the beauty of the youths, and enquired from what people

[1] See *Selected Homilies of Ælfric* (Sweet), p. 57, 2nd edition.

they were brought. He was told that they were from England, and that their nation was as manly as it was beautiful. Again Gregory enquired whether the people of the land was Christian or heathen. He was told they were heathen. Gregory sighed long and deeply, and said 'Alas, that men of so fair complexion should be subject to the black devil!' Again he asked what was the name of the people from which they came. It was answered him that they were named Angles. Then quoth he, 'Rightly are they called Angles, for they have the beauty of angels, and it behoveth such that they be companions of angels in heaven.' Once more Gregory enquired what was the name of the province from which the boys had been imported. He was told that the inhabitants of the province were called Dere. Gregory answered: 'Well are they called Dere, seeing that they have been saved from wrath [*de ira*] and invited to the mercy of Christ.' Yet again he enquired: 'What is the name of the king of the people?' It was answered him that the king was called Ælle. Thereupon Gregory played on the name with his words, and said: 'It behoveth that Alleluia be sung in the land, to the praise of the Omnipotent Creator.

Earlier in the same discourse Ælfric remarks, 'many holy books relate his [Gregory's] holy life and conversation, and also the *Historia Anglorum*, which King Alfred translated out of Latin into English. The book speaketh plainly enough concerning this holy man.' Here we have a clear intimation that a translation of the Venerable Bede's *Ecclesiastical History* was one of Alfred's 'achievements.' It would savour of disingenuousness to read into the passage the meaning that Alfred merely caused the work to be translated, but in attributing to the King personally the execution of a task which might have been carried out by others, it is possible that Ælfric was mistaken. As there is extant a translation of the *History* in the vulgar tongue, it has been very generally assumed that this is the translation of which Ælfric speaks. Mr. Miller, however, who edited the work for the Early English Text Society, entitles it cautiously 'The *Old English* Version of Bede's

Ecclesiastical History of the English People.' There is an air of non-committal about this description, which prepares us for a critical discussion not too favourable to the claim advanced on the King's behalf. Mr. Miller is ready to recognize Alfred's influence and inspiration—he thinks he may have been behind the undertaking—but that is as far as he is able to go. This judgement is not, like some, a capricious or arbitrary pronouncement born of an idle desire to upset pious beliefs, but founded on a careful and conscientious investigation of the text. The result of this study was to disclose the presence of Mercian features in the vocabulary, which appear to be inconsistent with Alfred's authorship, but quite consistent with the theory of a previous version in an Anglian dialect, of which these peculiarities are traces, or of a Midland writer, who handled the West-Saxon speech as Livy did Latin, and so originated the term 'Patavinity.' Apart from linguistic considerations, the version does not conform to the King's ordinary methods as exhibited in his other translations, and notably in his Orosius. Ten Brink raises no question as to the soundness of the attribution, but even he is struck by the contrast thus presented. Narratives like those of Ohthere and Wulfstan are technically to be condemned in the context in which they occur, being excrescences for which a modern translator could plead no excuse, but the sternest critics could have found it reasonable if Alfred had supplemented Bede with a store of fresh data drawn from his personal knowledge, and relating more particularly to later periods and the southern portion of the kingdom. The German scholar's suggestion that the King had jotted down such particulars in his Handbook and deemed it supererogatory to state them twice over, does not carry conviction, and in any case does not account for the drastic abridgement of the *History*, of which whole chapters are represented by their headings. The test of style accentuates the feeling of uncertainty; and, if any conclusion may be deduced from it, it is that two minds were concerned in the translation, one having a preference for a strictly literal rendering, while the other had no objection to a degree of embellishment and indulged the national liking for pleonasm. The most faithful of all Alfred's translations is that of the *Pastoral Care*.

Mention has been made of Alfred's Handbook. Somewhat like Milton, the King made it a constant practice to copy or have copied for him, in a commonplace book, literary memoranda to which he attached special importance. Asser furnishes a pleasing picture of his master's eager pursuit of the best thoughts. Writing of the year 887, he says:

In the same year also Alfred, king of the Anglo-Saxons so often before mentioned, by divine inspiration, began, on one and the same day, to read and interpret; but that I may explain this more fully to those who are ignorant, I will relate the cause of this long delay in beginning. On a certain day we were both of us sitting in the King's chamber, talking on all kinds, as usual, and it happened that I read to him a quotation out of a certain book. He heard it attentively with both his ears, and addressed me with a thoughtful mind, showing me at the same time a book which he carried in his bosom, wherein the daily courses and psalms and prayers which he had read in his youth, were written, and he commanded me to write the same quotation in that book. Hearing this, and perceiving his ingenuous benevolence, and devout desire of studying the words of divine wisdom, I gave, though in secret, boundless thanks to Almighty God, who had implanted such a love of wisdom in the King's heart. But I could not find any empty space in that book wherein to write the quotation, for it was already full of various matters; wherefore I made a little delay, principally that I might stir up the bright intellect of the King to a higher acquaintance with the divine testimonies. Upon his urging me to make haste and write it quickly, I said to him: 'Are you willing that I should write that quotation on some leaf apart? For it is not certain whether we shall not find one or more other such extracts which will please you; and if that should so happen, we shall be glad that we have kept them apart.' 'Your plan is good,' said he; and I gladly made haste to get ready a sheet, in the beginning of which I wrote what he bade me; and on that same day I wrote therein, as I had anticipated, no less than three other quotations which pleased him; and from that time we daily talked together, and found out other quotations which pleased him, so that the sheet became full, and deservedly so; according as it is written, 'The just man builds upon a moderate foundation, and by degrees passes to greater things.' Thus, like a most productive bee, he flew here and there asking questions, as he went, until he had eagerly and increasingly collected many various flowers of divine scriptures, with which he thickly stored the cells of his mind.

Now when that first quotation was copied, he was eager at once to read, and to interpret in Saxon, and then to teach others; even as we read of that happy robber, who recognized his Lord, aye, the Lord of all men, as he was hanging on the blessed cross, and saluting him with his bodily eyes only, because elsewhere he was pierced with nails, cried: 'Lord remember me when thou comest into Thy kingdom!' for it was only at the end of his life that he began to learn the rudiments of the Christian faith. But the king, inspired by God, began to study the rudiments of divine Scripture on the sacred solemnity of Saint Martin [Nov. 11], and he continued to learn the flowers collected by certain masters, and to reduce them into the form of one book, as he was then able, although mixed one with another, until it become almost as large as a psalter. This book he called his ENCHIRIDION or MANUAL, because he carefully kept it at hand day and night, and found, as he told me, no small consolation therein.[1]

In these paragraphs the learned Gaul sets Alfred before us at the very outset of his career in letters. How belated he thought him may be gathered from the comparison with the thief on the Cross; and he palliates his backwardness by a threefold handicap—recurring attacks of a mysterious malady, the dread of which prostrated and paralysed him, the disturbed condition of his kingdom, ever the prey of

[1] Giles' tr.

piratical pagans, and the necessary cares of government. Alfred, however, had still thirteen or fourteen more years to live; and, although the age of forty is rather an advanced period of life for striking out on a new path, it was hardly an instance of the eleventh hour.

The extent of what Alfred accomplished in the allotted spell will never be known for certain. One of his admirers —Ethelwerd—cannot be acquitted of exaggeration. 'Lastly' he says, 'in the same year [900] King Alfred departed out of this world, that immoveable pillar of the Western Saxons, that man full of justice, bold in arms, learned in speech, and, above all other things, imbued with the divine instructions. For he had translated, out of Latin, *unnumbered volumes*, of so varied a nature, and so excellently, that the sorrowful book of Boethius seemed, not only to the learned, but even to those who heard it read, as it were brought to life again.'

It is doubtful whether Ethelwerd intended to convey by *numero ignoto* quite all that is signified by 'unnumbered,' but in any case the phrase denotes considerable activity with the pen. It is said that there is no royal road to learning, but Alfred appears to have discovered one. He himself acknowledges the help received from four eminent foreigners; to this William of Malmesbury adds, what would be hardly suspected from Ethelwerd's glowing eulogy, that 'Asser deciphered in plainer words the meaning of Boethius' books *De Consolatione*, which the King himself turned into the English tongue.' Thorpe goes so far as to suggest that Asser not only simplified the text, but prompted many of the additions to it. In the Englishing of Bede the Mercian words may be due to the participation of Mercian scholars in a translation to which the King contributed, perhaps, the largest share. Werferth, Bishop of Worcester, Plegmund, Archbishop of Canterbury, and

Æthelstan and Werewulf, the King's priests and chaplains, were all Mercians by birth. On the other hand, there can hardly have been a standard of purity in the use or rejection of particular words as belonging to this or that dialect; and as Alfred married a Mercian princess and books were constantly read to him by Mercian lips, his sense of provincialism must have tended to become obliterated. However that may be, it is evident that Alfred did not occupy the position of a common student. It will be best to regard him as the central figure of a great intellectual awakening, which he promoted by all the means in his power; and it is idle to question that amongst his talents were discernment and the accompanying gift of direct and perspicuous language. As far as can be judged, he was in no way behind the most elect spirits of his time in taste and the art of expression. We are told by William of Malmesbury that the King shortly before his death achieved a translation of the Psalter; and he is said to have rendered into English other parts of the Bible, excerpts from St. Augustine, Æsop's Fables, and a treatise on falconry. These, perhaps, were included in the *numero ignoto* of the Old English chronicler, but it may well be that the fame of the royal author attracted into its orbit productions with which he had not even a remote connection. Morbid vanity or downright roguery may have led Chattertons to alienate their mental offspring; or, again, waifs and strays of literature may have been given to a name which stood above all others as the palladium of pre-Conquest wisdom and learning. The eleventh-century *Proverbs of Alfred* exhibits him in the *rôle* of universal instructor of thanes, bishops, and bookmen.

> He wes king, and he wes clerk;
> Wel he luuede godes werk.

CHAPTER II

THE 'ANGLO-SAXON CHRONICLE'

ENGLAND is extraordinarily fortunate in possessing a history in the native language of the early ages of national life, which, singularly enough, is continued beyond the date of the Norman Conquest. No people in Europe can boast of a parallel record; and however defective it may be in certain respects, it is inspired by a love of truth—the prime virtue of any writings professing to be historical—and remains to this day the principal source from which we derive our knowledge of those troublous times.

The origin of the *Chronicle* has been constantly attributed to Plegmund, King Alfred's coadjutor, whom he raised to the see of Canterbury. This account cannot be accepted, but there are indications that zeal for this highly important branch of intellectual activity received a fresh impetus during the reign of the greatest of Anglo-Saxon monarchs, and, in the words of an able French writer, 'these chronicles were developed under his influence.' M. Jusserand speaks of 'chronicles.' Although it is usual to quote the compilation as the *Saxon, Anglo-Saxon,* or *English Chronicle,* the history has descended to us in no fewer than seven distinct forms, which are sufficiently independent to call for separate notice. Moreover, successive epochs, after a certain period, are treated by contemporary annalists. The whole is anonymous, and so the *Chronicle,* as the work of many hands, may well pass as a monument of the patriotism of generations of scribes, each of them content to add its tribute to the remembrance of England's past, and then die and be forgotten.

Of the seven chronicles the most important, beyond doubt or question, is that of Winchester. The manuscript was presented by Archbishop Parker to the library of Corpus Christi College, Cambridge, where it is still preserved, and the oldest portion of it, which extends to the year 891, is in the handwriting of a single copyist, and not later than the tenth century. The MS. as a whole extends to 1070 in Anglo-Saxon, and to 1075 in Latin. The next in interest and importance is the Peterborough Chronicle, with the MS. of which the Bodleian Library was enriched by Archbishop Laud. Originally this ended with the year 1122, but was continued to 1154. Composed in the Abbey of Medeshamstede—the former name of Peterborough—it embraces a series of forged documents relating to ancient benefactions and grants of privileges to the foundation; and this feature has led to the utterly groundless and absurd conclusion that the *Anglo-Saxon Chronicle* was begun by the monks of Peterborough. The conclusion is absurd because the great fire of 1116, which destroyed the minster, destroyed also most of its muniments and literary treasures. As part of the work of reparation, about the year 1121 the monks set about the composition of a new chronicle, for which materials were drawn from various sources, the annals of Winchester, the annals of Abingdon, and the annals of Worcester, of which last they appear to have possessed themselves of a version extending to the year 1107. The *Peterborough Chronicle* continues the narrative not only to the date of its commencement, but without serious interruption to 1131. The final instalment—from 1122 to 1154—seems to have been accomplished after an interval of several years during which the ingress of Norman idioms became more pronounced.

Between the oldest and youngest of the family of chronicles intervene the remaining five, two of which, and those the most noteworthy, have been already named. The Abingdon and Worcester MSS., both of which are contained in the Cottonian Library, and marked Tiberius B i and B iv respectively, extend, the former to the year 1066, and the latter to the year 1079. Worcester, it will be remembered, was the see of Werferth, the friend of King Alfred, and the translator of St. Gregory's *Dialogues.* A prelate of this type was likely to leave his mark on those who served the cathedral, and it was during his time that commencement was made of a chronicle relating to events in Northumbria and Mercia. In 1016 these annals were incorporated with those of Winchester, and brought down to the current year—the year in which Æthelred II died, and Canute began his reign. The Danish ascendancy made no difference as regards the language of the country, West-Saxon being still used for legal and official purposes, but the establishment of a foreign dynasty was bound to have a depressing influence on a people distinguished above all others for its love of liberty. Between the dominance of the Danes and the disintegrating victory of the Normans occurred an interval which, though not without disquieting omens, was more agreeable to the patriotic temper than the era which preceded or that which was to follow. Godwine is too great as a man, a warrior, and a statesman to be compared with Byrhtnoth, but the spirit of that hero seems as if reincarnated in the famous earl, from whose loins sprang the last of our native kings. The Worcester annals during these decades reflect the gladness of the English restoration; and the narrative waxes more lively and lifelike as it recounts the fortunes of the resolute chief, who, more than any other man of his nation, staved off the impending doom of Norman despotism. An account is given of the battle of Hastings, and of William the Conqueror, of whose character there is presented a very just and discriminating estimate. The annalist remarks with admiration on this monarch's inflexible maintenance of the King's peace, which enabled a man to travel unmolested through his kingdom with his bosom full of gold, and would not suffer any one to slay another, no matter how great an injury had been inflicted on him.

Closely allied to the *Worcester Chronicle* are the annals compiled at Abingdon Abbey. The latter are actually based partly on the Worcester annals, and partly on a transcript of the Winchester annals made at Canterbury, and extending to the year 997; but the chronicle, like that of Worcester, is enriched with much independent material. This remark applies, in each case, more particularly to the later years. Begun about 1046, the *Abingdon Chronicle* was continued for ten years, after which there was a cessation of historical industry until the days of Harold. Mention is made of the march against Sweyn and the hard-won victory at Stamford Bridge, and then there is again silence.

We have referred to a Canterbury transcript of the Winchester annals. This MS. is one which formerly belonged to the Abbey of St. Augustine in that city, and is now in the Cottonian Library (Tiberius A vi). As we have seen, it extends to the year 997. Another copy (Otho B xi), which was continued to 1001, perished in the fire at Ashburnham House in 1731. This formed the basis of Wheelocke's edition, printed at the end of his folio edition of Bede's history, and published in 1643 at Cambridge.

Lastly, there is the bilingual chronicle of Canterbury. During the former half of the eleventh century, the Winchester MS., which afterwards passed into the possession of Archbishop Parker, found its way to Canterbury, and soon after the elevation of Lanfranc to the metropolitan see, additions were made to it in the shape of eleven scattered, but highly important, notices relating to the period 1005-70. In the last of these notices an account is given of the Norman prelate and the contention between him and Archbishop Thomas of York.

It must be plain, on comparing these accounts, that, while several versions of the *Chronicle*, and indeed most, have claims upon our attention, as providing supplementary or alternative narratives, the Winchester annals occupy a unique position; they are the ground, the chief corner-stone of the whole historical structure. That being the case, it will be expedient to re-examine the subject more closely, and place in evidence the various phases that marked the evolution of this central and standard record. In the first place something must be said in explanation of the fact that the chronicles are impersonal, and, while sometimes broadening out into all the fullness of national memorials, at other times shrink into the petty insignificance of mere local registers. This peculiarity will cease to excite wonderment when we are informed of the probable origin of the chronicles. A seventeenth-century scholar—Gibson—refers to an account supplied by Walter Bower, the continuator of Fordun's *Scotichronicon*, from which it appears that in the monasteries of royal foundation in England, whatever worthy of remembrance occurred in the neighbourhood was committed to writing, that such records were compared with each other at the next synod, and that out of them were composed the chronicles. It is well known in connection with necrologies that a strong tie of brotherhood united the monasteries and capitular bodies of the realm, which were in incessant communication with each other; and thus in time records which in their inception had been conventual, synodal, or provincial only, would come to fulfil the higher function of preserving the memory of national events. The variations between the different chronicles cannot disguise their general resemblance, which appears to be due to a spirit of fellowship and co-operation, or, in other words, to an extension of the practice already noted as existing within certain confines.

That Winchester should have led the way in the formation of a national chronicle appears quite reasonable when we recall that it was the capital of Wessex, and therefore more in contact with the court than those cities which were simply ecclesiastical centres. Much time, however, was to elapse before annalists acquired an historical conscience. Not that they perverted the truth—only that the earliest entries are, to a distressing extent, jejune and desultory. As time went on a notable improvement took place. There were fewer gaps; notices became fuller, more explicit. Still something was wanting to stimulate ardour to the highest pitch, and that was a just pride in the national greatness. The glorious reign of King Æthelwulf evoked this feeling, which is likely to have been fostered by Bishop Swithun. Under the direction of that enlightened prelate, or at his instigation, the annals were remodelled. It has been conjectured that an amalgamation of the Winchester and Canterbury chronicles occurred at this time (855). Anyhow, many omissions were filled up, and very occasionally the dry enumeration of facts is interrupted with a story. The older edition did not extend in a backward direction beyond the seventh century; the new version traced the course of events to an epoch much more remote—the advent of Hengest and Horsa and the first landing of the allied peoples. This information would have been drawn in the main from oral traditions and popular minstrelsy.

There are some odd things in this fresh compilation, such as the attribution to Æthelwulf of a pedigree reaching back to the Jewish patriarchs and terminating with Adam. This is reproduced in Asser's Life of Alfred, and, absurd as it seems to us, was to all appearance gravely received and transmitted as authentic and official.

From 866 to 887 the continuation of the *Chronicle* bears signs of being left to a single writer, who was able to link up the incidents of the terrible struggle with the Danes in regular sequence; and the vicissitudes of some years are recorded at some length. But the style is still annalistic; the subject-matter alone is important, and eloquence, we might think, deliberately eschewed.

In 991 a second revision was carried out on precisely the same lines as the former. Defects were made good, and the record now included an account of the island in pre-Saxon times to the year 60 B.C. In the nature of things this prologue must have been derived from written, that is, Latin, sources. It has been assumed in some quarters that those sources were the works of Bede chiefly, but it turns out on investigation that the *Ecclesiastical History* has been used only in the accounts of the earliest inhabitants of Britain and Ireland. Elsewhere the principal authority is Eusebius, and it is only in places where the *Chronicle* adds to or departs from his statements that Bede is called—always tacitly—into requisition. Dates are computed according to the reckonings of Eusebius and Orosius, who calculate a space of 5,198 years from the Creation to the Birth of Christ. These observations are intended to apply to the portion of the *Chronicle* antecedent to the year 449.

From 449 to 597 the *Chronicle,* far from depending on Bede, contains matter relating to Wessex, a part of England of whose history the Northumbrian writer knew exceedingly little. With this and some Kentish narratives the section is almost exclusively occupied. For the ensuing period, as far as the year 731, at which the *Ecclesiastical History* ends, this was undoubtedly the chief source, since there are few statements in the *Chronicle* that may not be found in the older work. There are a few. Of the years 603, 616, and 617, for example, the Peterborough MS. has accounts derived from some other authority. Certain of the earlier MSS., also, comprise additions from unknown sources—we may take as instances the entries for the years 693 and 710—and elsewhere, as Florence of Worcester observes, there are actual deviations from Bede's record.

From 732 to 845 the *Chronicle* is itself the fountain-head of all that is known of that long period. From 851 to 887 Asser's Life of Alfred is an affluent, whole passages being transferred to the *Chronicle* with few variations. In the following century the process was reversed, Ethelwerd turning the English chronicle into mediaeval Latin. From the year 1001 onwards the divergencies between the different MSS.—those, that is to say, that transcend that period—become more frequent and more pronounced. The Abingdon and Worcester chronicles are most harmonious, but even they exhibit marked discrepancies. The former, for example, contains Mercian accounts of the years 1046, 1048, 1049, and 1053, which the latter is without.

One or two questions are raised by what has been stated in the foregoing paragraph. The first regards the historical accuracy of the *Chronicle.* And here it must be remarked that the MSS. we possess manifestly suffer from 'clerical errors' and editorial lapses, some of which, especially those of a chronological nature, are radical and vitiate the entire set, whilst others, affecting one or more versions, may be corrected by the various readings shown by the chronicles themselves, or by the Latin compilations of Florence of Worcester and Simeon of Durham. In translating from the *Anglo-Saxon Chronicle* those estimable writers doubtless had access to MSS. no longer extant, and both can be proved to have resorted to authorities other than the *Historia vel Chronica hujus patriae.* At this distance of time the assertions that can be best tested are those which refer to celestial phenomena. Correct notices of eclipses of the sun are given under the dates 538, 540, 664, and 733. In the two latter cases the day and the hour are named by Florence, but omitted in the *Chronicle.* Again the *Chronicle* speaks of an eclipse of the moon as occurring in 795. Simeon of Durham places the event in 796, and this is correct. An error of this description might arise from carelessness on the part of the transcriber or from the entry having been made after a considerable interval.

We have pointed out that the MSS. were periodically revised and enlarged, and that items omitted in the earlier editions were supplied in the later. We have seen also that poetical fragments are inserted here and there in the narrative. These are found under the dates 937, 941, 958, 973, 975, 1011, 1036, and 1065. Examination of these verses renders it evident that the compositions were not made in the years to which they are assigned. That on the accession of Edgar, for instance, appears in the text under the year 958, in which that monarch ascended the throne, but it is demonstrable that it was not penned at the time, since allusions occur to his subsequent conduct and character. In a similar way, that on his death, which happened in 975, is relegated to the year in which the event befell. The poem, however, cannot have been a contemporaneous production, otherwise we should not have been told that the demise took place, *according to the calculation of those skilled in numbers*, in the month of July.

Another question of great interest is whether the chronicles were originally written in the native tongue or in Latin. No decisive answer can be returned to this inquiry, but it is significant that in the case of other nations histories that were the work of ecclesiastics were composed in Latin, the language of the Church. Bede and Ethelwerd before the Norman Conquest, and Florence of Worcester, Simeon of Durham, and others after that event, follow the general rule in such matters; and it seems more than likely that, in their earliest forms, the various local chronicles with which we have been dealing were in Latin, from which they were translated into English. The very meagreness and simplicity of the notices has been supposed to favour this view. If we accept the use of Latin as normal, and that of the dialects as exceptional, for historical purposes, how are we to account for the revolution to which the *Anglo-Saxon Chronicle* bears witness? The explanation is not far to seek. It is summed up in the single expression 'Alfred.' It would indeed have been singular, if at a time when that great man and great monarch was labouring to promote the diffusion of knowledge by translations of Bede and Orosius, annalists should have persisted in the employment of a language unintelligible to the mass of his subjects, whose interests were now to be considered. Once established, the usage was confirmed and may be said to have died hard, perishing at last of the decay of Old English through the loss of its grammatical inflexions and changes in its vocabulary.

This loss must have occurred through the adoption of

English by the Normans, who did not assimilate its grammar and idioms, or only to a partial extent. The *Peterborough Chronicle* reflects in some degree, the transition to Middle English. Down to the twelfth century the Old English speech is preserved with hardly a variation, except as regards certain interpolations in which the language is extremely corrupt. Some of the later annals exhibit a similar decline from the classical standard. Long ago it was remarked by Mr. English: 'We are not to take the last years of the *Chronicle* as a sample of the English of the time, but as a specimen of the broken English of a French monk.' Who was that monk? Sir Henry Howorth ventures to name him—one Hugo Candidus, or Hugh of the White Face, who was eye-witness of the fire already mentioned, and wrote a Latin history of the Abbey, which corresponds with the contributions to the *Chronicle* possessing a Norman cast.

The general character of the *Chronicle* is disappointingly jejune, but this barrenness of detail is relieved in places, not only by poetical insertions, but by prose narratives. The most striking, and certainly the best known, is the story of the desperate fight between King Cynewulf and the Ætheling Cyneheard, which may have been derived from a ballad, and forms the subject of an early interpolation. The event occurred in 784, and under that year it is recorded in the following simple terms:

> In this year Cyneheard slew King Cynewulf, and he was there slain and eighty-four men with him; and then Beorhtric succeeded to the Kingdom of the West-Saxons.

Who would suspect, on perusing this formal entry, the high romance which it enshrouds, and is displayed in a tale of heroism inserted, out of its place, in a notice of the year 755. Let us turn to it:

An. DCC . LV. In this year Cynewulf and the West-Saxon 'witan' deprived Sigebryht, his kinsman, of his kingdom for his unrighteous deeds, except Hampshire; and that he held until he slew the aldorman who had longest remained with him. And then Cynewulf drove him into Andred; and he there abode until a herdsman stabbed him at Pryfetes flôd (Privet); and he avenged the aldorman Cumbra. And Cynewulf fought often in great battles against the Brito-Welsh.

And about thirty-one winters after he had the kingdom, he would drive out an ætheling, who was named Cyneheard, and Cyneheard was Sigebryht's brother. And he then learned that the King, with a small company, was on a visit to a woman at Merantûn (Merton), and he there beset him, and surrounded the bower before the men discovered him who were there with the King.

And when the King perceived that, he went to the door, and then gallantly defended himself, until he looked on the ætheling, and then rushed out on him, and sorely wounded him; and they were all fighting against the King until they had slain him. And when by the woman's gestures the King's thanes had discovered the tumult, they ran thither, whoever was ready, and with all speed. And to each of them the ætheling offered money and life; and not one of them would accept it; but they continued fighting until they were all slain, save one, a British hostage, and he was sorely wounded.

When in the morning the King's thanes, who had remained behind, heard that the King was slain, they rode thither, and Osric his aldorman, and Wigferth his thane, and the men whom he had previously left behind, and found the ætheling in the burgh where the King lay slain; and they had locked the gates against them, and they went thereto. And he then offered them their own choice of money and land, if they would grant him the kingdom; and made known to them that their kinsmen were with him, who would not forsake him. And they then said, that to them no kinsman was dearer than their lord, and that they would never follow his murderer. And they then offered that they should go from him uninjured; and they said that the same had been offered to their companions, who before had been with the King. They then said that they no more minded it 'than did your companions who before had been with the King.' And they then were fighting about the gates, until they followed in and slew the ætheling and the men who were with him, all save one, who was the aldorman's godson; and he saved his life, although he had been repeatedly wounded. And Cynewulf reigned thirty-one winters, and his body lies at Winchester, and the ætheling's at Axminster; and their direct paternal kin goes to Cerdic.[1]

---

[1] Thorpe's tr.

CHAPTER III

HOMILIES AND HOMILISTS

In the ninth century Alfred laboured for the welfare not of the State alone, but of the Church; in the tenth century Dunstan entered into his labours. The great Archbishop is remembered for his antagonism to ecclesiastical laxity and strenuous devotion to the Order of St. Benedict, but he did not pass by the interests of the layfolk and cordially encouraged the work of translation. In his projects of reform he was ably seconded by Æthelwold, Bishop of Winchester, who has bequeathed to us an English rendering of the Rule of St. Benedict, and an historical disquisition on the Church of England. The joint influence of these eminent prelates resulted in the multiplication of sermons in the vulgar tongue, of which the earliest are those known as the *Blickling Homilies*.

This name was bestowed on them for the reason that the MS. was retrieved in Blickling Hall, Norfolk, and the identity of the author is shrouded in mystery. Even the time of the writings is not quite certain. It is true that Sermon XI—that on Maundy Thursday—mentions the year 971, but the date of the MS.—all that is really involved—may not have been coincident with that of the compositions themselves. One thing seems fairly plain, and that is that the *Blickling Homilies* are older than those of Ælfric, whose vocabulary has a modern look in comparison with Alfred's, and whose style shows a marked improvement on that of the writers of the preceding century. His sentences are less complex, but more compact and consecutive. The *Blickling Homilies*, on the other hand, preserve the old traditions of intricate constructions and few effective conjunctions. The vocabulary is archaic, including many terms not used by Ælfric but discoverable in contemporary verse.

The prose of the *Blickling Homilies* is distinctly poetical. 'Many passages,' it has been well said, 'read in a translation, might easily be taken for extracts from poems.' Nor is it only the language that trenches on the province of verse; rhythm and alliteration are imported, though not usually with anything like the same degree of stringency. The following quotation from Sermon X in the Blickling collection will serve to illustrate these features.

> Nu is æghwonon hream & wop, nu is heaf æghwonon & sibbe tolesnes, nu is æghwonon yfel & slege, & æghwonon þes middangeard flyhþ from us mid mycelre biternesse & we him fleondum fylgeaþ & hine feallende lufiaþ.
>
> Now there is lamentation and weeping on all sides; now there is mourning everywhere, and breach of peace; now is everywhere evil, and slaughter; and everywhere this world fleeth from us with great bitterness, and we follow it as it flies from us, and love it, although it is passing away.[1]

In Sermon X the Blessed Virgin is addressed in the words, 'The redness of the rose glittereth in thee, and the whiteness of the lily shineth in thee,' while in a brief, fragmentary discourse our Lord is described as 'se goldblosma' (the golden flower).

The word 'homily,' like the word 'catechism,' is apt to

[1] Morris' tr.

suggest the driest sort of spiritual instruction. Probably this is due to the collection of plain sermons prepared at the time of the Reformation, which movement made a sensible abridgement of the sensuous and imaginative elements in the conduct of church services. The homilies with which we have to do preceded that 'necessary evil,' as Coleridge calls it, by many centuries; and, accordingly, the Old English writers were at liberty to sweeten their teachings with the mead of Christian mythology. For the purpose of edifying the rustic audiences, for whom these sermons were specially designed, the apocryphal gospels stood on the same plane as the canonical scriptures; and the lives of the saints, including English confessors, were deemed legitimate topics for the pulpit, as their festivals came round. Homilists strove to interest, to adapt themselves to, rude and childish minds, and so they told stories, painted portraits, and overlaid their discourses with extravagant, highly-coloured frescoes of scenes and shrines. The preachers were perhaps as credulous as their hearers. In many instances they had no means of checking received accounts, and their standard of probability, determined by religious enthusiasm, was very different from that of more critical ages. The Blickling sermon on Ascension Day contains the assertion that 'those say, who have travelled thither [to the Holy Land] and come hither again, that the spot whereon our Lord last stood on the earth in bodily fashion, ere He ascended in His human nature into Heaven—that it is even now at the present day very highly honoured with many divine glories before the eyes of men.' This forms the preface to a vivid piece of description, which must have held congregrations spell-bound.

We learn also that the spot is on the summit of Mount Olivet; also that there is there built round about the spot a great and glorious church; and its circuit is wrought basket-wise, in the most beautiful and sumptuous manner that men can devise it. Then there are three porches built round the church, and all those very handsomely wrought above and roofed over. But the great church, which stands there in the midst, is open above and unroofed, because our Lord would that to the eyes of those men who believingly came thither and visited the holy place, the way might always become familiar to look up to heaven, whither they knew that the Lord had bodily ascended. And though the house itself is open overhead and not covered up, as I before said, yet it is ever by the grace of God protected above from all bad weathers, so that no rain or tempest is able to enter in. And ever since this house (or the place) was built there no one has ever been able to overlay the footsteps themselves, neither with gold nor silver, nor with any worldly ornaments, but whatsoever man may lay thereon, the earth herself immediately casts it from her, back into his face, and not for any interval would she have it upon her; nor would she accept any worldly decoration, since the holy feet of our Lord stood upon her. Wherefore there is built in the large church round about the footsteps [an enclosure] somewhat wider than a bushel basket, as high as a man's breast; it was first made of green copper, now it is ornamented with gold and silver. On the western side there is a moderate-sized door, through which a man's head and shoulders may enter, so that one may do obeisance to the footsteps, and kiss them; and many men, those who may obtain leave to do it, take the mould from the footsteps, that they may have it for a relic, and thereby many diseases and ailments are cured, when the mould is taken away. . . .

Moreover, there hangeth also, placed over the footsteps, a large lamp that is always filled with oil, as often as is needful, and is ever burning day and night for the honouring of those footprints. There are also in the great church built about this spot eight windows, very large, made of glass, and at each one there hangs a lamp, ever filled with oil and burning all night through the windows, as is the nature of oil to shine brighter than a wax taper. And not only does the light shine over the hill whereon the church is built, but also the city of Jerusalem, which is a mile westward from that spot, so that every night, in every quarter of the city, the light may be shining from the holy place. . . .

And now, dearest men, although we are not now at the holy place that I have spoken of, nevertheless we may in these places in which we now are, become good and meet before our Lord, if we now in our life-time do what is true and right.[1]

It may be noted that there are many quotations from the Vulgate, which are sometimes translated, sometimes not. The writer abbreviates either by adding *etcetera* after the opening words, or inserting *usque* before the last word of the sentence. There was no English 'authorized version.'

Anxious as the homilists were to please, they did not fail in their proper function of admonishing the flock of Christ. For a specimen of the impressive eloquence with which they pressed home the lesson, 'Set your affections on things above, not on the things of the earth,' we may turn to the sermon entitled 'Sawle þearf,' or 'The Need of the Soul'—one of the Blickling collection.

Dearest men, consider that ye are frequently toiling and always solicitous about the things wherewith we should fill and adorn our body; but it shall happen after a few days or a few years, that the same body shall be in the tomb, eaten and devoured by worms. Wherefore we have much more need to trouble ourselves about the need of our soul, which shall be present in heaven before God and His angels. 'I entreat you,' said Augustine, 'that ye go to the tombs of rich men, and then ye may see a plain example [of the vanity of riches].' They were wealthy in this world, and their riches were very many in lands and in vineyards; and their store-houses were filled with manifold riches, and their bliss and their amusements were very abundant. Behold now diligently, that all is gone from their eyes. They had many adornments of precious garments. They had also wives and concubines, and their lustful indulgences, and feasts, and sports, and excessive drinkings, and

---

[1] It may be of some interest to state the probable origin of this story. This was a narrative in Abbot Adamnan's *De Locis Sanctis*, itself derived from the itinerary of Arculf, a Frankish bishop, who had visited Jerusalem. (See *Adamnani de locis sanctis libri tres ex relatione Arculfi*, Migne's *Patrol.*, vol. 88.)

foolish and thoughtless embraces. And divers blisses they had in their drinkings, and their morning and evening feasts they mingled together. . . .

But whither have gone the wealth and the adornments or the vain pleasures? or whither have gone the great things that encompassed and surrounded them? And where are those who praised them, and spake to them flattering words? And where have gone the adorning of their houses, and the collection of precious gems, or the vast acquisition of gold and silver, or all the wealth which they daily more and more amassed, and knew not, nor took heed of the time when they should leave all? Or where have gone their wisdom and their ingenious skill? And where is he that hath given false judgements? And where is the splendour of their beds and their couches, or the manifold dissembling of their friends, and the great multitude of their servants, and the fretwork of their lamps which burned before them, and all the great crowds that went with and thronged about them? All these are now gone from their eyes.

But the preacher is not satisfied with rhetorical questions—he enforces his point by a grotesque story, a sensational tale, which is certainly apposite enough, and might strike one as expressly invented for the occasion. It is, we believe, a matter of dispute among divines whether our Lord's parable of Dives and Lazarus is a fable or a revelation of an historical drama. The narrative in the Blickling homily, which bears a certain resemblance to the Evangelical apologue, is plainly fictitious, and yet the miracle is no greater than many others commended to the acceptance of the faithful.

We may now hear related a story of a certain rich and influential man who possessed in this world great wealth and very splendid and manifold treasures, and lived a pleasant life. Then it happened that he died, and there came to him a sudden end of this transitory life. There was then one of his kinsmen and earthly friends that loved him more than any other man; and on account of longing and the sorrow caused by the other's death he could no longer stay in the country, but with a sorrowful mind departed from his native land and from his dwelling-place, and in that (foreign) land dwelt many years; and this longing of his never diminished, but much oppressed and afflicted him. Then after a time he began to long for his native land again, for he wished to behold again the tomb, and to see what he were like whom formerly he had often seen beautiful in face and stature. . . .

Then the bones of the dead man called to him, and thus said, 'Why hast thou come hither to see us. Now mayest thou see here a portion of dust, and the relict of worms, where thou previously didst see a purple garment interwoven with gold. . . . Remember this, and know that my riches that I had of yore are all vanished and come to naught, and my dwellings are decayed and perished. But turn thee to thyself, and incline thy heart to counsel and merit, that thy prayers be acceptable to God Almighty.'

He then, so sad and sorrowful, turned away from the dust-spectacle, and turned himself away from all the affairs of this world; and he began to learn and to teach the praise of God, and to love spiritual virtues; and thereby earned for himself the grace of the Holy Spirit and delivered also the other's soul from punishment and relieved him from torments.

The Blickling homilist, like many of his contemporaries, is impressed by the near approach of the year 1000, which he evidently thinks may be the time of the Second Advent, though he does not forget that this is a secret known to the Lord alone. In view of this contingency, he summons all—bishops, priests, and people—to repentance and amendment of life. He is persuaded that the coming of the great and terrible day cannot be long delayed, because the signs and tokens whereof the Apocalypse speaks —except that Antichrist has yet to be revealed—have been fulfilled, and five of the six ages of the world have already run their course. The end of the world must needs happen in the present age, of which, since 971 years have elapsed, the greater part is past. The other ages have been of varying duration, and no man can tell how long God may be pleased to constitute the present millennium; but the preacher will not allow his audience to take comfort in the fact. As an incentive to penitence, he draws lurid pictures of the impending Judgement and the sufferings of hell.

The English preface which Ælfric prefixes to his collection of homilies is full of the ideas of the imminence of Doomsday—he speaks of 'this time which is the ending of the world'—and the noxious part that Antichrist is to play in the penultimate scene. The date of Ælfric's homilies can be determined with tolerable exactness by a dedicatory letter addressed to Sigeric, Archbishop of Canterbury, whose occupancy of the see lasted from 990 to 995. It is perhaps on account of this extreme lateness that in the English preface the chief interest centres in the person, powers, and pretensions of Antichrist as the immediate precursor of the great day of account. If that time was as near as general expectation foreboded, then the appearance of the accursed seducer might be looked for at any moment. Ælfric therefore assumes the aggressive by illuminating cautions. He not only interprets the name, but describes the nature of the subtle and potent adversary. Just as Christ is truly God and man in one person, so Antichrist is a 'human man' and true devil. He is the *visible* devil.

As we have intimated, these homilies represent Ælfric's share in the campaign against the crafts and deceits with which this tempter will seek to ensnare the simple and unwary to their eternal perdition. By inditing them he discharges his conscience of an obligation imposed by the plain and reiterated commands of Holy Writ. 'It seemed to me,' he says, 'that I should not be guiltless before God, if I would not, either by speech or by writing, make known to other men the evangelical truths which Himself spake or thereafter discovered to holy doctors.' Ælfric, in turn, imposes a just obligation on any one who may desire to transcribe his books. He adjures him in God's name to produce correct copies, 'lest we should be censured by reason of careless writers.' Much evil is caused in this way; and if a man will be guiltless in God's judgement, he must rectify whatever he has distorted.

The Latin preface is quite different. It is an *apologia*, in which the writer defends his procedure and expounds his methods. At the outset he is proud to name himself the pupil of the 'kindly and worshipful' Æthelwold; and, after a formal greeting to the lord archbishop, he announces as his object the spiritual profit of those who cannot be instructed in any other than their native tongue. That this may be accomplished more effectually he eschews obscure terms, and uses simple English, the meaning of which may be readily apprehended by readers or hearers. Remembering perhaps Alfred's account of his manner of translating, Ælfric states that he has not everywhere rendered word for word, but meaning for meaning. The sense being the main thing, it was plainly necessary that no suspicion of heresy or heterodoxy should attach to those writers from whose works he borrows; he therefore records the names of Augustine of Hippo, Jerome, Bede, Gregory, Smaragdus, and Haymon as those whom he has followed, and whose authority is universally admitted by Catholics. Not only are passages of the Gospels unfolded, but also the martyrdoms or lives of the Saints, forty subjects being dealt with in the book containing the preface. Ælfric intimates that he has in hand another book which is to serve as a complement to the present volume. His notion is that the sets should be read in churches in alternate years so as to preclude the weariness that would be caused by too frequent repetition. He foresees two criticisms. One concerns the interpretation, because it is not always literal, or because it summarizes passages in the original. The other is that he does not in his discourses travel over the entire field of the gospels after the order of the church ritual. Ælfric does not meet the latter objection, but as to the former, his reply is that if any one is dissatisfied with his labours, he is welcome to construct for himself a book with a superior interpretation on such lines as commend themselves to his understanding. But he rightly deprecates unauthorized tampering with his own exegesis, the fruit of earnest study.

The practice which Ælfric contemplates points to a demand for ready-made sermons by lazy, ignorant, or inefficient clerks, and the low standard of attainments in the English Church made it eminently desirable. We are reminded of Sir Roger de Coverley's bargain with his chaplain.

> At his first settling with me, I made him a present of all the good sermons, which have been printed in English, and only begged of him that every Sunday he would pronounce one of them in the pulpit. Accordingly, he has digested them into such a series, that they follow one another naturally, and make a continued system of practical divinity.

Addison saw no harm, but rather much good, in a custom generally regarded as reflecting on the talent, zeal, and honesty of persons who have the cure of souls, for he proceeds:

> As Sir Roger was going on in his story, the gentleman we were talking of came up to us; and upon the knight's asking him who preached to-morrow (for it was Saturday night) told us, the Bishop of St. Asaph's in the morning and Dr. South in the afternoon. He then showed us his list of preachers for the whole year, where I saw with a great deal of pleasure, Archbishop Tillotson, Bishop Saunderson, Doctor Barrow, Doctor Calamy, with several living authors who have published discourses of practical divinity. I no sooner saw this venerable man in the pulpit, but I very much approved of my friend's insisting upon the qualifications of a good aspect and a clear voice; for I was so charmed with the gracefulness of his figure and delivery, as well as the discourses he pronounced, that I

think I never passed any time more to my satisfaction. A sermon repeated after this manner is like the composition of a poet in the mouth of a graceful actor.

I could heartily wish that more of our country clergy would follow this example, and instead of wasting their spirits in laborious compositions of their own, would endeavour after a handsome elocution and all those other talents that are proper to enforce what has been penned by greater masters. This would not only be more easy to themselves, but more edifying to the people.

Ælfric is very desirous that it should be understood that his sole purpose is the edifying of the people—not fame or reputation for great learning. As for easing the burdens of other priests by providing them with a stock of sermons, it appears from the English preface that many English books were already in circulation, but unhappily he had detected in them much error which unlearned men in their simplicity mistook for much wisdom. He makes honourable exception of the books which King Alfred judiciously translated from Latin into English, but, apart from these, the evangelical teachings in written form were available for those only who knew Latin.

Ælfric's implied condemnation of writings like the *Blickling Homilies*, which he may or may not have seen, strikes us as somewhat severe, but he was a typical product of the strict discipline and erudite traditions of the Benedictine order, in which he had been reared. Even his English style, so limpid and free from affectation, proves how diligently he observed the rule he had laid down for himself, to write in a strain that the meanest could comprehend. When he first comes to the word 'apostle,' though his sermon on St. Gregory shows it to have been anglicized, he interprets it as 'ærendraca.' In the same way 'disciple' is explained to signify 'leorningcniht.' There are many passages like 'þes dæg is gehaten *Epiphania Domini*, pæt is Godes geswutelung-dæg' ('This day is called

Epiphania Domini, that is, the day of God's manifestation').

It is a pity that we do not know more of Ælfric's personal history. From the fact that he describes himself as *alumnus Adelwoldi* we may infer that he was educated in the monastery school superintended by that eminent churchman. The opening lines of the English preface tell us something of his subsequent life.

I, Ælfric, monk and mass-priest, though more frail than becomes that estate, was sent in King Ethelred's days by Elphege, Æthelwold's successor, to a monastery that is called Cernel, at the instance of Æthelmær the thane, whose quality and excellence are known everywhere.

The sermon on the nativity of St. Edmund, king and martyr, opens with a paragraph which affords an interesting illustration of the manner in which Ælfric obtained some of his knowledge of the past.

A certain very learned monk came from the south over the sea from St. Benedict's place [1] in the days of King Ethelred to Archbishop Dunstan three years before he departed this life, and the monk was called Abbo. They remained in conversation until Dunstan had told about Saint Edmund, even as Edmund's sword-bearer had told it to King Athelstan, when Dunstan was a young man and the sword-bearer was a very aged man. The monk then put all the narratives in a book, and afterwards, when the book came to us, within a few years, we translated it into English, even as it stands hereafter. Within two years the monk went home to his monastery, and was soon appointed abbot in the same monastery.

Ælfric himself was destined to attain the same ecclesiastical rank. Although his life was consumed with literature and study, he did not fail to win powerful friends amongst the laity, who interested themselves in his pur-

[1] Fleury.

suits and saw to his advancement. Already a hint to that effect has occurred in the commencement of the English preface before quoted; and we may now trace his career in as much detail as our scanty information will allow. The Æthelmær there mentioned was the son of Æthelweard,[1] who, it is worthy of note, married a daughter of the heroic Byrhtnoth. At Æthelweard's suggestion Ælfric carried out the translation of various books of the Old Testament, but, on the whole, his relations with Æthelmær appear to have been more intimate and beneficial. In 1005 he was promoted to the abbacy of Eynsham in Oxfordshire. The monastery had been richly endowed by Æthelmær, most of whose later years were spent within its precincts; and it seems a fair assumption that to this nobleman Ælfric owed his introduction to other thanes—Wulfgeat, Sigwerd, and Sigewerth—to whom he addressed certain of his writings.

Ælfric's compositions were not all in English, for during his residence at Eynsham he penned a Latin biography of his earliest and best friend, a *Vita Ethelwoldi*, which he dedicated, very fitly, to Kenwulf, the occupant of the see of Winchester, which Æthelwold had once adorned. This sketch was not only an acknowledgement of the debt under which he rested to one whose precepts and example had coloured the whole of his life, but was designed quite as much for the spiritual improvement of the community of

[1] There were two Æthelweards. One, the King's high reeve, is stated in the *Anglo-Saxon Chronicle* to have been slain in Hampshire in an attempt to repel a landing of the Northmen in 1001. His son Æthelmær, ealdorman of Devonshire, surrendered to Sweyn at Bath, with the western thanes, in 1013. He was the father of the younger Æthelweard mentioned in the *Chronicle* under the year 1017: 'In this year Eadric an ealdorman was put to death, and Æthelweard, son of Æthelmær the great.

which he was the head. The date of Ælfric's decease cannot be ascertained, but he seems to have survived, at any rate, to the year 1014, since about that time he drew up at the bidding of Wulfstan, Archbishop of York, a pastoral epistle, or two pastoral epistles, known by the title of *Sermo ad Sacerdotes*.

Ælfric's existence was one of ceaseless intellectual toil; and, though he is remembered chiefly for his *Homiliae Catholicae* and his *Passiones Sanctorum*, these studies in divinity and hagiology were far from exhausting his activities. Here it is well to state that the second series of sermons promised in the preface were duly completed, and in a second edition of the work were inserted several additional homilies. Apparently at some time between the publication of his sermons and that of his Lives of the Saints, Ælfric's attention was drawn aside to educational requirements, and this led to the production of a Latin grammar derived from Priscian with an interlinear translation. Far more curious and original as an instrument of instruction is the *Colloquium Ælfrici*, the aim of which was to enable young scholars to acquire facility in Latin conversation by setting before them model dialogues on subjects of everyday experience. The Cottonian MS. (Tiberius A 3) is equipped with an interlinear gloss, which is wanting in the Bodleian copy, edited and extended by a namesake of Ælfric, but on various grounds may be accounted genuine. This composition is valuable for the insight it gives us into the various trades and occupations that were exercised by the dependents of an important religious establishment and others of like standing. It has the further merit of being decidedly amusing. Ælfric could not conceive of a trustworthy or efficient homilist who was not also a Latinist; and, as a specimen of the way homilists were, or might be, made, we may venture to quote the opening sentences of the colloquy, premising that *D.* stands for *Discipulus*, and *M.* for *Magister*.

We cildra bidda þe, eala Lareow, þæt þu tæce us sprecan
D. Nos pueri rogamus te, Magister, ut doceas nos loqui
* [rihte], forþam ungelærede we syndon, and gewæmmodlice
Latialiter recte, quia idiotæ sumus, et corrupte
we sprecaþ.
loquimur.

Hwæt wille ge sprecan?
M. Quid vultis loqui?

Hwæt rece we hwæt we sprecan, buton hit riht spraec
D. Quid curamus quid loquamur, nisi recta locutio
sy and behefe, næs idel, oþþe fracod?
sit et utilis, non anilis, aut turpis?

Wille [ge beon] beswungen on leornunge?
M. Vultis flagellari in discendo?

Leofre ys us beon beswungen for lare, þænne hit ne
D. Carius est nobis flagellari pro doctrina, quam ne-
cunnan; ac we witun þe bilewitne wesan, and nellan onbelædan
scire; sed scimus te mansuetum esse, et nolle inferre
swincgla us, buton þu bi to-genydd fram us.
plagas nobis, nisi cogaris a nobis.

Ic axie þe hwæt * sprecst þu? Hwæt hæfst þu weorkes?
M. Interrogo te quid mihi loqueris? Quid habes operis?

Ic eom geanwyrde monuc, and ic sincge ælce dæg seofon
D. Professus sum monachum, et psallo omni die septem
tida mid gebroþrum, and ic eom bysgod [on rædinge] and
synaxes cum fratribus, et occupatus sum lectionibus et
on sange; ac, þeah-hwæþere, ic wolde betwenan leornian sprecan
cantu; sed tamen vellem interim discere sermocinari
on Leden gereorde.
Latina lingua.

The master then inquires about the candidate's companions and elicits from him that among them are ploughmen, shepherds, oxherds, hunters, fishermen, fowlers, chapmen, shoemakers, salters, and bakers. One of each calling is addressed in turn, and catechized as to his mode of life. First, the ploughman, who murmurs at his hard lot. He has to set out at break of day, urge his oxen to the field, and harness them to the plough. However severe the winter, he dare not skulk at home for fear of his lord. Having yoked the oxen and fastened share and coulter to the plough, he is forced to plough a whole acre or more daily. He has a companion who is now hoarse with cold and shouting. He has to fill the stalls of the oxen with hay and carry out their dung.

'Hig, hig!' quoth the master, ' tis great trouble.'

'Yes,' replies the husbandman, ' 'tis great trouble, because I am not free.'

In addition to these grammatical labours, and probably about the same time, Ælfric gave himself to the task of formulating in English an astronomical treatise, in which he dealt with the division of the year, the stars, and certain atmospherical phenomena. Based on sundry compositions of Bede, the work never found a definite name, being variously entitled *De Temporibus*, *De Computo*, and *De Primo Die Saeculi*. Such exercises seem a little divorced from Ælfric's main purpose in life, and suggest that, being an excellent and versatile scholar, he was just then employed in the instruction of youth in the monastery to which he had been sent by Bishop Elphege. However, he was soon to return to more serious occupation.

In 996 Ælfric sent forth a new series of discourses, comprising some homilies of the ordinary kind, but composed for the most part of Lives of the Saints, of which there had hitherto been few examples in English. It is considered certain that two—that of St. Martin, in which he follows Sulpicius Severus, and that of St. Edmund, for which, as we have seen, he was indebted to Abbo of Fleury—are earlier than the remainder, of which Ælfric is accounted sole author. Judging from the content, it is probable that the work was intended primarily for conventual audiences, but the inclusion of similar matter in the previous compilation forbids the assumption that it was designed exclusively for their behoof.

Between the two collections there is this remarkable difference, that the former is pure prose, while the latter approximates to verse so nearly that Professor Skeat has edited it—in four volumes—for the Early English Text Society as Ælfric's *Metrical Lives of the Saints*. It is a curious problem that we have here. Noting, as is inevitable, the constant and almost continuous employment of alliteration, some scholars fail to discover any consistency in its application. They find 'the rime-letter of poetry, but without its metrical form.' They therefore hold this species of composition to be rather alliterative prose than actual verse.[1] The concluding piece, in Mr. Sweet's excellent *Anglo-Saxon Primer*—which he rather sarcastically prescribes for 'some of our Professors of and Examiners in the English language!'[2]—is Ælfric's Life of King Edmund

[1] It is only just to state that Dr. Skeat in no way lays stress on the metrical character of the *Lives*. He has simply reproduced the divisions into lines which he found in the Anglo-Saxon MS. and leaves the question whether in fact the compositions are verse or prose quite open.

[2] A capital instance of learned ignorance occurs in Ellis's notes on the *Battle of Brunanburh*. Reading 'beorna beah gifa,' he translates, 'of Barons the bold chief,' and justifies the rendering thus:

'(1) *Ballice* is boldly, Mar. xv, 43, in the Rushworth Gloss, and *bealh* varies little in sound from *beah*.

'(2) Whiter in his *Etymol.*, p. 347, gives *gevar*, *Chaldaic*, and thence deduces our corresponding *chief*, captain, etc. *g* and *c* are certainly letters of the same organ; and in Saxon *cafre* and *cafost* are chiefer, chiefest; and Matt. xxvii, 57, Gothic, *gabigs* is applied to Joseph of Arimathea, an honourable man.'—*Specimens of Early English Poetry*, i, 14.

Beah-gifa is, of course, literally 'ring-giver,' and so 'chief.'

which is there printed as prose, but if we select sentences at random and read them, guided by the alliteration, we shall soon become conscious of cadences, in which the alliterated syllables usually coincide with the main stresses. Take the following:

> Hwæt þa se flot-here ferde eft to scipe, and behyddon þæt heafod þæs halgan Eadmundes.
>
> Hie eodon þa endemes ealle to þæm wuda, secende gehwær, geond þyflas and bremlas, gif hie ahwær mihten gemetan þæt heafod.

We are forced to conclude that the *Lives of the Saints* betray a rude and irregular versification, and the only question is whether the author's aim was to write poetry or extremely artificial prose—artificial not in the sense that *Euphues* is artificial, but in admitting capricious obligations, in setting up rules and restrictions, which do not belong to the nature of prose as such. The style is as simple and unpretentious as that of Ælfric's earlier writings, and is certainly not tinged by the associations of the poetical forms that so curiously variegate the complexion of his periods.

Ælfric must have been widely recognized as a great force in the spiritual and intellectual life of his age and country. We find Wulfsige, Bishop of Sherborne, applying to him for a pastoral epistle to be addressed to the easy-going clergy of his diocese. Ælfric liked this commission so well that he was induced to return to the subject in a more methodical work entitled *Canones Ælfrici*, in which, somewhat as George Herbert in later days, he inculcated the duties of the priestly calling. Ælfric was especially intent on enforcing the need of celibacy, which was repugnant to many of the priesthood.

We have previously made mention of Ælfric's *Sermo ad Sacerdotes*, written at the instance of Archbishop Wulfstan in 1014. This, being divided into two parts, he designated as *duae epistolae*; and the contents of the discourse are practically identical with those of the earlier pastoral, but revised, enlarged, and rearranged. Originally in Latin, it was afterwards, at Wulfstan's request, translated into English, presumably because the majority of the clergy were not sufficiently versed in the former language to be able to reap the full benefit of the admonitions.

'To the distance from Rome,' says Lappenberg, 'and their slender dependence on the papal chair, the people of England are apparently indebted for the advantage of their having retained their mother tongue as the language of the Church, which was never entirely banished by the priests from their most sacred services. Their careless, sensual course of life, and perhaps the prejudice, which prevented them from learning even so much Latin as was requisite to enable them to repeat the Paternoster and Creed in that language, have proved more conducive to the highest interests of the country than the dark subtlety of the learned Romanized monk, pondering over authorities. Even the mass itself was not read entirely in the Latin tongue. The wedding form was, no doubt, entirely in Anglo-Saxon; and its hearty sound and simple sterling substance are preserved in the English ritual to the present day. The numerous versions and paraphrases of the Old and New Testaments made those books known to the laity and more familiar to the clergy.

Ælfric was an industrious contributor to the popularization of the Scriptures. It may be doubted whether translations were to be found in such plenty as is implied in the above passage, but it is certain that he was by no means a pioneer in the pious labour. When Æthelweard desired him to translate Genesis, he informed Ælfric that he was already in possession of a version extending from the story of Isaac to the conclusion of the book; all that was wanted therefore was the completion of the remainder, which Ælfric carried into effect, though with some few omissions. Translations of the other books of the Pentateuch appear to have been extant in a similar fragmentary form; and, in every instance, Ælfric used, when he did not actually reproduce, the renderings of his predecessors. His own versions took the shape of excerpts, and included the Books of Joshua and Judges, so that it is usual to refer to his work as a translation of the Heptateuch. About or soon after this time a complete English version of the Gospels made its appearance, and Thorpe, who published an edition of it (Oxford, 1842) terms it 'probably Ælfric's version.' This conjecture may be defended partly by the date of the MS. and partly by the fact that no writer can be named more likely to have undertaken such a work than the diligent Benedictine who is known to have Englished other portions of the Bible, and who, in his homilies, translates many passages of the New Testament. In the present state of our knowledge, however, we must be content to consider the Anglo-Saxon Gospels as anonymous.

The authorship of the versions of the Mosaic books, which came into Ælfric's hands, is doubtless beyond hope of discovery, but it is often possible to identify his own contributions by the love of alliteration which marks the latter portion of his career, in which these translations apparently fall. Before entering on the task, he had already incorporated in his Lives of the Saints extracts from the Books of Kings and Maccabees. On the other hand, it must not be overlooked that there exists a free translation of Job, which bears a striking resemblance to Ælfric's sermon on the patriarch in the second series of his Catholic Homilies, and is *not* alliterative. It may be an early experiment of Ælfric's, or it may not be his at all, but it does suggest the possibility that this writer may not always have felt it incumbent on him, even after his conversion to the alliterative principle, to adorn his prose with the tinsel of verse.

Here it will be opportune to glance back at the course of Biblical translation down to this epoch, so far as such a retrospect is possible. The paraphrases, to which we have allotted a special chapter, stand somewhat apart from the subject now under consideration for the reason that the motive in their case was the motive of all poetry—to please. Translation of the Scriptures is naturally dictated by a higher—the highest—purpose, and presupposes as the chief virtues in the translator adequate learning and unwavering fidelity to the Sacred Text. Having regard to the importance of the service, it is not surprising that the names of the most eminent writers and theologians in early times have been connected with it. Tradition attributes a metrical version of the Psalter to Aldhelm, who, though only his Latin poems survive, is said to have practised English versification. Thorpe, however, considered as 'possibly Aldhelm's' the translation in the Bibliothèque Nationale at Paris (MS. Lat. 8824), which he published under the title, *Libri Psalmorum cum paraphrasi Anglo-Saxonica* (London, 1835). The MS., which is of the eleventh century, comprises a metrical translation in the West-Saxon dialect—Aldhelm was Bishop of Sherborne—from Psalm li, 6, onwards, and a later prose translation of the first fifty. The metrical renderings of these psalms have not been entirely lost, since considerable remains have been preserved in an English Benedictine office dating from about the time of the Norman Conquest. The language of the translation, it may be observed, exhibits archaisms, which justify, to some degree, Thorpe's very cautious and quite conjectural attribution of it to Aldhelm. A metrical version of Psalm l in the Kentish dialect, with the translator's prologue and epilogue, is believed to be not later than the eighth century.

The celebrated 'Durham Book' (MS. Cott. Nero D iv)—

a codex of the Four Gospels with an interlinear gloss in English has been assigned to Ecgberht, Bishop of Lindisfarne, a lover of books and a younger contemporary and friend of the Venerable Bede, who laboured for the promotion of learning and Church discipline, and was rewarded with the archiepiscopal see of York. In point of fact, Aldred's Northumbrian gloss seems to be not earlier than the middle of the tenth century—the date also of the 'Rushworth Gospels,'[1] which are likewise equipped with an English interlinear version. William of Malmesbury informs us that Bede translated the Gospel of St. John; and the same authority credits King Alfred with an English rendering of some fragments of the Psalms. These statements, if they have any basis of fact, possess no more than historical interest, since the versions have perished. At the same time it is not an unreasonable supposition that the reign of Alfred, distinguished as it is for the revival of letters, may have witnessed some efforts at the Englishing of portions of the Bible in prose form: and if its latest editor be correct, the eleventh-century translation of the Gospels, which Thorpe ascribed to Ælfric, was originally put together in Alfred's time, and re-copied as popularized at the period of the second revival initiated by Dunstan.

To return to the subject of homilies. Perhaps the most interesting of all Old English compositions of the class is that called *Sermo Lupi ad Anglos quando Dani maxime persecuti sunt eos*. Although it bears a Latin title, it is in English; and the name 'Lupus' is a thin disguise of Wulfstan. The writer was, in fact, the prelate who commissioned Ælfric to shape for him the pastoral epistle before

[1] The Rushworth Gospels are so called because the MS., now at Oxford, belonged at one time to the eccentric historian, John Rushworth.

referred to and described. Wulfstan was Archbishop of York from 1002 to 1023, and during part of the time—till 1016—held the see of Worcester *in commendam*. Fifty-three of his homilies have been handed down, but hitherto only one of them has been published—the *Sermo* before mentioned.[1] Wulfstan is not to be compared with Ælfric in point of literary finish, but he had many of the qualities of a popular preacher. His writing is animated and picturesque, and the circumstances of the time were calculated to bring out those traits in perfection. More than once we have had occasion to allude to the visitations of the Northmen in quest of plunder or settlements. The appearance of these pagans was always alarming, but Sweyn's vindictive march through the heart of the kingdom in 1012 surpassed in cruelty all former expeditions. Wherever he came fields were wasted, villages burnt, churches ransacked, and the whole of the male population put to the sword. Wulfstan draws a terrible picture of these disasters, which he represents as retribution for the prevailing impiety and immorality, and as a foretaste of the yet worse calamities that will shortly be experienced in consequence of the coming of Antichrist and the world's end. His account of the degradation of his countrymen does not seem to be at all exaggerated, being amply confirmed by the laws of Ethelred. It is a shocking and almost incredible scandal that after centuries of Christianity there should have existed an inhuman commerce in which brother sold brother, father son, and son mother! The sermon was delivered in 1014, two years before the death of Ethelred the Unready.

What is the precise relation between homilies and lives

[1] Napier, however, gives sixty-two extracts from the remainder —some very short—in his *Wulfstan, Sammlung der ihm zugeschrieben Homilien*, etc. (Berlin, 1883).

of the saints? That they are related may almost be taken for granted from the fact that Ælfric's collections are made up partly of sermons and partly of the lives of martyrs and confessors. The truth is that from the earliest times the lives of the saints were read publicly as part of the Church service. 'The practice was to read the acts of those saints and martyrs who were to be commemorated in the liturgy of the day following, in order that the faithful might join in commemoration with memories refreshed.'[1] At a later period the acts were read after Prime in the chapter house—not in the church—and usually, it would appear, in an abbreviated form, as the auditors were presumed to be familiar with the legends, and needed to be reminded rather than instructed. It is clear that, in these circumstances, the auditors would have been monks. They alone also can have been present when the lessons for the second nocturn were read, these being taken from the Lives of the Saints. It is to be observed, however, that all Bede's sermons and many of Ælfric's were pronounced to monkish audiences; and when the scanty details of the legends were developed into a more complete narrative, and their moral and spiritual significance duly expounded, the distinction between such discourses and sermons based on Holy Writ became rather fine. Both classes of writings might be termed with equal propriety homilies. Dr. Herzfeld, the editor of an *Old English Martyrology*, observes: 'When we see how meagre and incomplete the accounts of the legends in our history frequently are, we may readily infer that they were mainly intended to refresh the memory of the preacher, and supply him with the groundwork of his sermon.'

[1] Smith and Chetham, *Dict. of Christ. Ant.*, ii, p. 1137.

The able scholar, whose words have just been quoted, has made a thorough study of the various matters connected with his subject; and although the *Old English Martyrology* has no great literary merit, it opens up bypaths which enable us to arrive at a truer conception of the state of learning and culture during the best periods preceding the Norman Conquest than would be possible apart from such researches.

Cockayne promulgated the theory that the *Martyrology* was produced in the time of Alfred and under his direction, but the supposition does not agree with evidence gathered from the work itself. The latest event recorded is the death of Abbot Hygebald, which occurred about A.D. 740. No mention is made of St. Boniface, the glory of the Anglo-Saxon nation; hence it may be judged that the compilation was completed some years before the death and canonization of the 'Apostle of Germany'—that is to say, a full century and more before the reign of Alfred. Originally, there is little doubt, it was a monument of Anglian industry, for Mercian forms yet survive in the texts, and, what is quite as significant, the English saints commemorated are almost without exception Mercian or Northumbrian.

The fact that the *Martyrology* is in English may be thought to indicate a limited acquaintance with Latin on the part of the monks in general, but no lack of linguistic talent or ecclesiastic learning can be charged against the authors of the work. Cockayne and Dr. Herzfeld, between them, have built up a formidable list of the sources from which the legends were derived. The former was convinced that the origin of stories like those of Milus and Senneus, Arsenius, Pelagia, and Martialis is directly Oriental. Herzfeld, on the other hand, is of opinion that such legends, as well as passages which appear to be of

Jewish origin, came through French channels.[1] Striking resemblances have been traced between the Old English text and portions of Greek legends (*e.g.*, those of Christopher, Marina, and James the Less), but here, again, Herzfeld is sceptical as to any direct influence. We have it, however, on the testimony of Bede, that Greek was not unknown in England in his time, so that there would be nothing surprising in an immediate indebtedness to Greek authorities. Further light on this subject will be forthcoming in the succeeding chapter.

Meanwhile, it is important to note among the sources the conspicuous place occupied by Bede. His metrical martyrology appears to have been used, and his *Ecclesiastical History* is cited again and again (*e.g.*, 2nd March of St. Chad: 'þæs wundor and líf Beda se leornere wrát on Angelcynnes bocum'). Bede, if the expression may be allowed, is dissolved into an Old English commission, of which the compiler or compilers of this work were members. They have drawn extensively on his writings—not only those referred to; and his treatise, *De Temporum Ratione*, more particularly the chapter on the characteristics of the months, has furnished material that makes interesting reading. The Old English names of the days of the week have been perpetuated, but this is not the case with the names of the months, two of which take us back to a then not very remote reign of paganism.

September.

On þæm nigoðan monðe on geare bið þritig daga. se monað hatte on leden Septembris ond on ure geþeode haligmonað, forþon þe ure yldran, þa þa hi hæðene wæron, on þam monðe hi guldon hiora deofulgeldum.

[1] There were no Jews in England prior to the Norman Conquest.

On the ninth month in the year there are thirty days. The month is called September in Latin, and in our language the holy month, because our ancestors, as long as they were pagans, used to sacrifice to their idols in this month.[1]

November.

On þam endlyftan monað on geare bið þritig daga. se monað is nemde on læden Novembres ond on ure geþeode blodmonað forþon þe ure yldran, þa hy hæðenne wæron, on þam monðe hy bleoton á; þæt is þæt hy betæhton ond benemdon hyra deofolgyldum þa neat þa þe hy woldon syllan.

In the eleventh month of the year there are thirty days. The month is called November in Latin, and in our language 'month of sacrifices,' because our forefathers, as long as they were pagans, always sacrificed in this month; that is, they dedicated and assigned to their idols the cattle they were going to give.'[2]

The literal meaning of 'deofulgyldum' is, of course, 'images of devils'; and account may well remind us of *Beowulf*—'swylc wæs þeaw hyra.'[3]

[1] Herzfeld's tr. [2] *Ibid.* [3] See p. 63.

CHAPTER IV

JOCO-SERIA

Let us now turn to a narrative drawn from one of the best known compilations of the Middle Ages—the *Gesta Romanorum*. It may seem that there can be no close connection between tales and homilies, save in the case of Lives of the Saints, but it is unquestionable that collections of the former were made expressly for the pulpit, and where such were lacking, other tales were freely introduced. Vincent of Beauvais tells us that in the thirteenth century it was customary for preachers to stimulate the attention of weary listeners by quoting Æsop's fables; and the *Gesta Romanorum* was used for the same purpose. The story-book was so named because each tale was assigned to some emperor of Rome, real or supposed; and it was often convenient to begin the application with the words, 'Beloved, the emperor is God.'

To modern readers perhaps the most familiar of the tales in the famous old collection is that of Apollonius of Tyre, because on it is founded the Shakespearean play of *Pericles, Prince of Tyre*. In the library of Corpus Christi College, Cambridge, which contains so many other good things, is the apparently unique, but unfortunately imperfect, MS. of an Old English version of this story. This was printed by the industrious Mr. Thorpe as a whole, and a short extract from it is one of the pieces in his

Analecta Anglo-Saxonica (pp. 108-9).[1] As the tale is a translation, it would be somewhat beside the mark to lavish words on its substantial merits or demerits, but all will unite in admiring the style of the Old English prose, which is extremely easy, fluent, and charming. The story is of late Greek origin, but it was obviously derived from a Latin source, and the oblique cases of the name 'Apollonius' occasion the translator some amount of difficulty. To-day a scholar would disregard the inflexions, but Old English has inflexions as well as Latin, and in the former as in the latter verbs and prepositions govern cases. 'To,' for example, governs the dative, so we find 'ða heo becom to Apollonio,' the Latin dative serving instead of the English. In one place, however, the translator forgets himself and makes an unsightly hybrid of his hero's appellation—'ða het se cyng sillan Apollonige þa hearpan.' These variations—'Apollonius,' 'Apollonio,' 'Apolloni'—must have been perplexing to the natives for whose benefit the translation may be presumed to have been made, but the deference thus paid to Latin endings is not shown to Greek proper names. If the inquiry were sufficiently germane, it would be an interesting philological or philosophical study to determine by what process 'Archestratus' was transmuted into 'Arcestrates,' and 'Apollo' into 'Apollines.' In both cases the errors appear to have been copied from the Latin model, and were likely to offend very few. Apart from learned names and less learned distortions, there is little or nothing to betray the hand of the translator; indeed, there is a strong Anglo-Saxon colouring in such phrases as 'ic hine gelaðode to ðisum urum gebeorscipe' and 'ðare hearpan sweg.' As for the treatment of Latin proper names, even Ælfric cannot avoid

[1] London, 1834.

some inconsistency, but he is rather more systematic and goes farther in the direction of Anglicizing appellations by employing the genitive 'es' and the dative 'e.' He, however, retains the Latin accusative 'um' ('Gregories,' 'Augustine,' 'Cuthbertum').

By a not uncommon artifice Ælfric occasionally poses his hearers with difficult questions, holding them in but momentary suspense, since he does not delay to furnish the answer. Thus in his sermon on the Creation he remarks: 'Some men enquire, whence comes the soul? whether from the father or the mother? We say, from neither of them; but the same God . . . who breathed into Adam's body, and gave him a soul, giveth souls to children.' The *Dialogues of Solomon and Saturn* are entirely composed of such questions and answers, Saturn being the disciple and Solomon the never-failing fount of wisdom. *Solomon and Saturn,* in its essence, is rather European than Anglo-Saxon, and it is worthy of remark that when Saturn's place was taken by Marcolf, the character of the composition underwent a radical change and Solomon was often made to look foolish. The French version was known to Rabelais, who affords an instance of the way in which the sage meets his match. 'Qui ne s'adventure n'a cheval ni mule, ce dict Salomon. Qui trop s'adventure perd cheval et mule, respondit Malcon' (*Vie de Gargantua*).

In the Old English dialogues there is nothing of this cynicism. They are a kind of cross between the catechism and Mangnall's Questions, except that the parts of teacher and scholar are reversed. The ten commandments are given—some of them in English only; others in Latin with an English translation. Most of the questions, however, are curious and trivial, *e.g.*, 'What bird is the happiest? The dove, because it betokens the Holy Ghost': and again, 'What water is the happiest? The river Jordan, because Christ was baptized in it.' Incidentally, there is disclosed a good deal of quaint lore derived from some other source than the Bible.

Tell me from what Adam's name was formed? I tell thee, from four stars.

Tell me, what are they called? I tell thee Arthrox, Dux, Arothalem, Minsymbrie.

Tell me, of what age Adam was, when he was created? I tell thee, thirty winters.

Tell me, of what height Adam was created? I tell thee, one hundred and twenty-six inches.

Tell me whither went the angels who renounced God in the kingdom of heaven? I tell thee, they were divided into three parts: one part He set in the drift of the air, another part in the drift of the water, and the third part in the abyss of hell.

Solomon is great on figures and statistics. He knows that Adam had thirty sons and thirty daughters. He knows the exact duration of our first father's punishment in hell—namely 5,228 years. It might have been expected that Adam's deliverance would come at the date of our Lord's 'harrowing' of hell. Christ's Passion is said to have occurred 6,158 years after the Creation, and Adam's life of toil and misery lasted 930 years. Solomon states that Adam was in hell those thousands of years for tasting the forbidden fruit of the fig-tree, and that on a Friday! From this compendium of useful and entertaining knowledge we learn that the reason why stones are barren is that Abel's blood fell on stones when Cain, his brother, slew him with the jaw-bone of an ass! Also, that the reason why the sun is red in the evening is that it looks on hell! There is one thing that even Solomon does not know. Asked to say where the sepulchre of King Moses is, he can only reply that it is near a house called Fegor, and there is no man who will know it before the Great Judgement.

Though pleased to regale his disciple with this feast of intellect, Solomon is always perfectly serious. 'What is the heaviest thing on earth?' he is asked. He answers: 'Man's sins and his Lord's wrath.'

The dialogue was a favourite mode of instruction in the Dark and Middle Ages. We have previously had an example in the dialogues of Gregory the Great. Alcuin, an Englishman, wrote Latin dialogues, and there are others of equal note, concerning which the reader, who is desirous of further information, may profitably consult Kemble's *Anglo-Saxon Dialogues of Solomon and Saturn,* which throws abundant light on the entire subject. Here it will be enough to state that there are actually two Anglo-Saxon dialogues. One, apparently rather older than the other, is furnished with an epic introduction describing the various countries through which Saturn has travelled, including *Marculfes eard.* This, by the way, is the sole allusion to Marcolf. The dialogue ranges over a number of topics of deep human interest, such as death and age and inequality of fortune.

The other and younger composition displays Saturn as a Chaldee—an eorl—who had made wide conquests in the field of knowledge, having imbibed the philosophies of Egypt and of Greece, the lore of India, and whatsoever might be gathered from the books of all the islands. His errand to Solomon is to obtain instruction as to the efficacy and virtue of the Paternoster. Following Runic example, Solomon personifies different syllables and demonstrates the mystic property of the Paternoster to cast out evil spirits.

From what has been said it is evident that Saturn is no ignorant or inexpert inquirer. He typifies the highest expression of pagan intelligence, and at first is by no means convinced of his inferiority to the Hebrew sage.

Indeed, the talk between them is represented as a contest of wits, or, in mediaeval parlance, a disputation—'Her kið hu Saturnus and Saloman fettode ymbe heora wisdom.'

The dialogues cannot, of course, be dated, but the style suggests that they are considerably older than the writings with which we have been dealing—older, indeed, than the time of Alfred. There is an evident affinity between them and the riddles of which mention was made in a previous chapter.

As a rule, medical treatises would be deemed too austere and abstruse to receive notice in a manual of literature, which is concerned with the emotional, moral, and spiritual elements in man rather than his physical structure. But exceptions there are always, and Anglo-Saxon leeches were not so deeply versed in the mysteries of their calling as to confine themselves to learned discussions in a professional *patois*. It is to be feared indeed that they were not very expert practitioners. Bede tells us that one of their number, Cyneferth, operated on Etheldreda, queen and abbess, for a tumour, but without success. Unluckily the *Liber Medicinalis* (Læce-bóc or Leech-book) was not likely to raise the healing art as exercised by the rank and file of physicians. It might provide them with agreeable recreation, but hardly more.

We have already had occasion to name the Rev. Oswald Cockayne, whose profound learning was tempered by a lively wit and a most unconventional style of writing. Probably his greatest service to Old English literature was a collection of medical works, which he edited for the 'Chronicles and Memorials' series, and published under the title of *Anglo-Saxon Leechdoms*. The work, which was issued in three volumes, comprises, in addition to full introductions, an *Herbarium Apuleii*, the first part of which is based on Apuleius and the second on Dioscorides, not, however, on the original text; a Læce-bóc, which consists of a treatise on medicine in two books, to which has been appended a third, of a more 'monkish' character; 'lacugna' (recipes), prognostics from dreams, star-craft (from Bede's *De Temporibus*), and charms. From this exposition of the contents it will be natural to conclude that the leeches of the tenth century were disinterested enough to apply themselves to the prevention of the ills of the flesh, not only to their cure; and that they believed in signs that would now spell quackery or an extremely dark understanding. We shall see how far this was the case.

The Læce-bóc probably belonged at one time to Glastonbury Abbey, but the original owner is named in the colophon.

Bald habet hunc librum quem Cild conscribere jussit.

Some have imagined that Bald is a shortened form of Æthelbald, but Cockayne will not hear of it. To him Bald is Bald—and a physician interested in the history and literature of his beloved art. 'We see,' he says, 'the Saxon leech at his studies.' The author—who may have been Cild, though it is more likely that this was the name of the penman, calligraphy being an accomplishment of which, in those days, any man might be proud—assumes that his readers will be leeches, not laymen. This is shown by the frequent repetition of the parenthesis, 'as leeches know.' It is clear that there had grown up among the Anglo-Saxon or related peoples a theory of therapeutics, partly traditional and partly extended by contributions from native practitioners, who had thereby rendered themselves famous. Thus we are told 'Oxa taught this leechdom,' and of another remedy it is said 'Dun taught it.' The system was essentially eclectic, since Scandinavian and even Gaelic formulae are quoted. Many prescriptions are sufficiently fantastic, and in recording one of them the writer cannot restrain his sense of humour.

Some teach us against bite of adder to speak one word, that is Faul; it may not hurt him. Against bite of snake, if the patient procureth and eateth rind, which cometh out of Paradise, no venom will damage him. Then said he who wrote this book, that the rind was hard gotten.

Either directly or indirectly, through Latin translations, the Anglo-Saxon medical writers became acquainted with the works of Trallianus, Paulus of Aegina, and Philagrius. It may be, directly, for Bede assures us that the pupils of Archbishop Theodore 'knew Greek and Latin as well as they knew their own mother tongue.'[1] The patriarch Helias of Jerusalem sought to aid the natives of this island in distressing cases. In an interesting letter to King Alfred, here cited *in extenso*, the venerable metropolitan refers to the internal and external uses of an inflammable substance of which much is heard in these latter times—not, however, in the same connection: 'Similarly also petroleum is good to drink simple for inward tenderness, and to smear on outwardly on a winter's day, since it hath very good heat; hence one shall drink it in winter; and it is good if for anyone his speech faileth, then let him take it and make the mark of Christ under his tongue, and swallow a little of it. Also if a man becometh out of his wits, then let him take part of it, and make Christ's mark on every limb, except the cross upon his forehead, that shall be of balsam, and the other also upon the top of his head. All this Dominus Helias, patriarch of Jerusalem, ordered one to say to King Alfred.'

Cockayne's third volume comprises a vast number of prognostics from dreams, some of which are apparently

[1] *Eccl. Hist.*, iv, 71.

reasonable, others the reverse. 'To see oneself in prison betokens some kind of bother or trouble'—this we should call very reasonable. In other instances the rule of contraries is observed. It was the recognized office of dragons to guard hidden treasure, and thus, by a natural association of ideas, it is affirmed 'If you see a dragon flying over you, it betokens a hoard of gold.'[1]

The Anglo-Saxons doubtless believed in literal dragons; at any rate, their faith could receive stories quite as wonderful as the fabulous accounts of fire-drakes—that of the mandrake, for example. In a Cottonian MS. is an illumination representing a dog drawing a plant out of the earth. The accompanying text explains the operations thus:

> This plant, which is called Mandragora, is great and glorious in appearance, and it is efficacious. Thou shalt take it in this manner. When thou comest to it, thou wilt perceive it because it shineth in the night even as a lamp. When first thou seest its head, bind it very quickly with iron, lest it flee from thee. Its virtue is so great and glorious that it will flee away very quickly from an unclean man, when he cometh to it. Therefore bind it, as we said before, with iron. And thou shalt dig about it in such wise that thou touch it not with the iron; but thou shalt zealously dig up the earth with an ivory rod, and when thou seest its hands and feet,[2] bind them. Take then the other end, and bind it to a dog's neck, so the dog be hungry; after that cast meat before him, so that he may not reach it without pulling up the plant with him. Concerning this plant, 'tis said it hath such great virtue that whatsoever thing draweth it up shall immediately be circumvented in the same manner. Therefore, as soon as thou seest that it is pulled up, and thou hast power over it, take it immediately into thy hand, roll it, and press the juice from the leaves into a glass vessel; and when need cometh upon thee that thou help any man therewith, help him in this manner: against head-ache, etc.

[1] See p. 67.

[2] The root of the mandrake often divides in two, when it presents a rude resemblance to the human figure.

CHAPTER V

THE GREAT LATINISTS

ANYONE who undertakes to treat of Old English literature finds himself confronted at the outset by a curious, and to some extent embarrassing, anomaly. On the one hand, we have verse and prose of high quality that are anonymous; on the other hand, writers of European celebrity known only for their Latin compositions. These writers were schoolmasters in more than one sense. In the sense which primarily concerns us, they exerted enormous influence on the intellectual development of the entire nation. Their matter was freely appropriated, their methods imitated by younger admirers, who used the vulgar tongue. Many instances have been given of these obligations, but we have still to dispose of the question whether the original writers should be classified according to their nationality, or according to the language in which they expressed themselves. To us it appears impossible to set down Bede's *Ecclesiastical History*, for example, as a monument of Anglo-Saxon letters; and yet it would be manifestly incongruous to ignore those master minds except for casual allusions differing in no way from similar references to Continental scholars. In these circumstances a middle course seems reasonable; and brief historical notices of the fathers will probably suffice.

The earliest of them is Aldhelm. As he died in 709,

he belongs mainly to the seventh century. He succeeded his Celtic master, Maidulf, founder of Malmesbury Abbey, and was subsequently raised to the see of Sherborne. Aldhelm's style, which he himself described as either *verbosa garrulitas* or *garrula verbositas*, is believed by some critics to have had a profound effect on Cynewulf, whose English exhibits the same wordiness; and it may be noted that just as Cynewulf occasionally employs rime, so Aldhelm employs alliteration—as an ornament. He was a facile writer of Latin, and amongst his productions is a riming epistle in which he gives a lively account of a journey in Cornwall. His *De Laudibus Virginitatis* was one of the sources of the Old English martyrology. His *Ænigmata,* prefaced by a letter to 'Acircius,' in which he discourses on prosody and other topics, were initiated from Symphosius, and were themselves copied in the English riddles of the Exeter Book.

Bede also belongs in part to the seventh century (673?-735). His literary remains—the fruits of a large leisure—are remarkable for their voluminousness and variety. His minor writings comprise scholastic treatises, including a *De Arte Metrica,* which possesses considerable interest. Amongst other points he discusses the novel principle of rhythm that had displaced the old classical metres, especially in the hymns of the Church. Whilst recognizing the irregularities of the *vulgares poetae,* Bede is sympathetic towards the new sort of verse, and warmly commends the Ambrosian hymn:

> Rex aeterne Domine,
> Rerum creator omnium.

His dissertations on spelling and biblical tropes and figures are less attractive.

Bede wrote a number of scientific works, which were

much appreciated by later writers.[1] In *De Natura Rerum* he treats of the elements, comets, winds, the Red Sea, the Nile, and Mount Etna. In *De Temporibus* he is concerned with leap-year, the month, the week, the solstice. In *De Temporum Ratione* he speaks of the Greek, Roman, and English month, the moon and its influence, the epact (*i.e.*, the excess of the solar month over the lunar month, and of the solar year over the lunar year), Easter and so forth. Bede's masterpiece is, of course, his *Historia Ecclesiastica Gentis Anglorum*, a work which will never become antiquated. It is not a critical or philosophical work, but it is transparently honest and sincere. Bede cites his authorities. Down to the arrival of St. Augustine these are chiefly well-known historians like Orosius, Gildas, etc. After that date he depends on documents, recollections, traditions. In one place he gives a description of Paulinus based on the narrative of one who had seen him. Bede wrote, besides, commentaries on the Gospels, homilies, a life of St. Cuthbert (in prose and in verse),[2] and the Lives of the Abbots of Wearmouth and Yarrow. He was one of those Anglo-Saxon scholars who knew Greek, since he made use of a Greek text in his comment on the Acts of the Apostles.

Boniface (680?-755), who was born at Crediton, in Devon, is best remembered for his missionary labours among the Old Saxons. In one of his Latin letters he implores a correspondent to send him the homilies of Bede, of whose death he has just been informed. Boniface was the author of Latin riddles.

The name of Alcuin (735?-804) is indelibly associated with that of Charlemagne, at whose court he passed many

[1] See above, pp. 224, 234.

[2] From these two lives Ælfric entirely composed his alliterative homily on St. Cuthbert: 'Us sæde soðlice Beda.'

years. He was of York, and his English name was Ealhwine, but in the academic society of which he was a distinguished member in France, he was dubbed Horatius Flaccus. He composed works on the trivial arts (*i.e.*, grammar, rhetoric, and dialectic)—all of them in dialogue, and in one the disciple is no less a personage than Charlemagne. Somewhat similar is his debate between Winter and Spring—esteemed the best of his poems. The latter include a life of St. Willibrord (to whom he was related, and whose memory he has also handed down in prose), the story of York, and an elegy on the ruin of Lindisfarne, which had been burnt by the Danes. Alcuin, however, appears to better advantage in his lighter pieces, his epigrams, epistles, etc., which are a faithful mirror of the world in which he moved, and remind us of another and earlier guest of France—the courtly Fortunatus.

In conclusion, it will, we think, be conceded that Old English literature deserves the attention not only of the philologer and the antiquary, but of the lover of *belles lettres.* If *Beowulf* makes the strongest appeal, Cynewulf by his weirdness, and Ælfric by his sense of style, his mastery of elect prose must command the respect of all who know how to value originality and talent. On this point, however, we do not insist so much as on the utility of Old English literature as the reflection of a change from the fierce barbarism of the North to the Christian civilization which slowly permeated the mind of the nation. Regarded in this light, the study of Anglo-Saxon writings is of extreme interest; and as literature gains in importance the more it typifies the thought of an entire people, this circumstance will atone for the relative paucity of biographical details due to various causes, and, most of all, to the blushing lowliness of the vulgar tongue.

SOME LEADING DATES

A.D.
449. First landing of the English in Britain.
597. Mission of St. Augustine.
664. Cædmon at Whitby.
668. Theodore consecrated Archbishop of Canterbury; died 690.
709. Death of Aldhelm.
734. Death of Bede.
755. Death of Boniface.
757. Offa, King of Mercia; died 795.
787. First landing of the Danes in England.
793. Sack of Lindisfarne by the Danes.
804. Death of Alcuin.
849. Alfred born; King of Wessex, 871; died 901.
937. Battle of Brunanburh.
957. Edgar, King of Mercia; consecrated King at Bath, 973; died 975.
961. Dunstan, Archbishop of Canterbury; died 988.
963. Æthelwold, Bishop of Winchester; died 984.
990. Sigeric, Archbishop of Canterbury; died 995.
991. Battle at Maldon; death of Byrhtnoth, ealdorman.
1023. Death of Wulfstan, Archbishop of York.
1066. Battle of Hastings.

INDEX

CHISWICK PRESS: PRINTED BY CHARLES WHITTINGHAM AND CO.
TOOKS COURT, CHANCERY LANE, LONDON.

Birthdays
[illegible]
[illegible]
Bible
Confirmation